Leadership from Bad to Worse

Advance praise

"PAY ATTENTION. With this simple advice, Barbara Kellerman's latest work, *Leadership from Bad to Worse*, conveys the powerful message that followers bear the ultimate accountability for the quality of our leaders. And usually that's us. Using four brilliant profiles, two CEO's and two heads of state, Kellerman examines and reveals the unique circumstances, but common DNA, shared by bad leaders, but reminds us that the ball's in our court."
—**Stanley McChrystal**, Founder & CEO, McChrystal Group, General, US Army (Retd.)

"Barbara Kellerman's brilliant and blistering analysis is required reading and a cautionary tale to pull back from what is left of the brink."
—**Julia Hobsbawm**, award-winning business writer and
Bloomberg commentator

"*Leadership from Bad to Worse* is an impressive contribution to our understanding of what Barbara Kellerman calls the 'dark side of the human condition', the pathologies of bad leadership. Its distinguishing and commendable strength is its synoptic approach, exploring both bad leaders and bad followers in contexts ranging from politics to the workplace. Her innovative account of the four phases of corruption, where both leaders and their enablers descend from bad to worse, provides a new perspective for appraising and hopefully mitigating the ever-present dangers posed by leaders who go bad and then get worse."
—**Professor Haig Patapan**, School of Government and
International Relations, Griffith University

"A brutal but alas accurate depiction of the human parasites that cause most of the world's big problems. In her usual direct, brave, and humorous style, Barbara Kellerman has managed to produce yet another leadership masterpiece: an outstanding book!"
—**Dr. Tomas Chamorro-Premuzic**, Professor of Business Psychology at
Columbia and UCL, author of *I, Human: AI, Automation,
and the Quest to Reclaim What Makes Us Unique*

"Bad leadership—leadership that undermines democracy or distorts capitalism—doesn't just happen. As Kellerman points out in her invaluable book, it progresses in distinct phases that become more dangerous over time. But Kellerman is too astute an observer of leadership and followership simply to offer a stark warning. She insists that we all have a responsibility to stop or at least interrupt the downward spiral. No easy solutions, of course. Instead, an original and important look at how bad happens and how perhaps to preclude it."
—**Bert Spector**, Professor Emeritus, D'Amore-McKim
School of Business, Northeastern University

"Leaders inspire and captivate us, for better or worse. In her brilliant new book, Barbara Kellerman shows exactly how we get to worse, in unfolding stages that may appear harmless at first. For anyone concerned about the current state of leadership in business and society, *Leadership from Bad to Worse* will show you the signs to look out for—and correct—before it is too late."
—**Herminia Ibarra**, The Charles Handy Professor of
Organisational Behaviour, London Business School

Leadership from Bad to Worse

What Happens When Bad Festers

BARBARA KELLERMAN

OXFORD
UNIVERSITY PRESS

OXFORD
UNIVERSITY PRESS

Oxford University Press is a department of the University of Oxford. It furthers
the University's objective of excellence in research, scholarship, and education
by publishing worldwide. Oxford is a registered trade mark of Oxford University
Press in the UK and certain other countries.

Published in the United States of America by Oxford University Press
198 Madison Avenue, New York, NY 10016, United States of America.

Library of Congress Cataloging-in-Publication Data
Names: Kellerman, Barbara, author.
Title: Leadership from bad to worse : what happens when bad festers / Barbara Kellerman.
Description: First edition. | New York, NY : Oxford University Press, [2024] |
Includes bibliographical references and index.
Identifiers: LCCN 2023046739 | ISBN 9780197759271 (hardback) |
ISBN 9780197759295 (epub) | ISBN 9780197759301 (ebook)
Subjects: LCSH: Political leadership. | Leadership. |
Organizational behavior. | Capitalism—Social aspects.
Classification: LCC JC330.3 .K43 2024 | DDC 324.2/2—dc23/eng/20231107
LC record available at https://lccn.loc.gov/2023046739

DOI: 10.1093/oso/9780197759271.001.0001

Printed by Sheridan Books, Inc., United States of America

"How did you go bankrupt?" Bill asked.

"Two ways," Mike said. "Gradually, then suddenly."

—Ernest Hemingway, *The Sun Also Rises*

Books By Barbara Kellerman

The Enablers: How Team Trump Flunked the Pandemic and Failed America, Cambridge University Press, 2021

Leadership and Lust: Power, Money, Sex, Success, Legitimacy, Legacy (co-author with Todd Pittinsky), Cambridge University Press, 2020

Professionalizing Leadership, Oxford University Press, 2018

Hard Times: Leadership in America, Stanford University Press, 2015

The End of Leadership, HarperCollins, 2012

Leadership: Essential Selections on Power, Authority, and Influence (editor), McGraw-Hill, 2010

Followership: How Followers Are Creating Change and Changing Leaders, Harvard Business School Press, 2008

Women and Leadership: State of Play and Strategies for Change (coeditor with Deborah Rhode), Jossey-Bass, 2007

Bad Leadership: What It Is, Why It Happens, How It Matters, Harvard Business School Press, 2004

Reinventing Leadership: Making the Connection Between Politics and Business, State University Press of New York, 1999

The President as World Leader (coauthor with Ryan Barrilleaux), St. Martin's, 1991

Leadership and Negotiation in the Middle East (coeditor with Jeffrey Rubin), Praeger, 1988

Political Leadership: A Source Book (editor), University of Pittsburgh Press, 1986.

Women Leaders in American Politics (coeditor with James David Barber), Prentice-Hall, 1986

The Political Presidency: Practice of Leadership, Oxford University Press, 1984

Leadership: Multidisciplinary Perspectives (editor), Prentice-Hall, 1984

All the President's Kin: Their Political Roles, New York University Press, 1981

Making Decisions (coeditor with Percy Hill et al.), Addison-Wesley, 1979

Contents

Prologue

The Present

Bad leadership and its conjoined twin, bad followership, are as ubiquitous as they are pernicious. They are everywhere: in business and government, in religion and education and the military, in democracies as well as autocracies. It's why I've been interested in "bad" for years. In 2000 I wrote an essay titled "Hitler's Ghost: A Manifesto."[1] In 2004 I published a book titled *Bad Leadership: What It Is, How It Happens, Why It Matters*.[2] And in 2021 I came out with *The Enablers: How Team Trump Flunked the Pandemic and Failed America*—a book about bad followers.[3]

What I never could have imagined is that within months of my conceiving of and then writing the present book—about how unless bad leaders are stopped or at least slowed, they will inevitably, inexorably get worse—would come an earthshaking event that exemplified my point. It was the first war on European soil since the end of the Second World War.

"Putin's war," it's been called. Russian president Vladimir Putin's invasion of Ukraine on February 24, 2022. The war is evidence of how a leader who had long behaved badly—who was long unbound either by the rule of law or by the international order—would in time behave more badly. During the entirety of Putin's more than two decades in office, he displayed an insatiable appetite for both great power and great wealth. But his cravings and the criminalities they necessarily entailed remained unchecked. No great surprise, then, that his bad behavior did not over the years change for the better. Instead, it changed for the worse.

Putin is typical. He did not metamorphose from one kind of leader to another kind of leader overnight. To the contrary. His trajectory from bad to worse was gradual. Early in his tenure as president of Russia, beginning in 1999, Putin made clear that he was prepared to use all-out force to destroy, even to kill, to get what he wanted when he wanted it. On his orders renegades in Chechnya, a republic of Russia, were wiped out; Chechnya's capital city, Grozny, was bombed; and the Chechen people were compelled to become vassals of the Russian state.

Notwithstanding the early evidence of his extreme brutality and rampant corruption, Putin was left alone, free to continue to lead as he saw fit. It explains why over time Putin became increasingly greedy and autocratic and why over more time he became more dictatorial. In 2004 he scrapped local elections. In 2006 two of his most prominent critics were mysteriously murdered. In 2007 he delivered a ferocious speech in Munich that signaled his hardened position vis-à-vis the West, especially the United States. In 2008 he used the Russian military to impose his will on an independent state, Georgia. In 2011 and 2012 he crushed his opposition, ordinary Russians who took to the streets to protest him and his government. And in 2014 he invaded and then annexed Crimea, simply seizing it from Ukraine. It was this event—to which the West did not respond in any serious way—that triggered what became a chronic conflict in eastern Ukraine.

In 2015 he intervened militarily in the war in Syria, which included leveling the ancient city of Aleppo. In 2020 his agents tried again, once more unsuccessfully, to murder his single most prominent and politically dangerous opponent, Alexei Navalny. In 2020 Putin arranged for the Russian Duma to eliminate term limits, which meant he could run again for president in 2024 and, potentially, hold office until 2036. And in 2022, pursuant to Russia's invasion of Ukraine, he instigated what an essay in *Foreign Affairs* described as a "new police state," with methods reminiscent of Joseph Stalin's.[4]

About Putin's trajectory from bad to worse, three comments. First, it provides clear evidence that during his decades-long tenure in office he changed. Former national security advisor Condoleezza Rice put it this way: "I've seen Putin go from a little shy to pretty shy, to arrogant, and now megalomaniacal."[5] Second, it reminds us that until Russia invaded all of Ukraine, the changes in Putin elicited no significant resistance or repercussions either within Russia or without. Third, given that over more than two decades Putin's leadership was permitted to go from bad to worse, and then to still worse, it was probable, even predictable, that eventually it would become evil. Evil leadership, as I have defined it, is when the leader and at least some followers commit atrocities. They use pain as an instrument of power. The harm done to men, women, and children is severe rather than slight. The harm can be physical or psychological, or it can be both.[6] Putin's war exemplifies evil leadership. Putin's war is why in March 2023, just over a year after the war began, the International Criminal Court issued an arrest warrant for the Russian president for war crimes.

But to witness the progression from bad leadership to worse, Americans are not limited to looking abroad. They can look at home. In recent years liberal democracies, including but not limited to the United States, have been bedeviled by what is widely perceived as bad leadership and followership. Leaders of every stripe on a slide of disrespect and disrepute. And followers of every stripe on a slide of disappointment and disillusion.

The presidency of Donald Trump—judged by many, including professional historians, to be one of the worst in American history—is an example.[7] His tenure in the White House was a menace as serious as it was unforeseen. A menace to American democracy that came out of left field, or seemed to, at least in part because neither the American people nor the leadership industry typically pay bad leadership close, careful attention.

Which is ironic, given that most Americans are now persuaded that bad leaders are inevitable. Only 46 percent have a positive view of big business.[8] Fully 65 percent of Americans believe politicians run for office to "serve their own personal interests."[9] And more generally, "Americans have an overwhelming lack of trust in key groups of people who are in positions of power including . . . K–12 public school principals, journalists, military leaders, police officers, leaders of technology companies and religious leaders."[10] But while most Americans think bad leaders inescapable, they—we—usually assume that though those leaders are bad, they are not *that* bad. Most strikingly, until recently we have taken our political system for granted, presuming that autocratic leadership, fascist leadership, could never and would never happen here in the United States of America. And until recently we have taken our economic system for granted, presuming that corporate leaders would restrain themselves, never get to the point of being so rich and powerful that a single individual—think Elon Musk—could ever or would ever be dominant in the marketplace, cyberspace, and outer space.

Like Putin's time in the Kremlin, Trump's time in Washington testifies to the point I make in this book. Trump too went from bad to worse. To take perhaps the most obvious example, the tens of thousands of outright lies that he told during his four years in the White House ultimately culminated in the Big Lie. The lie that it was not Joe Biden who won the 2020 presidential election but Donald Trump. The lie that led to the January 6, 2021, attack on the U.S. Capitol. The lie that, along with the relentless pressure on Vice President Mike Pence not to certify the results of the election, constituted a blatant and malevolent, if ultimately failed, coup attempt. The lie led to widespread worry that Madisonian democracy was genuinely in peril.

Though Trump was the first president in American history to be twice impeached, he was twice acquitted by the U.S. Senate. These "botched" attempts to oust the chief executive "laid bare the fundamental weakness" of Congress's oversight power, while ensuring that Trump's term in the White House was neither seriously interrupted nor effectively impeded.[11] It's why he and his followers epitomize the trajectory that I describe in this book. Once bad leadership and followership set in, as they did during the first year of Trump's tenure, bad became worse. And then—as he descended into blatant racism and antisemitism, and into warnings of "death and destruction" should things fail in the eyes of the law to go his way—still worse. It was a logical if not entirely predictable outcome of this sequence that in time, some two years after he left the White House, Trump became the first former president to face criminal charges. By the end of summer 2023 he had been charged in fully four separate criminal cases. He was accused, for example, by the Department of Justice of willfully retaining national defense secrets in violation of the Espionage Act, making false statements, and a conspiracy to obstruct justice.

Inevitably Trump's bad leadership was in tandem with bad followership. Most importantly, he elicited and enlisted those I label "enablers." Enablers "are followers who allow or even encourage their leaders to engage in, and then to persist in behaviors that are destructive."[12] Like bad leaders, bad followers, with enablers at the top of the list, change. Over time they metastasize. They get worse unless, until, somehow they are stopped or at least slowed.

The process of going from bad to worse tends to be steady, not sudden or hasty. But once bad has burrowed in, it digs in deep and then deeper, making it finally very difficult to extract or excise. In other words, once the system is close to being completely corrupted, it's late, maybe even too late. By then bad leaders and their followers are so entrenched that they control the system itself, which is why at this point the only way to totally get rid of bad is to totally get rid of everyone involved.

This book looks at how bad leadership and bad followership evolve. As we will see, sometimes bad is obvious almost from the get-go; other times it reveals itself only slowly, surreptitiously, occasionally even imperceptibly. In any case, bad leadership and bad followership go through *four phases of development* as they worm their way deeply and completely into the group or organization of which they are a part. One purpose of this book is, then, to serve as an early warning system. It anticipates that by breaking bad leadership and followership into phases—each worse than the one before—their progression will be easier to predict and detect. And easier, therefore, to stop or at least slow *before* they turn toxic.

The trajectory from bad leadership to worse is not limited to the public sector, of course. It applies equally to the private sector, where leaders such as WeWork's Adam Neumann, Wells Fargo's John Stumpf, Uber's Travis Kalanick, and Purdue Pharma's Sackler family members similarly went from being bad to being worse. Hence the focus in this book is on leaders in both government and business. This is not to say that other leaders in other areas, say, education or religion, are unimportant or less prone to the decay to which I allude. But leaders who are presidents, especially of sizable countries, and CEOs, especially of sizable companies, are usually very powerful and, therefore, very well chronicled. The book zeroes in on four leaders who are exemplars—leaders who, though they might have been in some ways good, ultimately were bad as I define the term (about which more in Chapter 3).

I do not single out leaders only in democracies or only in autocracies. While people in the West, especially Americans, tend to think that leaders in autocracies are prone to being bad while leaders in democracies are prone to being good, it is not nearly so simple. True, Americans associate democracy with freedom and independence, and autocracies with controls and constraints. Better, therefore, we assume, to live and work in a democracy than in an autocracy. But, as we will see, that is not necessarily the case, or at least not in every instance or in every way. We cannot count on leaders, or for that matter on followers, anywhere to be always or even mostly good. It's the nature of the human condition to be good sometimes—and not good sometimes. And, as we will further see, unless bad leaders (and their followers) are corrected, their errors will be compounded. They will go from being bad to being worse.

Part I of the book sets the stage. It's a general discussion of the phenomen in question, beginning with a chapter on democracy and capitalism because these linchpins of good governance have been obviously in decline. Democracies are far more fractious and perceptibly less effective than they used to be, hapless in addressing many of our most pressing problems. Capitalism has been on a similar trajectory, seemingly powerless—certainly in the United States—to remove or even restrain what has become the most obvious thorn in its collective side, inequality in income and in wealth.

Leaders and their followers are responsible for these declines, which brings us to Chapter 2, a discussion of leadership and followership in the twenty-first century. In recent decades leadership has changed significantly, and followership has changed even more. There is, further, a relationship between democracy and capitalism, on the one hand, and leadership and followership, on the other. For example, one of the reasons democracies have been decreasing in number while autocracies have been increasing in number is that followers have changed. For reasons ranging from the nature of twenty-first-century parenting to the nature of twenty-first-century media (especially social media), followers are less conforming and more demanding, which is precisely why leaders not committed to democracy try largely or even entirely to control them. And one of the reasons capitalist systems are viewed as less attractive and socialist systems as more attractive, notably among young Americans, is that leaders have changed.[13] Over time they have become less civic-minded and more self-interested—or at least we perceive them as such.

Chapter 3 tries (though I confess at the outset that it succeeds only in part) to make meaning of being bad. I wrestle with questions like these: What does it mean for a leader or a follower to be "bad"? How can we make sense of being bad if your bad leader (or follower) might well be my good one? Why even take on bad leadership and followership given the complexities they inevitably evoke and the challenges they invariably present? And what does leadership going from bad to worse even look like? Whom exactly is it worse for? The leader? Their followers? Both? Others?

Chapter 4 is centered on the four phases of development. Bad leaders, and bad followers, are not born fully formed. What do they look like at the outset? Most start by being good in some obvious ways, or at least not bad in every obvious way. As indicated, what happens after that is that they change. Some change from being more obviously good than bad to being more obviously bad than good. Others change from being a bit bad some of the time to being a lot bad most of the time. Finally, in the final phase of the four-phase process, they all go from being obviously bad to being obviously worse.

But what's that about? If it's correct to say that bad leaders get worse over time if left unchecked, why don't we followers check them? Why do we give leaders license, implicitly or explicitly, to behave badly and then to behave worse?

Part II of the book seeks to answer questions such as these. It consists of four chapters—or four stories, or four cases—about four leaders and their followers. Two of these leaders are in the political realm, two in the corporate one. One is German, one Turkish, one American, and one Chinese. Three are men; one is a woman. Three are in capitalist countries; one is in a communist country. They are diverse, but the diversity is not statistically significant. Here are the criteria on which the four leaders were selected: (1) each had to be contemporary; (2) each had to have been in a top leadership post for at least five years; (3) each had to have a record of leadership that was well documented; (4) each had to have been clearly consequential; (5) each had to have been in some obvious way bad; and (6) each had to have had followers who similarly were visibly bad.

Part III of the book digs deeper into each of the four phases of development. Each chapter is about a different phase: from bad leadership and followership as embryonic to bad leadership and followership as full-grown and full-blown. From leadership and followership that are at least slightly benign to leadership and followership that are clearly malignant and often toxic.

The book concludes with the Epilogue, to bookend the Prologue. The Prologue is an introduction that pertains to the present. The Epilogue is an exhortation that focuses on the future. It gets to the heart of the matter. Can knowing that bad leadership is a process prompt us to stop it—maybe even reverse it? Can we, in other words, change our ways to inhibit or even halt an otherwise inexorable progression?

Knowledge is power. In this case our power can and should spring from the knowledge that bad leadership and followership are not static. They develop over time, they go from bad to worse. But they go from bad to worse *only* if we allow it. If, in contrast, bad leaders and followers are checked before they corrupt, at least before they corrupt completely, the outcome can be different.

PART I
LOOKING IN

1

Democracy in Decline and Capitalism in Question

Rarely in the history of American democracy has there been such uncertainty about its viability. The same applies to American capitalism. It too is under scrutiny as it has not been since at least the Great Depression, almost a hundred years ago. There is of course a connection between the two. Failures of capitalism create uncertainties in democracies. And deficiencies in democracies raise concerns over capitalism.

In the United States, democracy and capitalism have been in tandem since the beginning of the Republic. In fact, the ideology undergirding both is essentially the same, the one a reflection of and companion to the other. Democracy celebrates the rights of individuals, including the right to be relatively free and unfettered politically. Capitalism celebrates the rights of individuals, including the right to be relatively free and unfettered economically. America's political creed embodies and embraces ideals such as freedom, equality, and independence. America's economic creed embodies and embraces ideals such as liberty and individuality, essentially the right of any single individual to reap what he or she has sown and then keep it.

Not for nothing was Nobel Prize–winning economist Milton Friedman's classic book—since 1962 it has sold over a half million copies—titled *Capitalism and Freedom*. Not for nothing did he extol the virtues of both and their interdependence. It is impossible to have capitalism without freedom, Friedman argued. Similarly, it is impossible to have freedom without capitalism. Economic and political freedom were, he claimed, irrevocably entwined, each one dependent on and sustained by the other.

Over the years some of Friedman's ideas have been discredited, or at least questioned. Moreover, the practices that he preached have been modified not only in the United States but elsewhere in the world as well. It is now widely agreed that to have a maximum of political freedom, some constraints on economic freedom are necessary, such as the levying of taxes. One could even argue that in the United States the related debate is central to the political

divide: how much government intervention should there be not only to stabilize the economy but to equalize it? The relatively hard right, including
libertarians, say none or nearly none. The relatively hard left, including progressives, argue the opposite, that significant government intervention is not
only desirable but necessary to bring a semblance of equality and equity to
American democracy. They further argue that without greater equality and
equity, democracy will crack and, in time, break.

Americans at the top of the economic ladder generally refuse, at least publicly, to admit to the connection between capitalism and democracy. Though
some of the rich, especially the ultra-rich, are known for their philanthropy,
there is no evidence that most or maybe even any have an interest in seriously
changing the system that made them a fortune. This notwithstanding the fact
that since the 1970s inequality in the United States has become significantly
more extreme. Even the pandemic exacerbated the disparities. "Thanks to
stock market gains, stimulus and a pandemic recession that largely bypassed
white-collar jobs, Americans were able to save an estimated $2.5 trillion
more than usual since the pandemic began."[1] But these savings were accrued
nearly entirely by those who already were relatively wealthy. In mid-2021,
those who were not (the bottom 20 percent of households) accounted for
only a small fraction of overall spending, most of which was on basics such as
food and housing.

By 2023 the phenomenon was global. The world's rich had never been
richer. In fact, according to a global wealth report by Credit Suisse, the
wealthiest 1 percent owned about 50 percent of the money in the world,
while the poorest 50 percent owned about 1 percent.[2]

To claim that an imbalance as extreme as this one can possibly be healthy
for democracy is to whistle in the wind. Which raises questions about how
this happened. How did democracy decline? How did capitalism come
into question? Though there is no single answer, leaders—elites, people in
positions of authority—are the most visible of the various explanations.
More than anything or anyone else, they, and their followers—followers have
an impact even when they are passive as opposed to active—are responsible
for where we are and for why we are where we are. This particularly applies
to leaders in government and in business. In the United States, certainly, it
is they who perpetuate the political system. In the United States, certainly, it
is they who perpetuate the economic system. Moreover, wittingly or unwittingly, they collude. America's government leaders work hand in glove with
America's corporate leaders to sustain the status quo. Such change as does

come about invariably is a consequence of pressure from below, from ordinary people (followers) who for one reason or another, or for more reasons than one, are sick and tired of the status quo.

Democracy in Decline

Since the presidency of Donald Trump, the level of anxiety over the resilience of American democracy has reached a new high. Not since the Civil War, or perhaps the Great Depression, has democracy in the United States seemed so precarious. Not because of a threat from without, but because of a threat from within. The United States is so riven by division, including about what is truth and what is falsehood, that hope for America as a durable democracy in which reasonably honest and competent government is a given has flickered. There have been murmurings of civil war. And there was for a time certainly a significant increase in crime and gun violence, especially while Americans "grappled with an unfolding pandemic, deep political divisions and social unrest, economic disruption and social isolation."[3]

Some of the high anxiety was as personal as it was political—a particular response to President Donald Trump. But Trumpism and everything that it implied outlived Trump in the Oval Office not only at home but abroad as well. Many of the doubts and much of the despair that came to be associated with the apparent decline of democracy are global. Which is to say that liberal democracies around the world have been affected by dysfunction and afflicted by decline. Years before Trump was even elected, political sociologist Larry Diamond watched democracies around the world experience what he called a "mild but protracted democratic [not economic] recession." But after Trump became president it became clear that democracy everywhere, including in the United States, was in trouble. Diamond ultimately concluded that, "We can now talk of a [democratic] crisis."[4]

Freedom House is a nonprofit, nongovernmental organization that is best known for assessing the political freedoms of countries around the world. Its reports are relied on by journalists, academics, and policymakers interested in determining how civil liberties are trending. If you happen to prefer democratic forms of government to autocratic ones, the news out of Freedom House has not of late been good. In recent years democracies have "sustained heavy new losses" in their struggle against autocracies."[5] Moreover, in recent years strongmen such as Xi Jinping and Vladimir Putin have tightened their grip on power; illiberalism has risen from Hungary to Turkey; and resistance to autocracies has met with violent repression from Syria to Belarus, from Myanmar to Hong Kong.

The real story of democracy in decline, however, is not about any given date or disaster, including a public health disaster such as the pandemic. Rather, it is about change over time, which is why the more important story is that 2021 was *the sixteenth consecutive year of decline in global freedom.* As Freedom House put it in 2022, "The long democratic recession is deepening." Specifically, there are three indicators, each of which is directly on topic, about leaders who went from bad to worse. First, there was an increase in the number of authoritarian leaders; second, there was an increase in the number of authoritarian leaders who are more repressive now than they were earlier in their tenures; and third, there was an increase in the number of democratic leaders unable to satisfy their followers, who for their part are increasingly fickle and fractious.

While India is the largest example of a country in which democracy recently was degraded—under the leadership of Prime Minister Narendra Modi, the world's most populous democracy is judged no longer "free" but only "partly free"—it is China and the United States that most dramatically illustrate the trajectory to which I refer.

China's president Xi Jinping has become more authoritarian—and then, as we will see, virtually totalitarian—with every year that he has been president, starting in 2013. Moreover, contrary to what the West had hoped, he has extended and expanded his realm, which now includes Hong Kong, with possibly Taiwan next in his sights. Further, not only did the Chinese government become more oppressive in its domestic policies—its efforts to contain COVID were draconian for years, for example—but it became more aggressive in its foreign policy. Previously content to stay within the confines of whatever they deemed their national borders, more recently Chinese officials have embarked on markedly more assertive strategies and tactics abroad, ones that leave an imprint far from the Chinese mainland. China currently has the world's second-largest military budget (after the United States) and the world's largest navy. It has strengthened its nuclear stockpile and developed more sophisticated missiles. It has increasingly inserted itself in multiple multilateral institutions. It has started to play a role on the global stage, such as when it brokered the restoration of diplomatic relations between Saudi Arabia and Iran in 2023. It has aligned itself openly and repeatedly with Russia, notwithstanding the latter's attack on Ukraine. And its Belt and

Road Initiative—"President Xi Jinping's signature foreign policy under-taking and the world's largest infrastructure program"—has led to Chinese investments in some seventy countries around the world, including in Latin America and Africa.[6]

Freedom House does not spare the United States. In 2021 it gave what was once the world's most admired democracy an unambiguously bad review. "The parlous state of US democracy was conspicuous in the early days of 2021 as an insurrectionist mob . . . stormed the Capitol building and tem-porarily disrupted Congress's final certification of the [2020 presidential] vote. This capped a year in which the administration attempted to under-mine accountability for malfeasance . . . amplified false allegations of elec-toral fraud . . . and condoned disproportionate violence by police in response to massive protests calling for an end to systemic racial injustice."

Tellingly, it was a prominent scholar of Nazi Germany and the former Soviet Union who first sounded the alarm about fascism in America. Yale historian Timothy Snyder detected early in Trump's tenure that he had the stuff of a despot, so Snyder wrote a small, slender volume that became an unlikely bestseller. It was titled *On Tyranny: Ten Lessons from the Twentieth Century*.[7] Snyder warned Americans that they had to be vigilant, hence his ten lessons included "do not obey in advance," "defend institutions," and in-sist on "the truth."

After the January 6 insurrection, but before Joe Biden was inaugurated, Snyder wrote another piece, this one about what had transpired during the three preceding years. Snyder concluded that during the time Trump was in the White House the United States had come dangerously close to an "abyss," largely though of course not entirely because Trump was our first "post-truth president"—a president who had chipped away at the rule of law and spoken not facts but fictions.[8] I earlier indicated that the frequency with which Trump lied was astonishing. Not so much because he was relentless and shameless but because so many Americans were willing to tolerate and even embrace his fabrications. The Big Lie was no more than, and no less than, the inevitable culmination of the habitual lying that preceded it.

Anne Applebaum, an American expert on Russia and Eastern Europe, wrote another important book on the general subject, *Twilight of Democracy: The Seductive Lure of Authoritarianism*. It appeared in 2020 and was similarly a response to the presidency of Donald Trump and similarly a warning to those who continued to believe that it—authoritarianism, fas-cism—"can't happen here." Like Snyder, Applebaum was alarmed by what she considered the unwarranted, unwanted complacency of the American people, Americans unwilling or maybe unable to see that the United States, like any other democracy, is vulnerable to an attack from within. The United States, she wrote, "may be doomed . . . to be swept away into irrelevance. It is possible that we are already living through the twilight of democracy; that our civilization may already be heading for anarchy or tyranny . . . ; [that] advocates of illiberal or authoritarian ideas . . . will come to power in the twenty-first century, just as they did in the twentieth."[9]

In 2020 Donald Trump failed to win a second White House term. Instead, Joe Biden—a seventy-seven-year-old Democrat with a long career as a public servant and a reputation as a centrist of considerable integrity and moderate temperament—was elected president. Moreover, by implementing a COVID-19 vaccine program with rapidity and efficiency early in his tenure, Biden seemed initially to suggest that the U.S. government could still work. But it did not take long for him too to run into political trouble: specifically, his decision only months after he took office to withdraw all American troops from Afghanistan seemed a mistake from which his administration might not recover.

Even so, Biden managed to chalk up several major legislative accomplishments during his first few years in office. Moreover, several of his foreign policy initiatives were similarly impressive, among them his leadership of the Western alliance in resisting Russia virtually immediately after its attack on Ukraine. Still, the warnings about American democracy in danger did not abate. Among the various reasons was Trump's staying power—or, better, the staying power of Trumpism. In mid-2021 at a meeting of the Republican faithful in Florida, members of the audience referred to Trump's erstwhile vice president, Mike Pence, as a "traitor" for certifying that Joe Biden won the 2020 presidential election. And well into 2023, notwithstanding his rampant vitriol (exacerbated by his fear of the long arm of the law), Trump was still far in the lead among Republicans expected to run for the White House in 2024.[10]

Whatever the outcome of the 2024 presidential election, many if not most Republican voters and many if not most Republican elected officials are likely to remain loyal to Trumpism, if not to Trump specifically. This means the United States is destined to remain for a time badly fractured. Americans had been forewarned. As Steven Levitsky and Daniel Ziblatt pointed out in their widely read 2018 book, *How Democracies Die*, there is nothing in the U.S. Constitution or in American political culture to immunize the American people against a democratic breakdown.[11] Moreover, any such breakdown was not going to be announced by the ring of a gong. If democracy eroded, it would happen slowly but impactfully. In their recent book, *Tyranny of the Minority*, Levitsky and Ziblatt extended their argument more specifically to blame the American Constitution for allowing minorities routinely to thwart majorities. For allowing systemic impediments such as the electoral college and gerrymandering in the extreme.[12]

Over the last couple of decades many reasons have been given for the decline of democracy. In fact, the more obvious its palpable precariousness, the more the reasons proliferated. Here are some of the most persuasive. First is the diminishment of trust in democratic governments and their attendant institutions, especially though not exclusively in the United States. Second is the worldwide weakening of democratic norms and the concomitant rise of isms such as nationalism and populism. Third is the rise in the number of illiberal democracies, in which elections take place but are rigged, in which civil liberties are scarce, and in which corruption is rampant. Fourth is what Shoshana Zuboff termed "the knowledge coup," in which mega tech companies such as Meta, Alphabet, and Amazon became empires of their own, rivaling in power democratically elected governments.[13] Fifth is what political scientist Tom Nichols has called "the narcissism pandemic."[14] He refers here not to narcissism in leaders but to narcissism in followers, ordinary people who are much preoccupied with themselves and little occupied with the welfare of everyone else.

Finally is what in 2012 I referred to as "the end of leadership." In my book of that title, I described the historical trajectory in which over the last several hundred years, starting especially with the Enlightenment, leaders have grown weaker and followers stronger.[15] In fact, the recent rise of strongmen around the world, political leaders who exert complete control or try to, is a product of the end of leadership. The more political leaders are threatened by their followers, the more leaders of countries other than robust democracies tighten their grip on their people.

Arguably the single most important reason for the decline or crisis of democracy is the inequality that has been a hallmark of democracies in the late twentieth and early twenty-first centuries. I refer to the extreme and still growing inequality of opportunity and, in consequence, in income and wealth. These inequalities impinge obviously on other inequalities, such as those of class, gender, and, above all, race. In the United States, on which I focus in the next section, the inequalities have become so extreme as to raise fundamental questions about the system itself. Questions about capitalism—about whether, as Friedman had it, capitalism and freedom are not only *not* inextricable but even compatible. As economist Anat Admati summarized the problem, "the forces of 'free-market capitalism' have undermined and overwhelmed democratic institutions, leading to intertwined crises in both capitalism and democracy."[16] No wonder several smart books have been written in recent years "noticing that the relationship between democracy and capitalism has gone haywire."[17]

The United States we now know is in good company. There is a "well-established global pattern of democratic backsliding" that is the consequence of leaders having gone from good to bad and then from bad to worse—and of followers putting up with whatever their leaders did.[18] Trouble is that while the "global pattern" illuminates the problem, it does not address it.

Capitalism in Question

In the United States, on which I focus in this section, the disparities between the rich (including the super-rich and the mega-rich) and everyone else have widened in recent decades and then widened some more. The progression has been relentless, to the point of becoming offensive and then to many, if not most, infuriating. This headline, from the *Wall Street Journal* on May 16, 2022, is typical: "Pay Packages for CEOs Rise to Record Level." It was the sixth straight annual such record. Along similar lines, in 2022 *Forbes* again published a World's Billionaires List. It had grown to an astonishing 2,668 names. Moreover, as French economist Thomas Piketty has pointed out, usually the super-rich get still richer. "Past a certain threshold," he wrote, "all large fortunes, whether inherited or entrepreneurial in origin, grow at extremely high rates, regardless of whether the owner of the fortune works or not."[19]

It's the unfairness that rankles. For the rampant inequalities reflect not just the American economy gone askew but American politics as well. Politics that more than before are fueled by big money, by dark money, and by a system of campaign financing that other liberal democracies find laughable if not scandalous.

America's political divides, its culture wars, its economic uncertainties, and its financial insecurities go a long way toward explaining ills that include rises in disinformation and misinformation; rises in nationalism and populism; rises in racism and hate crimes; and rises in restiveness, restlessness, and resentments, especially among those who feel they've been left behind. The increase in the numbers of hate crimes is indicative. In 2021, America's sixteen largest cities saw a 44 percent jump in these sorts of offenses, with the trend continuing and even accelerating into 2022. Groups singled out for attack included but were not limited to Black Americans, Jewish Americans, and Asian Americans. Reports of hate crimes against Asian Americans increased fully 343 percent from 2020 to 2021.[20] Reports of hate crimes against Jews in New York increased 41 percent in 2022 from the year before.[21]

Ironically, policies that would at least start to address the insidious inequalities would be easy enough to implement. For example, while the idea of imposing a wealth tax (a higher income tax rate) on the richest Americans and the richest American companies triggers sharply opposing views among the political and financial elite, it does not do the same among the public. President Donald Trump strongly opposed a wealth tax and labeled it socialist, and "few of the super-rich seem to think about paying tax as anything other than a personal assault."[22] In contrast, progressives such as Senators Bernie Sanders and Elizabeth Warren have long supported such legislation. Meanwhile, there is considerable consensus among the American people: they clearly and consistently side with Sanders and Warren.

Most Americans favor proposals that have the rich paying more. A 2020 Reuters/Ipsos poll found that nearly two-thirds of respondents supported the proposition that the more people had—especially those at the top—the more they should pay and the more they "should contribute an extra share of their total wealth each year to support public programs." Moreover, this was a view not confined to Democrats. While support for the idea among Democrats was stronger, at 77 percent, 53 percent of Republicans felt the same.[23] Still, because the U.S. government is in important ways in disrepair, passing legislation that even a great majority of the American people favor—think gun control—has become difficult and in many cases impossible.

Given that the systems of democracy and capitalism are stuck, it's no surprise that as the disparities have continued to escalate, the furies have started to dominate. Even mainstream publications such as the *New York Times* now have editorials with titles such as "The Tax Pirates Are Among Us." They point out that "generations of policymakers haven't shown much interest" in getting everyone to pay their fair share.[24] Moreover, who would deny that "dramatic increases in executive remuneration since around 1990 have contributed to the sense of unfairness and to spite"?[25] Astronomically high incomes are seen as a reflection not of achievement but of overweening power and unmitigated greed.

In part the furies have been fueled by the increase in information. We know more now than we used to about how much the rich are getting away with. For example, in 2021 ProPublica revealed that it had obtained "a vast cache of IRS information" showing that billionaires many times over such as Jeff Bezos, Elon Musk, and Warren Buffett had paid shockingly low federal taxes for years—and sometimes had paid not a dime. In 2007 Jeff Bezos (by then already a millionaire many times over) paid nothing in federal income taxes. In 2018 Elon Musk, soon to become the richest or second-richest man in the world, similarly paid the Internal Revenue Service nothing. And in recent years others among the fabulously and famously wealthy—such as Michael Bloomberg, Carl Icahn, and Donald Trump—essentially did the same. Taken together, ProPublica claimed, the information it acquired demolished "the cornerstone myth of the American tax system: that everyone pays their fair share, and the richest Americans pay the most. The IRS records show that the wealthiest can—perfectly legally—pay income taxes that are only a tiny fraction of the hundreds of millions, if not billions, their fortunes grow each year."[26]

Information and commentary such as these raise important questions. For example, in the current political climate, can capitalism even begin to level the playing field? What more precisely is the relationship between the fraying of democracy and the failures of capitalism? And why have the American people supported "generations of policymakers" who have not just allowed inequity to increase but encouraged it? Let's be clear: *America's political leaders have enabled America's corporate leaders to get what in many cases is a free ride. And America's corporate leaders have enabled America's political leaders to get what in many cases is a free ride. Of course, for leaders to be ineffective, unethical, or both requires followers who tolerate or even support them.*

Not for nothing did the Council on Foreign Relations decide in 2021 to try to identify threats to "democracies around the world and outline steps that [people] in the United States and other countries can take to reverse the erosion of democratic norms and values."[27] And despite heartening evidence that in recent decades childhood poverty has been significantly reduced, a report published in 2021 by the Children's Defense Fund nevertheless concluded that millions of Americans were failing to participate in the prosperity that capitalism is supposed to generate: "Today's median Black family owns $3,600—just 2 percent of the median white family's wealth. The median Latino family owns $6,600—only 4 percent of that of the median white family."[28]

The pandemic exacerbated inequalities—again, wealth especially—not only domestically but globally. Everywhere the already quite wealthy were the greatest beneficiaries of policies intended to mitigate the effects of the pandemic. Put directly, in most countries COVID-19 widened still further the gap between the rich and the poor. It should be noted, though, that other developed countries, notably in Europe, perform better on equality measures than does the United States. Due to the greater redistribution of wealth between the top 10 percent and the bottom 50 percent, Western European countries continue to lead on equity in income. The United States, meantime, shows "a significant rise in the concentration of incomes, unseen in other countries."[29] Small wonder that *Financial Times* columnist Rana Foroohar worriedly wrote in 2023 that overweening corporate power had become a "kitchen table topic in America."[30]

To understand why inequality is so much worse in the United States than it is in Western Europe, we need to take a second look at America's corporate leaders, specifically CEOs who reap humongous benefits from the chasm in pay between them and those in their employ. If you believe in even a semblance of fairness, the numbers are awful. As journalist Peter Eavis put it, "even in a gilded age for executive pay," 2020 was a "blowout year."[31] Eight of America's top-earning executives earned more than $100 million—but more to the point was the gap between superiors and their subordinates, between leaders and their followers. In 2022 the ratio of pay between a CEO and a typical worker soared to 399 to 1, the highest on record.[32] In the forty years between 1978 and 2018 CEO pay rose an astounding 1,007.5 percent, while during the same period the rise in pay for the average American worker was a puny 11.9 percent.[33]

With the wealth gap getting greater with every passing year, two more points particularly pertain.[34] The first is that philanthropy is not an equalizer. Philanthropy is not tantamount to changing the system. One could even argue it contributes to preserving it. Bill Gates has become emblematic of the ultra-rich philanthropist who works hard to benefit the planet. For example, Gates and his former wife, Melinda French Gates, spend billions of dollars each year (and have done so for years) to fight disease and poverty not only at home but abroad. Much better, obviously, than not. But in addition to the personal and political issues raised by the fact of two people having so much money and so much power, there are systemic issues. For example, when wealthy people donate money they can take a deduction on their federal income tax return—thereby they contribute less to our national coffers. Additionally, huge philanthropies sometimes are impediments. Precisely because of its enormous size, the Bill and Melinda Gates Foundation dominates the global health landscape, not always a good idea, especially when it impinges on local decision-making.

A second important point is that extreme inequity in wealth and income is tied to extreme inequity in power. I refer here specifically (though not only) to the massive difference in power between corporate employers and their employees. It's a syndrome for which Amazon became for a time the emblem. Amazon is either the largest or second-largest private employer in the United States.[35] So it matters that the company was long known for fostering an "ultracompetitive workplace where employees were obsessively measured against one another and encouraged to trample their way to the top."[36] Nor was Amazon in any other way generous—it was as stingy in its pay and benefits as in its working conditions. In striking contrast, its founder and longtime CEO, Jeff Bezos, became world-famous for being, among other things, one of the world's richest people (or, depending on the price of Amazon stock, *the* richest).

Amazon became, in short, the archetype of what critics of capitalism were angriest about. Hubert Joly, former chairman and CEO of Best Buy, is one of the few leaders in corporate America who has spoken up and spoken out on this issue. For years Joly has argued that American capitalism needs to be fixed. It needs to end profit maximization at all costs, restore the social contract between employers and their employees, and develop "an approach to business that takes human dignity as a starting point."[37]

But Joly's is an uphill battle. Even during the pandemic, Amazon continued to track every minute of warehouse shifts.[38] No wonder its workers got fired in humongous numbers—and no wonder its workers quit in humongous numbers. It got so bad that Bezos's announced departure as CEO was accompanied by a bit of a turnaround. For whatever reasons—among them, no doubt, the increasingly bad publicity and the threat of unionization—toward the end of his tenure as CEO he finally made a few concessions. Bezos was now committed, he announced in April 2021, to having Amazon become "Earth's best employer." What exactly this meant remains to be seen. Still, the company promised to install some new safety initiatives and implement some new diversity plans. Moreover, raises were announced, such as in an Amazon warehouse in New York City, one of the most expensive places in the country in which to live. How much was the raise? Hourly wages were increased by 50 cents.

To say that democracy is in decline and capitalism is in question is not to say this decline is irreversible or that the question is unanswerable. Most observers considered the results of America's 2022 midterm elections a sign of democratic life. And one could argue that at the top of President Joe Biden's initial agenda was to restore both the resiliency of liberal democracy and the functionality of market capitalism. Still, it did not take long for him to realize how difficult this would be, even after the pandemic had been largely vanquished and even after he had scored major legislative victories. For we live in a time in which we who live in liberal democracies, especially the United States, chew up our leaders, especially political leaders at the national level. Because our level of skepticism is high and our level of cynicism even higher, and because our national discourse is coarse and our social media even coarser, we make it hard for them to succeed. Young people have become so estranged that at best only half of them vote, and many do not even identify with capitalism.[39] In a recent poll more college students called themselves socialists than capitalists.[40] To say that capitalism has lost its sheen is, in short, a failure for which the leadership class is largely responsible.

Here is an extreme example of what's gone wrong. More than one-quarter of the world's billionaires live in the United States. Sometimes we know what they are thinking and doing. But mostly we do not. Mostly we have no idea of the impact they have because they deliberately engage in "stealth politics." As one of the authors of a book titled *Billionaires and Stealth Politics* framed the problem: "What we see basically is a class of people who have more money than God, who are very politically active in relatively unknown ways and who we have reasons to believe have been politically influential and have used their political influence in ways that don't really serve the interests or preferences of what most Americans want."[41] Stealth politics are often conducted at the state and local levels, where many important issues are decided without scrutiny by the national media, and where dark money plays an outsized role.

It's time, then, to acknowledge the obvious. America's leaders have failed in two critical ways. They have failed to sustain American democracy by better maintaining trust in government. And they have failed to sustain American capitalism by better maintaining trust in business. There are, of course, countless exceptions to these general rules. There are smart, honest, and hardworking public officials. And there are smart, honest, and hardworking corporate executives. But far too many political leaders have a lust for power, which explains why they enable the palpable decline of democracy. And far too many business leaders have a lust for money, which explains why they enable the palpable inequality of capitalism.[42]

Additionally, they collaborate. By working together implicitly or explicitly, political and business leaders are equally to blame for weakening the American edifice and undermining the American experiment. By failing year after year to fix what's broken, both contribute to America's political stresses and economic strains. One of the most obvious ways in which they are yoked is through the huge sums of money now needed to fill campaign coffers. The problem can be traced to the Supreme Court's 2010 decision in *Citizens United v. Federal Election Commission*, which freed corporations to fund without limits political candidates and campaign committees that meet just a single criterion: they promise to do the industry's bidding.[43]

Rana Foroohar has pointed out that while America's "economic illness," including high inequality and economic insecurity, is often blamed on bankers, the truth is that politicians on both sides of the aisle are also responsible. Specifically, she calls out "government leaders, policymakers, and regulators" who care more about "markets operating smoothly" than about the general welfare.[44] It's why leaders in government and business—both part of the problem—must both be part of the solution. As Jonathan Levy argued in his recent book, *Ages of American Capitalism*, "to repair the broken link between capitalism and democracy, what politics must do is get out in front of capital at the beginning of the economic process, in order to reshape its end."[45]

None of this is to say that followers are exempt from blame. While leaders in government and business have let us down, we the American people have let ourselves down. We contribute to the decline of democracy and the inequalities of capitalism by being insufficiently interested in and informed about civics, not much committed to the ideal of the common good, and passive citizens instead of active ones. For example, just over half of Americans know there are three branches of government.[46] Just over half of Americans can answer basic foreign policy questions.[47] Just 20 percent of Americans trust the government to "do the right thing" always or most of the time.[48] And though voter turnout has increased in recent years, it remains low compared with many other countries, including most Western democracies.[49] We have become increasingly self-interested and decreasingly public-interested. (Christopher Lasch's seminal 1979 book, *The Culture of Narcissism*, remains depressingly relevant.) We have become astonishingly tolerant of too many lies and too much money. We have gotten caught in the vise of toxic technologies.[50] And we have become inured to public discourse that is mean and mean-spirited; to fractured government; to divisions between races, classes, and genders; and to a leadership class so rich and powerful it seems as out of touch as it is out of reach.

The United States' descent from reasonably healthy democracy to measurably less healthy democracy, and from reasonably equitable capitalist state to measurably less equitable capitalist state, has been gradual. Nevertheless, it's been perceptible. Increasingly the United States has separated itself from countries such as Germany and France, in which public and private sector leaders more consciously collaborate to achieve social goals.

By many measures the United States continues to thrive and even to excel. Still, it's impossible to be a sentient American over the age of, say, forty, without a visceral as well as intellectual grasp of how the quality of life in America has diminished in recent decades: the crumbling of public works, the proliferation of mass shootings, the poor performance of schools. The reasons are multiple. But they certainly include too many leaders and too many followers who have stood by and done nothing as good became bad and bad became worse.

2

Followership and Leadership in the Twenty-First Century

After the worst of the pandemic was over, some employers (leaders) told some employees (followers) to get back to work—*in the workplace*. Some employees said fine. They were good with it. But others said not so fine. Having gotten used to working remotely from wherever they chose, usually though not always from home, they found they liked it. They found they had no interest whatsoever in returning to the not-so-good old days, which in most cases meant returning to the office five days a week, seven hours or so a day, in addition to what often was a long commute. So they said no, subordinates refusing to do what their superiors told them to do. It was primarily for this reason that more American workers quit their jobs in 2021 than at any other time in at least twenty years. A survey conducted by Prudential Financial confirmed that fully one-quarter of respondents said post-pandemic they would look for a new and better job, with many citing work–life balance among their top priorities.[1] The phenomenon became known as "the great resignation" or "quiet quitting."

There was more than one reason so many employees gave so many employers an ultimatum: *greater flexibility or I'm out*. Still, their attitudes were indicative. While leaders still have the most power and, given the positions they hold, the most authority, followers have more influence in the present than they did in the past. They—followers, stakeholders—are why Jeff Bezos and the company he led, Amazon, underwent a conversion from notoriously bad employer to, he insisted, "Earth's best employer."

Leadership and followership are like everything else: they change. Leadership is not what it was twenty years ago any more than it is what it was two hundred years ago. The same holds for followership. In fact, it's precisely because followers have changed that leaders have had no choice but to change along with them. It's also why leaders going from bad to worse is inseparable from followers going from bad to worse, even when they do so reluctantly.

Because followers in democracies have become increasingly entitled and emboldened, leaders in democracies now have one of two choices. To keep followers in line they must either be more oppressive and repressive than they were even a decade ago, as is the case in autocracies. Or, as is the case in democracies, they must pull back and accommodate to the new reality—in the workplace, for example, the changing balance of power between employers (leaders) and their employees (followers). Leaders must give their followers at least a little more leeway, a little more of a voice, a little more room to breathe.

Changes in how we think, in what we believe, and in how we behave do not happen overnight. They are gradual. Moreover, explanations of why they happen are invariably complex, not simple. Still, in the Western world it's easy enough to point to the Enlightenment as the originator and still primary explicator of our changing conceptions of leadership and followership.[2] Enlightenment thinkers such as John Locke, Montesquieu, and Mary Wollstonecraft, all of whom sought to curtail the powerful for the benefit of the powerless, are key to understanding the revolutionary upheavals of that period, especially in the late eighteenth century. The American and French Revolutions—and documents such as the American Declaration of Independence—were based on the proposition that those in positions of power and authority had to be brought down at least a notch, at least, while those who were not had to be brought up at least a notch, at least. Now everyone was entitled, in theory, to life, liberty, and the pursuit of happiness. Now the primary purpose of government was, in theory, to protect these entitlements.

The nineteenth and twentieth centuries were more of the same: the weak pushing on the strong. Whether slaves or serfs, workers, women, colonized peoples, or queer people, every one of these previously oppressed populations pressed the privileged to give them what they had come to believe they were owed. The rights revolutions of the 1960s and '70s—civil rights, women's rights, gay rights, even animal rights—were emblematic of the trend. And they were a reminder that shifts in power between leaders and followers are part of a timeless process, with the utopian, egalitarian endpoint remaining always out of reach.

In the second and third decades of the twenty-first century the pressures exerted by those at the bottom on those at the top continued unabated. Large numbers of Black Americans participating in newly revitalized social justice movements, especially after the murder of George Floyd. Large numbers of

women embracing the #MeToo movement, some generally, others specifically to press claims against men they accused of sexual assault, abuse, or harassment. And in the wake of changes in the law as well as in the culture, such
as the legalization of gay marriage, transgender individuals coming out of the
dark and into the light. Each of these is evidence of the evolution to which
I allude: the previously nearly entirely powerless taking on the previously
nearly entirely powerful. Nor is this phenomenon of follower empowerment
limited to any one county or region of the world. Harvard professor Erica
Chenoweth has calculated that "worldwide, we're living in a time where we've
seen more revolutionary movements using protest and nonviolent action
more generally . . . than we've seen at any other time in the past 120 years."[3]
This is not to say that these movements and protests are always successful; far
from it. Still, they are part of twenty-first-century political life.

Notwithstanding the inevitable fits and starts—such as, in the United
States, the Supreme Court's reversal in 2022 of the right of all American
women to get an abortion—the implications of the increased impact of
followers on leaders have been profound. This applies, obviously in different
ways, to both democracies and autocracies.

In the classroom I, the instructor, the professor, am now judged by,
evaluated by, my students. In the workplace leaders and managers are now
judged by, evaluated by, not only their leaders and managers but also their
peers and subordinates. Moreover, now when we want an opinion or recommendation, we are as likely to turn to our equals as to experts. Want to see a
movie? For a recommendation or suggestion, might as well ask a friend or
check out Rotten Tomatoes. Want to eat at a good Italian restaurant? For a
recommendation or suggestion, might as well check out Yelp or TripAdvisor.
No need anymore for experts—peers are in, authority figures such as professional reviewers are out.

Think of how museums have changed. In the old days, up to five or ten
years ago, American museums were led by their directors. It was they who,
along with their boards and their team, were responsible for the day-to-day
management of the museum and for determining its strategic direction. That
was then. Now things are different. Just like other American leaders, museum
directors are expected now to follow the lead of their clients and customers,
their constituents, and their communities.

- In 2021 New York City's Guggenheim Museum began proactively to
  reach out to people with disabilities.

- In 2021 the Speed Art Museum in Louisville, Kentucky, featured an exhibition devoted to the memory of Breonna Taylor, a woman who was shot dead in her bed by local police.
- In 2021, the National Gallery of Art in Washington, D.C., announced it had changed its leadership team from being 100 percent white to being half people of color.
- In 2021 the Philadelphia Museum of Art concluded a major renovation and expansion. The museum's director, Timothy Rub, said the new design would make the museum an even "more integral part of the community it serves."
- In 2021 the newly appointed director of the Toledo Museum of Art, Adam Levine, announced a total overhaul of the museum's strategic plan. His intention, he said, was to ensure that its collection represented "the demographic makeup of the country." Levine wanted people who came to the museum to feel a "sense of comfort and psychological safety."[4]

The explanations for this democratization are not limited to changes in the culture and the law. They also include changes in technology. Changes in culture and technology are the two most important explicators of why we are where we are now. Changes in culture *entitled* everyone who wanted a voice to have one. Changes in technology *enabled* everyone who wanted to have a voice to have one.

Changes in technology tend to be fast, especially now. We saw this again in early 2023 when ChatGPT was overtaken by GPT-4 seemingly overnight. Changes in culture, however, tend to be slow. Only years later did we notice, for example, how extreme has been the change in attitude toward people in positions of authority. Whether in the street or in the classroom, in small groups or in large organizations, in education or in religion, in the public sector or in the private sector, or even in the military, we now recognize a dramatic decline in respect for authority as being everywhere in evidence. The rights revolutions of the 1960s and '70s accelerated this trend; even the ostensible return to law and order under President Richard Nixon did not reverse a process that was hastened by, among other things, the largest and longest antiwar movement in American history.

Changes in culture and technology additionally explain why the differences between democracies and autocracies are greater now than they were ten to fifteen years ago. Democracies allowed, maybe even encouraged, the cultural and technological evolutions/revolutions to become entrenched in ways that were largely unfettered. Autocracies, in contrast, did not. Increasingly they clamped down on changes in culture, especially if those changes threatened the government or party in power, and increasingly they clamped down on changes in technology, especially if those changes threatened the government or party in power.

China's control of the internet is now the most stringent and sophisticated in the world, as is President Xi Jinping's use of technology to control the Chinese people. Russia too has become increasingly repressive, especially but not exclusively since the start of the war in Ukraine. In 2011 and 2012 social media facilitated large protests across Russia, particularly in Moscow. Since those disruptions, President Vladimir Putin came down far harder on his opponents, and he tightened the government's control of the internet. Of course, once the Russian parliament ceased to be a fully independent body, "it became easy for the Kremlin to pass laws and regulations to grant itself sweeping powers to control the digital domain."[5] As further evidence of Putin's tightening iron grip, his archenemy and single most prominent opponent, Alexei Navalny, has been poisoned and repeatedly imprisoned.

Followership in the Twenty-First Century

Before we liberal democrats celebrate the distinction between democracy and autocracy, we should be clear: the extreme democratization to which I refer—which was and still is enabled by changes in culture and technology—is perhaps the main reason for what has been repeatedly called "the crisis of liberal democracy." The fact is that democratic governance has become increasingly problematic and more difficult. Why? Because followers have become addicted to giving leaders, especially political leaders, a hard time—no matter what they do or how well they perform. Additionally, everyone now wants to be a leader; no one now wants to be a follower. *What America and the West more generally are experiencing, then, is as much a crisis of followership as it is a crisis of leadership.* Followers are chronically recalcitrant, reluctant, or even refusing to follow. In the old days, when the United States government told the American people they had to get vaccinated, overwhelmingly the American people got vaccinated without so much as a word of protest. Now, as often as not, the self takes precedence over the state which is as disliked as distrusted, and self-interest takes precedence over public interest.

Nor is this peculiarly an American phenomenon. Here's an indicator of the tenuousness of leaders even in venerable liberal democracies. Margaret Thatcher was prime minister of the United Kingdom for eleven years (1979– 1990), and Tony Blair for ten years (1997–2007). David Cameron was prime minister for six years (2010–2016), but his immediate successors, Theresa May and Boris Johnson, lasted only three years each (2016–2019 and 2019– 2022). And Johnson's successor, Liz Truss, was totally humiliated by barely surviving six weeks in office. She then was succeeded (in October 2022), by Rishi Sunak.

The U.S. Congress provides another example. For a decade at least it has been mostly an embarrassment, hopelessly outdated and frequently dysfunctional. The Senate used to be considered the "world's greatest deliberative body." Now it is afflicted by multiple ills, especially extreme partisanship, while at the same time being systemically stuck. How about this for an anachronism: two U.S. senators represent the just over 1 million people who reside in the state of Montana, and two U.S. senators represent the nearly 40 million people who reside in the state of California. Majority rule, anyone?

All too often, bipartisanship, cooperation, and compromise seem to be relics of yesteryear, with members of the House and Senate regularly refusing to go along to get along, to go along to get the work done. This has led to what sometimes seems paralysis. A proposal to create permanent legal status for immigrants brought to the United States as minors (a group known as the Dreamers) would pass overwhelmingly if Congress would only agree to have an up-or-down vote. But as columnist William Galston pointed out, for years neither party has let such a bill even reach the floor.[6] Similarly with gun control. In the wake of the 2018 school shooting at Marjory Stoneman Douglas High School in Florida, in which seventeen people were killed, fully 97 percent of Americans said they supported requiring background checks for all gun buyers.[7] But has Congress managed to pass even this single, modest gun control law? It has not. Though most Americans would welcome more agreement between Democrats and Republicans on this issue, as on many others, their elected officials seem more interested now in their own political well-being than in playing well with others.

Congress reflects Americans' attitude toward followers more generally. In short, being a leader is good, being a follower is bad. In part because of the approximately fifty-year-old leadership industry, which fuels our fixation on developing leaders, followers are devalued and even debased. We assume that being a leader is being successful. We assume that being a follower is being unsuccessful, or at least less successful. In the twenty-first century this message threads through American society. For example, the academy is replete with courses on leadership and virtually devoid of courses on followership.

The inattention to and lack of respect for followers is evident in the dramatic decline in the number of programs on civics, specifically in courses and curricula intended not so much to develop good leaders as to produce good followers. Responsible citizens. No wonder so many Americans cannot name the three branches of government. And no wonder so many Americans no longer trust either the federal government or the men and women who lead it. In 2021, only about one-quarter of Americans said they trusted the government in Washington to do what is right "just about always" (2 percent) or "most of the time" (22 percent).[8] (By 2022 the latter figure had dropped even further.) This is in contrast to when the National Election Study began asking about trust in government, in 1958. Then things were different. Then more than three times as many Americans trusted the federal government to do the right thing.[9]

In theory, Americans agree that participating in civic life is essential to sustaining their democracy. But what do they do—what do we do—to make this happen? Not much. Civics courses in grades K–12 have become less frequent, while leadership courses have become more frequent. The result? Lower levels of civic knowledge and skills. Lower levels of civic values and dispositions. And lower levels of civic behaviors.[10] Because Americans, like nationals of all countries, need a common cause, a shared narrative, and a conversation that is civil and respectful, obsessing about leaders at the expense of followers is costly. It fuels our fractiousness.

Democracy has been in decline, and capitalism has been in question, precisely because of this imbalance. On the one hand, followers have become much more important. But on the other hand, we followers are more widely ignored because in the main we do not tap into the power that could be ours if we made it ours. As the dramatic decline of unions in America testifies (despite a very modest resurgence in the recent past), follower power is uninformed and unorganized. People lack community. We are more divided than united. We vent online, as opposed to flexing our figurative muscles in ways that are productive. We tear down individuals and institutions, but we fail to capitalize on our collective clout.

Of course, there are important distinctions among democracies. The year 2023 saw enormous, extended (weeks and then months on end) demonstrations by infuriated followers in two of them: France and Israel.

A large majority of French people objected vociferously and sometimes even violently to President Emmanuel Macron's decision to raise the retirement age from sixty-two to sixty-four. And in Israel, a small country, hundreds of thousands of people took to the streets for months to protest Prime Minister Benjamin Netanyahu's plan to overhaul the Israeli judiciary.

Enormous, continuous, protests like these are precisely why autocracies have been proliferating—and getting more stringent. The "heady days of the so-called third wave of democratization" in the Middle East ended because leaders in the Middle East, for instance in Egypt, concluded that the only way for them to keep their followers in line was to threaten them if they resisted or refused. Thus the dreams of the Arab Spring ended in nightmares. In Syria, to take an extreme example, President Bashar al-Assad did what he had to do to hold on to power—his people, his country, be damned. It is estimated that about half a million people died because of Syria's civil war, and that about half of all Syrians had been displaced from their homes.

For years the Middle East was the rule, not the exception, when it came to autocracies. Autocrats nearly everywhere tightened their grip on power, while massive street protests in, for example, Belarus, Hong Kong, and Myanmar met with violent repression. Similarly, as political scientist Pippa Norris pointed out in 2021, illiberalism rose in "Brazil under President Jair Bolsonaro, in Hungary under Prime Minister Viktor Orban, and in the Philippines under President Rodrigo Duterte."[11] (By the end of 2022, Bolsonaro had been voted out of office and Duterte had retired from presidential politics. But it was not at all clear that in either Brazil or the Philippines anything fundamental had changed.)

In short, the receding of democracy and the progression of autocracy were organic responses to followers becoming more demanding. For a quarter century Russian human rights lawyer Ivan Pavlov was left essentially alone by the regime, relatively free to protect scientists, journalists, and others in the opposition from being swept up by the security state. But at the start of Putin's third presidential term, in 2012, which coincided with growing Russian unrest, things changed. Whereas Putin once saw Pavlov as an adversary, he now saw him as an enemy. In 2021, after Pavlov agreed to defend the most politically threatening of Putin's opponents, Navalny, Pavlov was himself arrested.[12]

The willingness of autocrats to exert political pressure, sometimes in the extreme, obviously has had consequences. One of them is that autocracies have given democracies a run for their money because followers in democracies are difficult to lead and manage, while followers in autocracies are much easier to handle. Political scientist Yascha Mounk made this point, noting that "dictators have learned to use digital tools to oppress opposition movements in sophisticated ways," and so the results of their oppression often have been not failure but success. By suppressing dissent, dictators have free rein, which has led in some cases, most impressively in China, to a resurgence of authoritarianism. As Mounk put it, "The story of the last two decades is not just one of democratic weakness; it is also one of authoritarian strength."[13]

What is obvious is that leaders in democracies follow their followers in ways that leaders in autocracies do not. Largely this is a good thing. We want leaders to listen to their followers. But we need to be clear-eyed. There are costs to weaker leadership that stronger leadership does not incur. Moreover, in the end we want leaders able to lead because we *need* leaders able to lead. Too much follower empowerment at the expense of too little leader empowerment makes people feel insecure, uncertain, rudderless. As Sigmund Freud observed in the early 1920s, groups seek stability; they need it, they want it. Freud went even further, writing, maybe warning, that we have an "extreme passion for authority," a "thirst for obedience."[14]

Leadership in the Twenty-First Century

There's no need for further comment on leaders in autocracies at this point in the book. I already made clear that to attain and then to sustain control over their followers, autocratic leaders must clamp down, generally hard. But what about leaders in democracies? How can they lead? How can they get followers to go along—followers who are so much coarser and more clamorous now than they were in the past?

The answers to questions like these are neither obvious nor easy, and they depend of course on the context. Leaders in business are different from leaders in government, and leaders at Volvo face issues that are different from those facing leaders at Ford. Still, all democratic leaders face some of the same challenges, perhaps foremost among them the changing relationship between leaders and followers. One of the most striking examples of a clueless, hapless twenty-first-century leader—someone who completely failed to appreciate that times were changing—was British prime minister David

Cameron. He failed to understand that whatever his power and authority were worth, they were worth much less than they used to be.

It was Cameron who was nearly single-handedly responsible for the debacle that was Brexit. Notwithstanding his own strong preference for having Great Britain remain in the European Union (EU), and although as prime minister he was not politically or constitutionally obligated to call for a referendum on Brexit, he did so anyway. It was Cameron's clever idea to put his leadership to the test by calling for what was effectively an up-or-down vote on his country's membership in the EU. He did so because he mistakenly believed that most voters would follow where he led. He thought he could secure a convincing majority for Great Britain remaining in the EU—apparently not even imagining that many of his followers might choose, on this all-important issue, *not* to follow.

The referendum on Brexit was held on July 23, 2016. The results of the vote were approximately 52 percent in favor of leaving the European Union, approximately 48 percent against. After the outcome of the referendum was announced, the prime minister was irretrievably humiliated. His resignation was effective immediately.

Though the long-term consequences remain still unknown, the costs incurred by Cameron's obtuseness could well be even higher in the future than they already have been. In 2023 Bloomberg estimated that Brexit was "costing the UK economy £100 billion a year ($124 billion), with the effects spanning everything from business investment to the ability of companies to hire workers."[15] The divorce proceedings—which involved between four and five years of painful, all-consuming negotiations—were wrenching in themselves.

Cameron's experience was evidence of how followers in liberal democracies have become a force with which leaders in liberal democracies must reckon. Donald Trump's fervid followers, his "base," were the bedrock on which his presidency stood. And they were the reason previously establishment, centrist Republicans were slavishly loyal to a man many if not most personally disliked and politically disrespected.

Follower power similarly explains why in the state of Massachusetts in 2021, nearly one-fifth of mayors chose not to run again.[16] Why in 2018 the U.S. Congress had the third-highest turnover rate in over forty years.[17] And why the turnover among America's CEOs has been high and getting higher. In January 2019, 219 CEOs stepped away from their posts, a striking 40 percent increase over the year before.[18] In October 2021 the number of CEO resignations was fully 54 percent higher than during the same month a year earlier.[19] Plus by 2022 it had become clear that CEOs were leaving their posts at younger ages and after shorter tenures.[20] Presidents of colleges and universities were similarly eager to get out—or similarly vulnerable to being pushed out. Not long before the COVID-19 pandemic struck, there appeared an article titled "Leadership Turnover Creates Surge in Search for College Presidents."[21] And in April 2022, after the worst of COVID was over, there was this article: "Riding the Wave of College Presidential Turnover."[22]

Finally, follower power explains this small but telling sequence of events. In 2022 New York University terminated its contract with a highly eminent professor of organic chemistry, Maitland Jones Jr. Why? Because large numbers of his students loudly objected to his being their instructor (82 out of his 350 students signed a petition against him). Why? Because they claimed Jones's course—widely considered a gateway to medical school—was too hard. The question of blame, or responsibility, does not concern us here. What does concern us is the overarching point. As the New York Times summarized it, "The entire controversy seems to illustrate a sea change in teaching, from an era when professors set the bar and expected the class to meet it, to the current more supportive, student-centered approach."[23] This particular change is indicative of a more general one—a change in the relationship in democracies between the supposedly powerful (leaders) and the supposedly powerless (followers).

None of this is to suggest that being a leader—a person in a position of authority—has lost its allure. Quite the contrary. The flourishing leadership industry is testimony to the fact that a lot of people pay a lot of money hoping to become a leader or to become a better leader than they already are. Rather, it is to point out that being a leader in the present appears to be considerably less rewarding than it was in the past. Not financially, obviously. Leaders in every sector of the economy, not just private companies, are being paid far, far more in the present than they were in the past—including presidents of colleges and universities. But rewards other than money have become harder to come by—and the job itself has become harder. In short, *the benefits of being a leader notably in liberal democracies have decreased, while the costs of being a leader notably in liberal democracies have increased.* Leadership has become less exalted an enterprise, one of the reasons leaders feel less obliged to behave well and more inclined to behave badly.

What, specifically, are the benefits that have vanished or been diminished? Some center on lifestyle, especially since leading in democratic systems has become more draining, more time-consuming, and more public. This while especially since the pandemic, more people are more eager to strike a balance between their lives inside the workplace and their lives outside. But some of the benefits that have vanished or been diminished relate to the decline of authority. Leaders just don't get the respect they used to. Their authority counts for little and sometimes nearly nothing.

Usually there is conflation and confusion around the three words "power," "authority," and "influence." I define "power" as A's capacity to get B to do what A wants, by any means necessary. I define "authority" as A's capacity to get B to do what A wants, because of the position that A holds or the credentials that A has. And I define "influence" as A's capacity to get B to do what A wants of B's own volition, because B has been persuaded by A to respond as A prefers. In each of these cases the leader (A) gets the follower (B) to do what the leader wants and intends. While the outcome is the same, the reason for the outcome, the explanation for why A prevailed over B, is different in each situation.[24]

These distinctions matter because in general leaders in democracies have less *power* than they used to. And because in general leaders in democracies have less *authority* than they used to. The implications of this are considerable. Because leaders have less power and authority now than before, they can no longer so easily punish their followers for not following—and they can no longer so easily reward them if they do follow. This puts a premium on leaders who are good at exercising *influence*—who are good at persuading their followers to go along of their own volition, or what the followers *think* is their own volition.

It's become routine for subordinates to in some way assess their superiors. This in itself is an important shift in the workplace dynamic between leaders and followers. When I first became a professor, I was never formally evaluated by my students. Moreover, in antediluvian times students called me Professor Kellerman, or maybe Dr. Kellerman. Those days are long gone. By the first and certainly second decades of the twenty-first century they were likely simply to call me by my first name, Barbara. This might seem a small thing, a trivial change. But it is not. This collapse of the distance between teacher and student—this leveling of the playing field between me (ostensibly the leader) and my pupils (ostensibly the followers)—is nothing short of an indication that we are living in a time in which power has been reduced and authority diminished.

Let's be clear: most leaders *like* having power and authority. For one thing, power and authority make it easier to lead, much easier. Having power and authority is also gratifying in itself. In general, people get pleasure from having more power as opposed to less. And in general, people get pleasure from being higher on the relevant ladder—whether it's the economic ladder, the social ladder, or the professional ladder—as opposed to lower. Suffice it to say, though most would not so admit, that leaders have good reason to lament the day when "command and control" went out and "flattened hierarchies" came in.

The other side of the coin is the costs incurred—the costs of leading in the present compared to the costs of leading in the past. Leading is harder now, and it's rougher. Leaders have become easy targets. Slings and arrows come at them from every direction, most frequently via social media, launched by those willing (and sometimes eager) to take them on or even take them down.

It was humiliating for the CEO of Royal Dutch Shell, Ben van Beurden, to have his company slapped with a court order forcing it to cut its carbon emissions. It was humiliating for the CEO of ExxonMobil, Darren Woods, to have shareholders vote to place on the board activists who had charged that the company was being put in mortal peril because of its continuing reliance on fossil fuels. (The vote was described as a "stunning defeat" for Woods.)[25] It was humiliating for the CEO of Starbucks, Howard Schultz, who had long played the progressive, to have to plead with his workers not to unionize— and then in 2023 be accused by the National Labor Relations Board of leading a company that had engaged in "egregious and widespread misconduct" to prevent unionization.[26] It was humiliating for the CEO of JPMorgan Chase, Jamie Dimon, to be slapped down by shareholders who resisted the board's proposal to give him a pay package they judged excessively high and undeserved. (The shareholder vote was nonbinding; nevertheless, it was at the time a stinging rebuke to both Dimon and the board.) It was humiliating for the CEO of Disney, Bob Chapek, to be kicked out of his post only to be immediately replaced by, of all people, his predecessor, Bob Iger.

Somewhat similar are the cases of the many leaders pushed out by followers emboldened by the #MeToo movement. In 2018 the *New York Times* calculated that at least two hundred prominent men had lost their jobs after public allegations by women of sexual harassment.[27] And at about the same time *The Atlantic* counted at least twenty-five candidates for office who ended their political campaigns after related charges.[28]

Nor was an accusation of blatant misconduct the sole criterion for severing a corporate connection. Especially for those at (or near) the top, the rules had not only tightened but changed. In 2019, Steve Easterbrook, CEO of McDonald's, was fired for having a relationship with a subordinate that by all accounts was consensual. The McDonald's board nevertheless concluded that Easterbrook had violated company policy by "dating or having a sexual relationship" with an employee with whom he had some sort of "reporting relationship."[29] And in 2022, Jeff Zucker, CNN's CEO, was pushed out, ostensibly for the same reason: for having a consensual relationship with one of his colleagues who, while technically a subordinate, was by all accounts a powerful executive in her own right.

In 2021 the *Wall Street Journal* featured an interview with Rich Lesser, described as a "CEO whisperer." Lesser, who was chief executive of Boston Consulting Group for nine years, made a career out of advising CEOs across America. What Lesser said to his clients echoes what I argue here. Three key points.

- Times have changed. Leading today is different from leading yesterday— it's more difficult. Lesser: "The CEOs I talk to have so much more on their minds" than they did "even five years ago." CEOs are "dealing with things that together have made it a much harder job than it was."
- Followers, stakeholders of every stripe, have become more entitled and emboldened. Lesser: in today's world, CEOs "have to have a learning mind-set, which means [they] have to be ready to listen to people."
- It's rough out there—leading in a democracy in the third decade of the twenty-first century is not for the fainthearted. Lesser: "Now you're managing trade-offs across multiple stakeholders, often in ways that are hard to read, often with intense scrutiny around what you say and do."[30]

Lesser was not addressing a general audience. He was speaking to leaders in business, those at the top of the corporate ladder in Western countries, especially the United States. He was cautioning them that leading in the third decade of the twenty-first century is different from how it was even five years ago, and more difficult. It requires new and different skill sets—and new and different mindsets.

The point, though, is a broader one. It is that leaders—*all* leaders—in democratic systems must change because followers in democratic systems have changed. All leaders must now "listen to people." And all leaders must now manage "trade-offs across multiple stakeholders." Who are these multiple stakeholders? They are us. They are people with different priorities, preferences, and passions—and, increasingly, the temerity to carp and withhold their support. They are those whom leaders must bring along if they want to lead—as opposed to running into a brick wall. Think of the school principal who not that long ago had only to say "do this" or "do that" and it was done, but who now must accommodate a whole host of stakeholders including parents, teachers, students, the public, the press, and angry anonymous voices on social media.

Followers then—ordinary people in democratic systems—have their own role to play. Precisely because they, we, have more power and influence than we used to, we must participate in making the machineries of democracy and the mechanisms of capitalism run smoothly. Whatever the demands, both leaders and followers need to be involved because both are not only invested in the outcomes, but implicated.

3

Making Meaning of Being Bad

What exactly do we mean when we say a leader is "bad"? For that matter, what exactly do we mean—or, more precisely, what do *I* mean, since hardly anyone thinks of followers as being either good or bad—when I say a follower is "bad"?

When I wrote the book *Bad Leadership*, I wrestled long and hard with the word "bad." It seemed so feeble, so mundane, more appropriate to describing a naughty child than a leader, not to speak of a leader like Hitler. So I looked for synonyms, words that were more interesting and evocative but which could similarly capture what I had in mind. To my consternation, I found that most of these were equally dreary. Synonyms for bad—such as "inferior," "poor," "inadequate," "substandard," and "deficient"—didn't quite cut it.

Then I went to descriptors that were more powerful because they were more precise. "Evil" certainly captures bad leaders such as Bosnian Serb general Ratko Mladic or Russian president Vladimir Putin, just as "corrupt" captures bad leaders such as Enron CEO Jeffrey Skilling and Philippine president Ferdinand Marcos and "intemperate" captures bad leaders such as Washington, D.C., mayor Marion Barry and Italian prime minister Silvio Berlusconi. The trouble is that these words are too precise. Saying that someone is evil, corrupt, or intemperate captures a certain type, which in some ways makes the label useful. But in other ways it does not. It is not useful if you are trying—as I was in *Bad Leadership*—to analyze the gamut of bad leadership. Because bad leadership had been, and still is, so little explored, what interested me about bad leadership was *all* bad leadership. Bad leadership—and now bad followership—in its various incarnations and manifestations.

So here I am again, back to "bad." "Bad" still seems best, the best of the several synonyms, because it is boundless. It is all-encompassing. "Bad" also seems best because its antonym, "good," is equally expansive, effectively infinite in its meanings. Childlike these words "bad" and "good" might be. But it cannot be claimed they are either elusive or evasive. To the contrary: they are simple, and they are clear. Both imply standards of behavior—which means they equally imply that these standards can be violated.

There are, however, three problems that inevitably arise when we deal with descriptors such as "good" and "bad." Moreover, these problems are not trivial.

The first is that humans are not widgets. They are flesh and blood, with hearts and minds, which makes them not simple things but complex beings. It is not, for example, uncommon for leaders to be bad in some ways and good in others. Leaders are not gods. They, like us, are mere mortals. This means they are a mix. Bad and good thread through leaders just as they thread through everyone else. President Richard Nixon will forever be saddled with the scandal that was Watergate. But in some ways, in some important ways, he was a good president, initiating and implementing what most would consider at least some good public policies at home and abroad. How then to assess Nixon in office? Do we shy away from judging him a bad leader because as president of the United States he did some good? Or do we flat out declare him a bad leader because what stands out, what he will most be remembered for, is not only his role in the war in Vietnam but also his role in Watergate, now shorthand for clandestine and often illegal activities engaged in by Nixon himself and by important members of his administration?

No question—it's complicated. But should these complexities preclude us from rendering judgment? Should they stop us from taking on critical, existential questions such as: How does bad leadership happen? What explains followers who go along with bad leaders? Why has bad leadership been so resistant to remediation? What if anything can be done to diminish this resistance?

I have long argued that we—especially but not exclusively those of us who claim to be leadership experts—have a professional and even moral obligation to take on questions like these. Bad leadership along with bad followership is a disease, a social disease still begging to be addressed. To be clearly identified and carefully codified, to be deconstructed and reconstructed so that someday it can be at least diminished, if not abolished. Think of bad leadership as a virus that has continued ceaselessly, perniciously, to infect. Why then do we continue, like robots, to tolerate it, to accept it as inevitable? Why have we been so helpless in the face of so serious and relentless a threat?

Viruses will not be stopped unless we try to stop them. To take on bad leadership and followership we must stare them in the face and face them down. We must not be intimidated. We must be willing to take on the seemingly impossible by walking on the dark side. *We must try harder than we have heretofore to stop, or at least to slow, what has been hurtful and even lethal to the human condition.* Where to begin? How to wrestle bad leadership and followership to the ground? In this book I provide one answer. I extract from the historical record stories about bad leadership/followership from which there is something to be learned.

The second problem in taking on bad leadership is that the word "bad" can and should be used in two entirely different ways. Leaders and followers can be bad because they are *ineffective*. Or they can be bad because they are *unethical*. (Sometimes they are both.) The point was driven home to me years ago when to a good-sized audience I said something I thought both obvious and inarguable. I said, "Hitler was a bad leader." When the time came for the audience to comment on my remarks, a man's hand shot up. It was clear he would take exception. He pointed out, correctly, that between January 1933 and September 1939, the pre–World War II period, when Hitler was in his prime as German chancellor, he and his followers were extremely unethical. But at the same time, they were extremely effective. The man was right; I was wrong. I was wrong to paint Hitler and his Nazi followers with a single brush. Their strengths and their weaknesses were far too nuanced and complex than the word "bad," if broadly applied, could begin to suggest. It was a mistake I never made again. From then on, I always made clear what I meant. Was the bad leader (follower) ineffective? Or was the bad leader (follower) unethical? Or both?

To see bad leadership and followership more clearly, picture them somewhere along two axes. The first is from effective to ineffective. The second is from ethical to unethical. Thus, a bad leader/follower can be, for example, somewhat ineffective or extremely ineffective. Similarly, a bad leader/follower can be ethical but ineffective, or effective but unethical, or both ineffective and unethical. Sometimes, though, it's not so simple—sometimes the two axes intersect. For example, it is possible for leaders/followers to be so ineffective as to be also unethical. President George W. Bush's decision in 2003 to invade Iraq is an example. Even the most strident of his detractors never accused Bush of being unethical. However, given his deeply flawed decision to go to war, succeeded by his deeply flawed execution of the war, it could reasonably be argued that his decision to intervene militarily in Iraq showed him to be not only an ineffective leader but also, because of the horribly high costs incurred, an unethical one.

Complexities such as these are among the reasons bad leadership and followership have been sidestepped. Delving into one or the other, not to speak of both, is daunting, a deep dive fraught with uncertainties and ambiguities, high risks of misunderstandings, and the dangers of fierce disagreements.

Which brings me to the third of the three thorny problems that bedevil bad leadership/followership: what I consider bad might not be what you consider bad. And, obviously, vice versa. There are occasions, though not many, on which there is near universal agreement on what is "bad." For example, a genocidal leader is usually thought bad. And a corrupt leader is usually thought bad. But in liberal democracies our conceptions of "bad" and "good"—especially our assessments of who is a good political leader and who is a bad one—tend to be so subjective as to be divisive.

I write as a citizen of what is generally thought of as a liberal democracy, the United States of America. And I write in the third decade of the twenty-first century. This is not to say that the assessments I make, the analyses I provide, necessarily would be different were I living in another liberal democracy. But they almost certainly would be different were I living content-edly in an autocracy. Similarly, this is not to suggest that my assessments and analyses would be different had I written this book five years ago. But they probably would have been different had I written this book fifty years ago, not to speak of five hundred years ago. The point is that, to a degree at least, bad leadership is subjective. It depends not only on who is rendering judgment but also on where and when judgment is being rendered.

For Americans, Donald Trump is the most striking recent example of a leader many deemed bad and many others considered good. He was, he is, a highly controversial figure. Tens of millions of Americans think him a splendid leader who was a splendid president. Tens of millions of other Americans think him a terrible leader who was a terrible president, the worst in American history. Opinions such as these reflect our histories, ideologies, personalities, attitudes, and opinions. Given the United States is arguably more divided now than it has been since the Civil War, our views of who is a good leader and who is a bad one naturally differ, sometimes in the extreme. This applies equally to bad followers, about whom I wrote in my recent book, *The Enablers: How Team Trump Flunked the Pandemic and Failed America*. But I am under no illusions. I recognize how different our judgments and assessments are, how "bad" is subjective, not objective.

What then is to be done about these strong differences of opinion, even in the values we hold? Students of leadership and followership essentially have two choices. The first is to remain neutral, which is in keeping with the current climate of political correctness. In fact, students and faculty in institutions of higher education are alert to the dangers of being cancelled because they gave an opinion. The leadership industry is somewhat similar. By avoiding the problem of bad leadership nearly entirely, it avoids taking a position on who is a bad leader or a bad follower. But avoidance gets us nowhere. Never will the leadership industry contribute to forestalling bad leadership unless and until it comes to grips with it.

Which brings us to the second alternative for those of us with an interest in leadership, an interest that extends to bad leadership. That is to address it head-on—to take on bad leadership/followership with all the energy and intelligence at our collective disposal. What exactly do I mean by addressing it head-on? What I am suggesting is that leadership learners, whether experts or novices, draw on subjects such as history, philosophy, psychology, political science, sociobiology, and neuroscience to seek answers to questions such as these: How does bad leadership happen? What motivates followers to follow bad leaders? Why has bad leadership been so resistant to remediation? What can be done to diminish the resistance?

Ineffective Leadership/Followership

In *Bad Leadership* I divided bad leadership/followership into seven different types.

> *Type 1: incompetent leadership*—the leader and at least some followers lack the will or skill (or both) to sustain effective action. Regarding at least one major leadership challenge, they are not able to create positive change. Nor, for that matter, are they able to sustain a satisfactory status quo.
>
> *Type 2: rigid leadership*—the leader and at least some followers are stiff and unyielding. Although they may be competent, they are unable or unwilling to adapt to new ideas, new information, or changing times.
>
> *Type 3: intemperate leadership*—the leader lacks self-control and is aided and abetted by followers who are unwilling or unable to intervene effectively.
>
> *Type 4: callous leadership*—the leader and at least some followers are uncaring or unkind. Ignored or discounted are the needs, wants, and wishes of most members of the group or organization, especially subordinates.

Type 5: corrupt leadership—the leader and at least some followers lie, cheat, or steal. To a degree that exceeds the norm, they put self-interest ahead of the interests of others.

Type 6: insular leadership—the leader and at least some followers minimize or disregard the health and welfare of "the other," those outside the group or organization for which they are directly responsible.

Type 7: evil leadership—the leader and at least some followers commit atrocities. They use pain as an instrument of power. The harm done to men, women, and children is severe rather than slight. The harm can be physical, psychological, or both.[1]

Three of the above types fall under the rubric of ineffective leadership: *incompetent*, *rigid*, and *intemperate*. Two other types fall under the rubric of unethical leadership: *corrupt* and *evil*. The two remaining types, *callous* and *insular*, are more difficult to categorize, though they are usually unethical. The point is that bad leaders and bad followers come in different shapes and sizes, which is why they have not only different incarnations but also different implications.

Ineffectiveness can be contextually determined. For example, a skill set may be applicable and functional in one context but inapplicable and dysfunctional in another. It's why the trait approach to leadership—which, anyway, is dated—is misplaced. Much-touted traits such as intelligence, compassion, and creativity could matter a lot in one context but much less in another. One of the more extreme examples of the importance of context to leadership is the man once known as "America's Mayor," Rudolph Giuliani. Before September 11, 2001, Giuliani was the not very popular mayor of New York City. Moreover, years later, he became in many circles a laughingstock, even a grotesque, having morphed into a pathetic if tireless defender of President Trump. But on September 11, 2001, in the immediate aftermath of the attack on the World Trade Center, and for months and even years thereafter, "America's Mayor" was a hero. Giuliani's leadership traits and skills were at the time, in the days, weeks, and months after the attack, perfectly suited to a city and indeed a nation in crisis.

Ineffective leaders are everywhere. Sometimes they are so obviously and extremely ineffective we wonder how they came to be leaders in the first place. And sometimes they're just ineffective enough to interfere with their own best-laid plans to create change or even to sustain stability. Moreover, leaders can be ineffective for several reasons. Some leaders lack education, experience, and/or expertise. Other leaders lack drive, energy, or the ability to focus. Still others are insufficiently clever, flexible, or emotionally intelligent, or they lack whatever the requisite attribute is. Leaders also can be ineffective in different ways—from miscalculation to mismanagement, from carelessness to callousness, from being too risk tolerant to being too risk averse. Leaders can be bad at mastering information, at coping with complexity, at minding the store, or at making decisions under conditions of uncertainty. They might be bad at managing change, managing conflict, managing crises, or managing themselves. Or they may be unwilling or unable to employ necessary and appropriate leadership strategies such as envisioning, prioritizing, communicating, educating, inspiring, persuading, mobilizing, organizing, coalition building, listening, adapting, getting information, managing, delegating, coordinating, negotiating, implementing—you name it.

Ineffectiveness is not about willful, deliberate wrongdoing. But ineffective leaders and their followers do not accomplish what they want and intend— or even sustain a satisfactory status quo.

Here is a glaring, indeed horrific, example of ineffective—and yes, arguably, also unethical—leadership enabled by ineffective followership: Dennis Muilenburg, former CEO of Boeing, and others at Boeing who, when things threatened to go wrong, and then did, should have intervened. In October 2018, a Boeing 737 Max jet crashed off the coast of Indonesia, killing 189 passengers and crew. A few months later, in March 2019, a second Boeing 737 Max crashed, this one also killing all on board, 157 passengers and crew. Muilenberg was left to explain the calamity, clean it up, and, insofar as possible, compensate for it.

Subsequent investigations revealed that even though the 737 Max had a potentially fatal flaw, it had been cleared to fly by the Federal Aviation Administration (FAA). No question, then, that the FAA shared blame for the two disasters. Its outrageous laxness, especially after the first of the two planes crashed, is inexcusable. Nevertheless, most of the responsibility for what happened rests with the company. More specifically, it rests with Muilenburg, who throughout his tenure at the top cultivated a company culture so intent on remaining competitive that safety was compromised. As Peter Robison, an expert on the two crashes, put it, "The sloppiness started at Boeing, in the early compromises of the plane's design, and then in the loose ends left dangling in the final days of development."[2]

To compete more efficiently and effectively with its main rival, Airbus, Boeing sent the FAA a safety assessment report riddled with errors. The problem was the 737 Max had a new flight system that could, under certain circumstances, change how the airliner handled. The system was unique to this aircraft, which explains why pilots who were insufficiently trained on it could be caught off guard by the possibility of a sudden, unfamiliar, and unmanageable descent. After the two disasters an incident report filed with a NASA database quoted a pilot who was familiar with the situation: "It was unconscionable that [Boeing], the FAA, and the airlines would have pilots flying an airplane without adequately training, or even providing available resources and sufficient documentation to understand the highly complex systems that differentiated this aircraft from prior models."[3]

By the end of 2019 it was evident that Muilenburg had been an ineffective leader not only while the 737 Max was in development but also during the months that followed the second crash. In December 2019, a *New York Times* headline read, "At Boeing, C.E.O.'s Stumbles Deepen a Crisis." By then the 737 Max had been grounded, but Muilenburg's leadership during this difficult period was in every way also badly lacking. Moreover, his repeated attempts to apologize for the two disasters were counterproductive. His expressions of regret were described as "clumsy" and as "prolonging Boeing's reputational pain."

Muilenburg's performance in the aftermath of the crashes was as it had been before then ineffective every which way—and arguably unethical in some ways. He left lawmakers irate, and families of victims who "repeatedly confronted him with posters of the dead" not only deeply saddened but also extremely angry. By the end of the year Muilenburg was finally out, fired by Boeing's board, which until that point had stood by him even as he tried and failed to stabilize the company. When it was all over, it was clear that the 737 Max crisis was by far the worst in Boeing's up to then largely distinguished 103-year history.

In his book on what happened at Boeing, *Flying Blind*, Robison identified several culprits in the calamitous sequence of events. Among them obviously were Muilenburg and the FAA. But there were also people who worked at Boeing (followers) who suspected or even knew the development of the 737 Max was being rushed and who therefore suspected or even knew the aircraft was risky at best and dangerous at worst. Last, though not least, was Boeing's board. Not only did the board not challenge Muilenburg after the first of the two 737 Max crashes, *but it chose the months between the two crashes to reward him handsomely*: "Two months after the [Indonesia] crash, it awarded him the highest pay of his tenure: $31 million, including a $13 bonus for performance."[4]

Robison wrote that Boeing was guilty of "malpractice." Moreover, in 2022 the Securities and Exchange Commission finally charged Boeing with having "put profits over people by misleading investors about the safety of the 737MAX."[5] But the malpractice, greed, and guilt were not Boeing's. Boeing is a company. It is an abstraction. Malpractice, greed, and guilt are not abstractions. They are real-world manifestations of the human condition—in this case, that of Muilenburg and his minions.[6]

Unethical Leadership/Followership

Unethical leadership would seem easy enough to define and describe. But it is not. Even the experts have trouble agreeing on what precisely is meant by so common a conception. In her edited volume *Moral Leadership*, the late Stanford Law School professor Deborah Rhode wrote that "by definition, moral leadership involves ethical conduct on the part of leaders, as well as the capacity to inspire such conduct in followers." But what is "ethical" conduct? And how are "moral" and "ethical" distinguishable? Or are they synonymous? Rhode noted that both "moral" and "ethical" imply a "commitment to right action." But the meaning of "right" remains opaque and, as noted earlier, it is entirely possible, if not probable, that your "right" is different from my "right." Interestingly, though she titled her book *Moral Leadership*, Rhode admitted that there was a "lack of consensus" on what the term even meant. She additionally acknowledged that it was precisely this "definitional incoherence" that continued to muddy the waters.[7]

The difficulties of reaching consensus on apparently commonplace words such as "moral" and "ethical," especially as they pertain to leadership, are, predictably, aggravated by differences in contexts and cultures. Retired business school professor Kirk Hanson, a contributor to Rhode's book, wrote that "global moral leaders" demonstrate several key characteristics, one of which is "a personal commitment to a set of values that transcend a nation or culture." But again, values that "transcend a nation or culture" are few and far between—if they exist at all. Moreover, to every rule there are exceptions. One of the Ten Commandments is "thou shalt not steal." But are there circumstances under which stealing is morally (or, if you prefer, ethically) justified? After considering the question most people conclude the answer is yes. What's called the "Heinz dilemma," which asks if an impoverished man is justified in stealing a lifesaving but expensive drug to save his dying wife, famously exemplifies the quandary of moral ambiguity.

While most of the leadership literature focuses, obviously, on leaders, there is no reason whatsoever for followers to be exempt from being judged good or bad, ethical or unethical, or, for that matter, effective or ineffective. While some of the time followers have no choice but to go along with what their leaders want and intend—at least not without risking punishment if they fail to fall into line—other times they do have a choice. Which is to say that when the choice is theirs, followers, like leaders, are responsible for what they do and how they do it.

In another one of my books, *Followership*, I developed five simple axioms, each of which pertains here:

- When followers do nothing—when they are isolates, who in no way participate in the group or organization of which they are members—they are bad. Or, at least, they are not good.
- When followers support leaders who clearly are good—effective and ethical—they are good.
- When followers support leaders who clearly are bad—ineffective, unethical, or both—they are bad.
- When followers oppose leaders who are good—effective and ethical—they are bad.
- When followers oppose leaders who are bad—ineffective, unethical, or both—followers are good.[8]

To testify to the importance of these axioms, I return to the case of Boeing and the 737 Max. During the investigations that followed the second crash, it came to light that several engineers had expressed concerns about the aircraft dating back to 2016. One openly balked at management's demands for less stringent testing of the jet's new engines, demands that seemed to prioritize haste over safety. Greater scrutiny in the interest of greater security would have cost the company time and money. Which is almost certainly why the engineer who objected most strenuously to existing company policy was removed from his post—without management conducting the additional testing he thought essential.

Careful reporting led the *Seattle Times* to conclude in May 2019 that "many engineers, employed by Boeing while officially designated to be the FAA's eyes and ears, faced heavy pressure from Boeing managers to limit safety analysis and testing so the company could meet its schedule and cut down costs."[9] What does this say about some leaders at Boeing? At a minimum, it throws into question their priorities. And what does this say about some followers at Boeing? At a minimum, it throws into question their courage. After all, we're talking here about not one airplane crash but two, just months apart, in which 346 lives were lost.

Muilenburg clearly pressured his subordinates to conform to his time-table. And nearly all of Muilenburg's subordinates clearly fell into line. What more can be said about the engineers who took the extra step of raising a red flag? On the one hand, it could be argued that they did something—they raised a red flag. On the other hand, it could be argued that they did not do enough. They spoke truth to power within the company, but not loudly or forcefully enough to get a sufficient response. And, as far as is known, none of them blew the whistle outside the company—to, as an obvious example, the press. Would this have cost the whistleblowers? Probably. Most whistleblowers pay a high price for calling attention to wrongdoing. But then, where would we be without whistleblowers, without followers bold and brave enough to act in the public interest? Let's be clear: there are times when whistleblowers—obstreperous followers, followers who refuse to follow—save us from great harm.

After the fact, there was remorse. One Boeing employee was quoted as saying, "I still haven't been forgiven by God for covering up as I did last year." And after the fact, there was awareness: "Everybody had it in their head that meeting schedule was most important because that's what leadership pressured and managed." Were there times when the requirements hadn't been "fully checked"? Yes. And were there times when "the lowest ranking and most unproven supplier" won contracts "solely based on the bottom dollar"? Yes. [10]

Unlike ineffective leadership and followership, which are usually self-evident, unethical leadership and followership are usually in the eye of the beholder. They tend much more to be subjective. It's why some diehard Bosnian Serbs will go to their graves believing Radovan Karadzic, a civilian leader of the Serbs during the Bosnian War, and Ratko Mladic, a military leader of the Serbs during the Bosnian War, to be heroes, not villains. Of course, most of the rest of the world would beg to differ. Most of the rest of the world would concur with the verdicts of the International Criminal Tribunal for the former Yugoslavia. Both men were found guilty of war crimes—including crimes against humanity and genocide. (Though they appealed the verdicts, Karadzic and Mladic continue to serve life sentences.)

Donald Trump is estimated to have told more than thirty thousand lies—made more than thirty thousand "false or misleading claims"—during his four years as president.[11] Many Americans found this abhorrent, especially in a chief executive. After all, from early childhood we are taught never to tell a lie. But many other Americans thought Trump's frenzy of fabrication acceptable or even admirable. For whatever reasons, they excused behavior in the White House they never would tolerate in their own homes. That is evidence, if any were still needed, that while we can make some progress toward making meaning of being "bad," we can go only so far.

Given that "bad" sometimes—or mostly, or maybe even always—is a matter of opinion, I have no illusions. I know full well that whatever judgments I offer in this book, some will take issue. So be it. Better than remaining mute to self protect.

4

The Phases of Development

Developmental psychologists talk about "stages" of development. For example, there are, broadly, three such stages in childhood: early childhood, middle childhood, and adolescence. In adulthood, the number of developmental stages varies, depending on which expert is being asked. An example is Yale professor Daniel Levinson, who in the 1970s published *The Seasons of a Man's Life*. The book became a best-seller in large part because Levinson and his collaborators postulated that stages of development extend beyond childhood and adolescence into adulthood. Though his sample was limited in size and scope, Levinson described six stages of adult development, from early through middle adulthood. The sequencing of the stages was important. Like other developmental psychologists, Levinson found we cannot leapfrog over one stage to get to another—for example, from the first stage to the third. Each stage is a necessary precursor to the next.

Which brings us to the word "stage," as in "stages of development" and "stages of change." What exactly is a "stage"? The dictionary defines a stage as a period in a process that consists of two or more such periods, each period following the one that precedes it in a certain progression. In other words, stage theories *always* presume a certain order or sequence that, absent interruption, has a beginning, a middle, and an end. A stage is not, however, only a psychological phenomenon. It is also a physical one. For example, when a cancerous tumor advances, it is described as doing so in stages numbered from I to IV, with IV the most serious. Stage I means the cancer is small and in only one area. Stages II and III signify the cancer is larger and has spread into nearby tissues or lymph nodes. And stage IV indicates the malignancy has metastasized to other parts of the body.[1]

Though I write in this book about a progression that takes place in a certain sequence, "stage" is not the word I use. Instead, I use the word "phase." While dictionaries describe the two as being virtually synonymous, there is nevertheless a small but important distinction: "'stage' has a slightly stronger suggesting of planning, and of a beginning and end, whereas 'phase' is less clear cut."[2] This difference suits my purposes, for one of the problems associated with stage theories is that the stages are *not* usually clear-cut. So, avoiding the word "stage" and settling instead on "phase" is appropriate to a discussion such as this one, which is about a progression, but one impossible to pinpoint precisely. *A phase is a discernable, distinguishable part of a progression that takes place over time—a statement that applies absolutely to bad leadership, which, unless it is stopped, gets worse in a certain sequence.*

During each of the three phases that succeed Phase I, as described in this book, bad leadership is worse than it was during the preceding phase. Put differently, bad leadership does not happen overnight, especially not very bad leadership. Rather, it evolves, or progresses over time in phases that, when surfaced, shed light on how and why when leadership begins to get bad and how and why it invariably gets worse. *The point is that bad leadership is not static—it changes over time into something more deficient or even dreadful than it was before. It is a process that, if not in some way impeded or interrupted, develops its own momentum. In which case worse leadership follows bad leadership just as surely as night follows day.*

Bad leadership has a compound effect. It usually starts small, perceptible perhaps, but not remarkable, and in any case easy enough to discount or dismiss, at least initially. Then come changes that usually, though not always, are gradual. Thereafter they pick up steam. The pace of change accelerates and there is increased momentum, which is why what seemed at the start to be insignificant becomes over time more significant and, eventually, more malevolent. Small changes become big changes that then get bigger still. No wonder bad leadership can have calamitous consequences. If left to its own devices—no one or nothing to tamp it down or wipe it out—it can become over days, months, years more injurious and more dangerous.

For years I have described leadership not as a person but as a system. For example, in an article published several years ago I wrote, "Leadership is not about the individual man or woman. Leadership is, instead, a *system* that consists of three parts, each of which is *equally* important, and each of which impinges *equally* on the other two. The first part is the *leader*. . . . The second is the *follower*—the 'other' who the leader must engage or, at least, neutralize to advance his or her interests. And the third is the *context* or, better, *contexts*—within which both leaders and followers necessarily are situated."[3] Here the discussion will focus not just on the bad leader but also on the bad leader's followers, who often though not always also are bad, and on the contexts within which bad leaders and their followers are situated. These systems—consisting of leaders, followers, and contexts—proceed in their entirety from one phase to the next. It is not just the leader who changes over time, who progresses from one phase to the next. Followers change too, and so do the contexts within which leaders and followers interact. At no point are bad leaders separate from their followers. And at no point are either bad leaders or their followers separate from the contexts within which bad leadership happens.

I divide the progression of bad leadership to worse leadership into four phases. Because this is a discussion about the human condition, these phases are not precisely delineated. Just as there is no bright line between stages—between, say, a boy's early childhood and his middle childhood, or a girl's middle childhood and her early adolescence—there is no bright line between phases of bad leadership. Still, given that the progression is predictable, dividing it into phases serves several purposes:

- *Phases raise our consciousness.* Although phases are an artifice, the concept focuses the mind. This is helpful because although bad leadership is as ubiquitous as it is pernicious, it has been relegated to the margins of our collective concerns, notably in the academy and in the leadership industry.
- *Phases simplify a process that otherwise is exceedingly if not overwhelmingly complex.* They provide access to terrain so laden with variables it is dauntingly difficult to navigate. Phases make it possible for us to see the trees through what otherwise seems an impenetrable forest.
- *Phases enable us to cluster phenomena that otherwise seem randomly distributed.* They permit us to convert what first appears as an unholy mess into groupings that are coherent and consistent.
- *Phases enable us to chart change over time.* Changes in leadership and followership can be difficult to detect, for they are often incremental. It's one of the reasons bad leadership happens. The trajectories from good to bad and then from bad to worse are sometimes so gradual and seemingly inconsequential that we downplay or even dismiss them, even as they gather steam.
- *Phases force us to face the truth.* We are disposed to deny truths that are unpleasant or inconvenient. Similarly, we are disposed to assume that though bad things happen, they are less likely to happen to us than to someone else. Phases of change, in this case of bad leadership, make it more difficult for us to avoid that which in the fullness of time will be unavoidable.

- *Phases foretell an inevitable, inexorable progression.* The concept of phases presumes that Phase I is followed by Phase II, Phase II by Phase III, and so on—unless and until the progression is stopped, or it reaches its endpoint.
- *Phases have pedagogical purposes.* In theory they are instructive. They predict what will happen without an intervention. In practice they are normative. When bad leadership and followership happen, an understanding of the phases through which they evolve leads to the conclusion that it is better to do something than nothing, lest bad become worse. This book is not, then, simply an intellectual exercise. It is also a cautionary tale—a warning about what will happen if bad is left untreated and unimpeded.

Because developmental theories necessarily are imprecise, I could have divided the progression from bad leadership to worse into three phases or into five. The following sequence is thus not etched in stone. Rather, the four phases are indicators of what will happen if bad leadership is permitted to progress.

- *Phase I: Onward and Upward.* Leaders paint a picture of a future boundlessly better than the past. It is a near-utopian vision of promises fulfilled and dreams realized.
- *Phase II: Followers Join In.* Leaders energize and secure their base of support. Usually their followers increase in number, as does their level of involvement and commitment.
- *Phase III: Leader Starts In.* Leaders and their followers embark on, or more aggressively continue, a course that in some way is bad. It is the beginning of a process during which, if left unchecked, bad leadership will inevitably, inexorably, become worse leadership.
- *Phase IV: Bad to Worse.* Leaders and their followers extend and expand their commitment to being bad. Because at no point during the preceding stages has the process been effectively interrupted or impeded, the outcome is as inevitable as predictable. It is dismal.

To illustrate the four phases, I will sketch the history of Nazi Germany. Specifically, the history of Adolf Hitler (the leader), the Nazis (the followers), and Germany (the context) during the period 1923 to 1939, the eve of the Second World War. Why draw on an extreme example to make a point?

Precisely because the leader, the followers, and the context that was Germany of that time were atypical. Hitler and the Nazis were so bad they became prototypes or archetypes of leaders and followers who went horrifically wrong, who became evil. Moreover, during the years in which they gained traction, Germany provided exceedingly fertile soil for promises kept and threats made, ethics be damned.

The question has been asked thousands of times: How did it happen that a country as cultured as Germany, as developed as Germany, was vulnerable to a leader like Hitler? It's complicated, and there's no way of doing justice to the question here. But in the pages that follow I trace the progression. How Hitler and the Nazis went from being marginal to being central—first in Germany, then in Europe, finally in most of the rest of the world. And how, because they remained unchecked for years, by anyone or anything, either at home or abroad, Hitler and his followers were able to progress from bad to worse. And then to still worse.

Phase I: Onward and Upward

One of the ways leaders enlist followers is to promise them a present better than their past—and a future better than their present. All leaders do it, including bad leaders. But bad leaders make promises they cannot and sometimes should not keep. Hitler was no exception. From his earliest days as leader of the Nazi Party, he based his case on the premise and promise of miraculous progress for Germany and most, though not all, of the German people.

As always, context was key. When Hitler first emerged on the national scene in the early 1920s, Germany had been defeated and depleted. Germans were, moreover, humiliated and debilitated. They had lost the Great War. They were coping with rampant inflation. And their politics were tumultuous and ominous, with centrists being squeezed from the right and the left. Germany was, in short, exceedingly fertile soil for a man like Hitler, who came out of nowhere but delivered his messianic message with messianic zeal.

In the early 1920s Hitler made two major moves. First, he seized the leadership of the then fledgling National Socialist German Workers' (Nazi) Party. Then, not long after, he and a few other party stalwarts mounted a short-lived and ill-fated coup against the German government (the so-called Beer

Hall Putsch). Despite his failure and subsequent arrest, these two events catapulted Hitler to national attention.

His message remained the same from when he first became leader of the Nazi Party to when he became chancellor just over a decade later (1933). In this period—Phase I, Onward and Upward—Hitler promised the German people their much-cherished homeland would rise from the ashes of war to become first a great nation and then a world power. Promises like these, of a future almost unimaginably better than the present, played perfectly to the fears, frustrations, anger, and aggression of his audiences.

Throughout his political career Hitler's message, delivered in his signature, almost hypnotic oratorical style, had two parts. One part was negative and toxic, expressing hate of whoever or whatever was the "other," whether an individual, a group, a country, or a culture. Most infamously, Hitler despised Jews, who from the beginning were targets of his most venomous verbal assaults.

The other part of Hitler's rhetoric was positive, forward-looking. Even early on, when his power was only over the still tiny, still marginal Nazi Party, his fantasy of a better future was singularly glowing and grandiose. There was a kind of lunacy about it, so expansive, so grand was the picture that Hitler painted. Germans were the chosen people and Germany the chosen land. Germany was to be entirely rebuilt—physically, psychologically, spiritually. It would rise from the ashes of its recent history to transcend and ultimately to triumph over its enemies, domestic and foreign.

Finally, Hitler's message was about Hitler, *all* about Hitler. Repeatedly he insisted that he and only he, the leader, the Fuehrer, could lead his people out of the wilderness and to the promised land. He was a narcissist and megalomaniac, envisioning and promising a near-utopian German future over which he would reign for life.

The duality to which I refer—deadly toxicity on the one hand, romantic fantasy on the other—was captured by Ian Kershaw, one of Hitler's most eminent biographers. Kershaw notes that early on, Hitler's incessant scapegoating, not only of Jews but also of Germany's constitutionally elected government, was intended to assuage Germans' anger and restore their self-esteem. But Kershaw goes on to point out that along with the negativity and vengefulness were optimism and hope. Hitler promised an entirely new "national community" that would unite Germans as they had never been united before, and enable them to become stronger than ever and remain so forever.[4]

After Hitler became chancellor, his rhetoric became still more militant and messianic. He warned that any threat to his power would be dealt with summarily. And he claimed that Germany's transformation was now imminent. In a speech delivered to the German parliament two months after he took office, Hitler spoke of the "political purification of our public life." He promised that the "entire system of education" would be used to cleanse the German body politic through a "thorough moral purging." And he reminded his listeners of how reverence for great men, of which he was the paramount example, had to be "instilled once more in German youth as a sacred inheritance."[5]

Phase II: Followers Join In

When Hitler became chancellor in the early 1930s, Germany had approximately half a million Jews, most of whom were thoroughly assimilated into the German economy and into German society. Many had trouble taking Hitler seriously, and most dreaded the idea of emigrating—leaving behind homes and jobs, families, and friends—to accommodate a leader whose excesses they assumed would soon be curtailed. Most other Germans, of whom there were approximately 65 million, gravitated slowly but inexorably toward the Nazi Party. While committed leftists never made their peace with Adolf Hitler, in time most Germans, Catholics and Protestants alike, aligned with the Nazis either because they were genuinely supportive or because they saw no viable political alternative.

By the middle of the decade, the Nazis could boast of two major accomplishments. First, they had accurately read the mood of the moment. Most Germans had been deeply disappointed by parliamentary democracy. The toll taken by the Great Depression in addition to that of the Great War explains in large part why so many Germans considered that their democratic experiment had failed. They were looking for a savior, and that savior was Hitler. Second, the Nazis had successfully bestowed on Hitler the mantle of legitimacy. He had, after all, been legally appointed chancellor. And he had, after all, enacted some important, even critical laws. These included criminalizing criticisms of Hitler and of the Nazi regime he had successfully installed.[6]

Throughout the 1930s, Hitler's hold over the German people grew increasingly strong with every passing year. In time it became a stranglehold. But while he was clearly unethical, just as clearly he was exceedingly effective. At home and abroad Germans were feeling increasingly emboldened and empowered. By 1936 repeated reports of widespread unemployment had given way to repeated reports of widespread labor shortages. Jobs and incomes had bounced back (in part because of conscription). The availability of goods and services had increased exponentially. Germany's infrastructure was being visibly improved. And women especially were being catered to by the Nazi government, which offered incentives to all (Aryan) women who quit their jobs, got married, and gave birth to a child. In the parliamentary elections held in March 1936 the Nazis claimed to have received over 99.9 percent of the vote. While the results were not reliable, no one doubted the German people had voted overwhelmingly for Hitler and the Nazi Party.

During this same period, Hitler's foreign policies were every bit as bold and presumptuous as his domestic policies. Even before he became chancellor, he had made his positions clear. He would make Germany not only stronger but bigger. To these ends he would ignore the restrictions imposed on Germany by the Treaty of Versailles and would start rattling his saber. By 1938 he proved as good as his word—and then some. In March 1938 Germany seamlessly annexed Austria, and in October it swallowed the Sudetenland, previously part of Czechoslovakia.

None of the facts on the ground, however, can capture or convey what became in the 1930s a frenzy of support for Adolf Hitler from his many millions of followers. Though they escape us today, from his earliest days in politics his skills as an orator especially had a remarkably powerful effect. They turned skeptics into fans and fans into the most fervid of followers. In his autobiography, Hitler described his first public speech, which took place in a small room in Munich: "I spoke for thirty minutes, and what before I had simply felt within me, without in any way knowing it, now proved to be real. I could speak!"

Indeed he could. He could convert individuals, small groups, and large crowds into true believers. Here is one of his early converts, a well-connected man of some sophistication, after hearing Hitler talk: "My critical faculty was swept away. . . . I experienced an exaltation that only could be likened to a religious conversion. . . . I had found myself, my leader, and my cause." The legendary filmmaker Leni Riefenstahl, who directed two of the greatest documentaries of all time, *Triumph of the Will* and *Olympia*, both of which were Nazi propaganda, had a similar response. After hearing Hitler at the Berlin Sports Palace, she was swept off her feet: "It seemed as if the earth's surface were spreading out in front of me . . . spewing out an enormous jet of water, so powerful that it touched the sky and shook the earth. I felt quite paralyzed."[7]

Hitler's followers fell into different groups. They ranged from those who were closest to the Fuehrer and the most deeply devoted, his acolytes, to those who were "only" or "merely" bystanders, who went along with Hitler as a matter of course or convenience.[8] Still, whatever the differences among them, this second phase in the progression of bad leadership to worse leadership is all about ensuring compliance. Bad followers are essential to bad leaders. Without the former, the latter are powerless. Which is why looking at bad leaders without simultaneously looking at their followers is pointless.

Phase III: Leader Starts In

Some leaders become bad over time. Other leaders are bad from the get-go, from the minute they take power and assume authority. Hitler was in this second group. As we have seen, he never hid who he was, what he believed, his passions, his ambitions, or his vision of the future. In fact, he trumpeted each from the ignominious start of what became in time a meteoric political career.

Still, though his power was evidently expanding, into the early 1930s many Germans were either unable or unwilling to take Hitler seriously. They could not believe that this seemingly curious extremist upstart out of Austria could do what he said he would do. Moreover, they could not believe that so many Germans would become in such short order deeply dedicated Nazis, fervent followers of the Fuehrer. If some Germans had a hard time believing that Hitler was happening even as he was named chancellor, all Germans were struck by the alacrity with which he transformed their country. Hitler set about implementing his program immediately upon taking office. Moreover, because of the lack of impediments, either institutional or individual, his ability to do what he wanted when he wanted was stunning.

To be sure, in the weeks immediately after his appointment as chancellor, Hitler remained somewhat cautious, aware that the man who appointed him, the old but venerable General Paul von Hindenburg, was still around and could pose a threat. But the Fuehrer's early circumspection rapidly succumbed to his natural aggression. History testifies that within months of assuming power Hitler consolidated that power, even before winter 1933 turned to spring 1933.

He did so by outmaneuvering or simply squelching his political opponents, by solidifying his support among the German people, and, importantly, by catering to Germany's political, economic, and military elite. Hitler further compounded his power by exploiting the law. In short order he bent to his will not only Germany's political system but its legal system as well, all without running up against a single significant roadblock. In the wake of the Reichstag (parliament) fire in February 1933 he persuaded Hindenburg (who remained president until his death in 1934) to sign the Reichstag Fire Decree, thereby rescinding many of Germany's civil liberties. Then came general elections—elections that Hitler had called for and which enabled him to form a majority government. Finally, just two months after he became chancellor, Hitler got the government to pass an amendment to the Weimar Constitution. In what was effectively a single stroke, this amendment, the so-called Enabling Act, made it legal for Hitler and his cabinet to pass any law without the consent of either the president or the parliament.

It was clear, then, just weeks after the Nazis came to power, that Hitler's assertive, even aggressive strategies and tactics were singularly effective. As Kershaw summarized it, "Power was now in the hands of the National Socialists. It was the beginning of the end for political parties other than the [Nazis]." In no time flat Hitler had triumphed over his most strident political opponents. And in no time flat he had cowed many millions of Germans—supporters and opponents alike—into submission. Within three months of taking office Hitler achieved what many had thought impossible: he no longer had to rely on support from outside the Nazi Party to do what he wanted. So, though he was still not able to wield absolute power, the next "vital steps toward consolidating his dictatorship now followed in quick succession." During the spring and summer of 1933 Germans "fell into line behind their new rulers."[9] This progression continued for years thereafter, which is to say that what Hitler was allowed to start, Hitler was allowed to continue. It is this that explains why his bad leadership progressed—why it went from bad to worse.

Ironically, the law writ broad was among Hitler's most potent instruments of power. For example, the sole purpose of the Nuremberg Laws, which were passed just two years after Hitler came to power, was to address the "Jewish question." By reducing Jews to second-class status in a single stroke, the laws were a necessary precursor to the genocidal policies that followed several years later. The Nuremberg Laws consisted of two separate race-based measures. The first deprived Jews of their citizenship by designating them "subjects of the state." The second, the Blood Protection Law, was intended to ensure racial purity. It flat-out forbade marriage or sexual relations between Jews and "citizens of German or kindred blood."

Everything that happened in Germany during the years just before and after Hitler became chancellor raises again the inconvenient but necessary question of how exactly to define bad leadership. There is no doubt that Hitler was stunningly *effective* in his quest for power and authority, and equally effective in his execution of that power and authority, especially between 1933 and 1939. At the same time, he was *unethical* (assuming that dictatorial rule and race-based laws are considered unethical). Yet numberless Germans were fine with it—fine with Hitler and fine with what he did and how he did it. In fact, most Germans were not only compliant but enthusiastic supporters of the Fuehrer and of the Nazi Party.

Phase IV: Bad to Worse

Hitler was not over until he was over—until he was dead, in 1945, in the final months of the Second World War. He is the archetype of a leader who proceeded from Phase I straight through to Phase IV. He was not stopped within Germany. And he was not stopped in time outside Germany by other countries in whose interest it would have been to do so. It is this failure to intervene effectively and early that explains why Hitler's progression from bad leadership to worse, and then to still worse, went on for over a decade. It is this failure to intervene effectively and early that explains why his followers' progression from bad followership to worse, and then to still worse, went on for over a decade.

All along, of course, were some who did resist, a relative few who refused to follow. Within Germany they were Hitler's military and civilian subordinates, or ordinary people who refused to go where Hitler led. Some small number, horrified by Hitler, even tried to overthrow the Nazi regime; these few people ran the gamut, from amateurs at the one end—for example, brother and sister Hans and Sophie Scholl, students who led the White Rose resistance movement and who, for their troubles, were arrested in 1943 and executed four days later—to at the other end professionals, so to speak, for example, a few army officers who tried but failed to assassinate Hitler in July 1944. They included the man who led the attempt, army officer Claus von Stauffenberg, who was immediately caught and one day later shot by a firing squad.

Hitler's most prominent and vocal opponent outside Germany was Winston Churchill. In real time, in the mid- and late 1930s, Churchill warned loudly and often against Germany rising, against the growing Nazi threat. But nearly no one in Britain was listening. Until war broke out, nearly no one in Britain had the slightest inclination or intention of acting on what Churchill had to say. Three reasons why. First, he was at the time a marginal figure, a member of parliament and the establishment who was nevertheless, for various reasons, easy to dismiss. Second, no one wants to hear bad news. We are hard-wired to avoid bad news insofar as possible, for as long as possible. Finally, failure of the imagination is endemic to the human condition. It was difficult in the 1930s, not long after the First World War, even to conceive of a second. To conceive of a Nazi takeover of Europe by Hitler, still seen by most as more outrageous than dangerous.

Credit Churchill, who was not yet prime minister, with doing what he reasonably could. In a speech delivered in the House of Commons on November 12, 1936, he warned: "Owing to past neglect, in the face of the plainest warnings, we have now entered upon a period of [great] danger. . . . [D]uring this very period Germany may well reach the culminating point of her gigantic military preparations." And in another speech, this one delivered to parliament a year and a half later, on March 24, 1938, he cautioned whoever would listen about the fate of the Sudetenland. It contains one of the most powerful lines in the literature on leadership. Of Hitler, Churchill said this: "The story of this year is not ended at Czechoslovakia. It is not ended this month. The might behind the German Dictator increases daily. *His appetite may grow with eating*" (italics added).[10]

As history testified, in this respect Churchill was a prophet. Hitler's appetite did grow with eating. As it inevitably, inexorably, does with bad leaders. But the lesson had not been learned—which is why it took Germany's invasion of Poland, in September 1939, to ignite real resistance. That was the start of the Second World War, a war for which most of Europe and the United States were woefully ill-prepared, precisely because the leaders of countries such as Great Britain and France were unable or unwilling to grasp that Hitler would not stop unless and until someone stopped him.

The trajectory of the Second World War speaks for itself. No need here to chronicle it, even cursorily—except to say that only when Hitler made the fatal mistake of invading Russia (1941), turning his erstwhile ally Joseph Stalin into an archenemy, were the Allies finally able to gain ground.

Meantime, bad to worse was concretized in a thousand different ways, such as by the expansion in the size, number, function, and mission of concentration camps. The first such camp was established in 1933, to house people the Nazis deemed political prisoners, such as Communists and Jews. However, these early camps were not concentration camps, as the term came later to be used. Rather, they were detention camps, where so-called enemies of the state could be held without trial. This extrajudicial status—simply lock people up and throw away the key—made it easy enough for the camps to evolve, to go from bad to worse and finally to fatal.

By the mid-1930s there were new camps, more camps, some with names that later became infamous, such as, now in addition to one of the earlier, Dachau, Buchenwald, and Sachsenhausen. These camps were an upgrade, so to speak, from the earlier ones. They had barracks, guard towers, and barbed wire, and they functioned independently, outside the law. During the first six months of 1938 the population of these camps expanded threefold. Later that year came another massive influx, with, in addition to more Germans, Czech and Austrian anti-Nazis, and, of course, tens of thousands of Jews.

In the early 1940s some concentration camps went from bad to worse—they became extermination camps. The best-known of these, the largest and deadliest, was Auschwitz, in Poland. The Holocaust Memorial Museum estimates that 1.3 million people were sent to Auschwitz, and that of these approximately 1.1 million were Jews. In addition to the approximately 960,000 Jews who died on the spot, non-Jewish Poles, Roma, homosexuals, and Soviet prisoners of war were also murdered there.

It's what can happen when bad leadership and followership are permitted to progress unimpeded. Detention camps can become concentration camps. And concentration camps can become extermination camps.

***

To reiterate: the four phases of leadership from bad to worse are not clear-cut. They cannot be precisely delineated or distinguished. Rather, they are signs and symptoms of a steady and accelerating progression that is as inexorable as it is abominable. In Phase I leaders sell themselves and their wares. They use the force of their personality and the content of their rhetoric first to entice and then to enlist followers in what is depicted as a glorious cause. In Phase II followers buy what leaders sell. They join in and sign on for reasons ranging from genuine and unadulterated enthusiasm to fear and loathing. In

Phase III leaders, along with some of their followers, begin to behave in ways that are palpably bad. At this point some followers will peel away—but others will not, enabling the bad leader to stay the course. Phase IV is the endpoint, the point at which bad leadership has become worse leadership—and then, if nothing intervenes effectively, becomes still worse.

PART II
DIGGING IN

5

Martin Winterkorn, CEO of Volkswagen

The scandal at Volkswagen—tagged "Emissionsgate" or "Dieselgate"—broke in 2015. In no time flat it became grist for the mill of business school case studies. So astonishing was what happened at Volkswagen, an icon of a company headquartered in an icon of liberal democracy, it was hard to grasp how so tawdry a mess had so sullied the carmaker's reputation. Surely there was something to be learned by studying the case up close, by deciphering who did what, when, and why.

Volkswagen has a bad distant past. During its formative years, the early to mid-1930s, the company was publicly endorsed and financially supported by German chancellor Adolf Hitler, who dreamed of producing a "car for the people." Hence the name Volkswagen, or "people's car"—and hence Hitler's heavy investment in Volkswagen, which enabled it to grow initially and then to thrive. However, not long after the start of the Second World War, the production of the "people's car" came to a grinding halt. Instead, Volkswagen was charged by the Nazi government with manufacturing vehicles for the exclusive use of the German military.

To fulfill its wartime assignment, Volkswagen used slave labor. Historians have estimated that during the war fully 80 percent of the company's labor force came from concentration camps. To be sure, Volkswagen was hardly the only German company to exploit forced labor. As Jack Ewing, author of an authoritative book about the emissions scandal, pointed out, several companies that are among Germany's largest today, including Mercedes-Benz Group, BMW, and Siemens, were guilty of labor practices essentially identical to Volkswagen's.[1] Still, when the emissions story became a global scandal, the fact that some seventy-five years earlier Volkswagen had an ill-begotten past further besmirched its ill-begotten present.

Almost immediately after the war was over, Volkswagen began its steady ascent to what not many years later was a remarkable success. By the 1950s the company had already begun to export cars not only to countries within Europe but also globally. By 1964 Volkswagen was shipping 330,000 cars a year to the United States. In fact, its iconic Beetle became a reverse status symbol, especially in America—of all cars, it was the Beetle and its larger counterpart, the VW bus, that were most closely associated with the leftist counterculture of the late 1960s and early 1970s. The Beetle's small size, its unfamiliar and even odd appearance, and its modest price tag seemed to perfectly suit a generation that had eschewed the materialism of its parents but nevertheless needed wheels to get to places like Woodstock. As for the VW bus, as Jill Lepore remembered it some fifty years later, "You could smoke pot in it, or fool around. You could sleep there, on the cheap. You could plot revolutions, or you could store your surfboard."[2] Volkswagen sales peaked in the United States in 1970—the height of the heyday of hippies—when some 570,000 of its cars were sold to American buyers. The Beetle ultimately became the best-selling and longest-running car design in automotive history. It and the VW bus essentially propelled Volkswagen to the top ranks of the world's automakers.

But by the last decade of the twentieth century the company's time at the top was over, especially in the United States. While in Europe Volkswagen had continued to do well—government incentives in several European countries made its diesel models attractive to consumers—in the United States sales had fallen dramatically. Volkswagen was continuing to lose ground to Toyota and other Japanese carmakers, who boasted better production methods and superior supply chains. This was during a time when Volkswagen's workforce had ballooned in anticipation of an expansion that never happened. All of which explains why, when Ferdinand Piech took over at Volkswagen in 1993, there was wide agreement that the company was "badly in need of change."[3] Toyota and Honda had given the previously invulnerable German carmaker a run for its money, to the point where Volkswagen had dropped to a humbling if not humiliating fifteenth place in sales in the largest car market in the world, the United States.

Phase I: Onward and Upward

The chairman of the executive board of Volkswagen, Ferdinand Piech, was endowed with a formidable family pedigree—and a formidable professional pedigree. He was the grandson of Ferdinand Porsche, the automotive engineer originally tasked by Hitler with taking the lead on developing the "people's car." And he was the son of Anton Piech, who had married

Porsche's daughter, Louise, and who himself had led Volkswagen between 1941 and 1945.

Ferdinand Piech was not, however, just a member of a remarkable automotive family. He was in his own right a superb automotive engineer—as well as an intensely ambitious and ferocious corporate leader and manager. It is Piech who is credited with Volkswagen's resurgence in the late twentieth and early twenty-first centuries, a consequence both of his aggressive moves into new and expanded markets and of his transformation of both Volkswagen and Audi into brands that were more clearly upmarket. Piech's status was such that in his obituary, *The Guardian* wrote he would "go down in history as an automotive legend, in the same class as Gottlieb Daimler, Henry Ford and Kiichiro Toyoda."[4]

Piech's reputation as something of an automotive genius was matched by his reputation as an exceedingly demanding leader and manager. He was known for being angry, aggressive, fierce, and frightening. Any subordinate who made the same mistake twice was summarily fired—Piech's tolerance for anything less than excellence was nearly none. *Wired* magazine described him as "an autocrat's autocrat."[5]

No surprise, then, that during the late 1990s and early 2000s Volkswagen's leadership was other than optimal. Piech's heavy-handed, commanding, and controlling leadership and management style was increasingly out of step with the changing times. This while the company's governance structure was a "strange mix" of family control, government ownership, and labor. (Employees at Volkswagen played a relatively large part in running the company, for like in all German companies, half the seats on its twenty-member supervisory board went to representatives of labor.)[6] The impact of Volkswagen's ineffectual and increasingly outdated management style during the years that Piech was in charge is difficult to overstate. The lack of an internal watchdog, and the disinclination of board members to challenge those at the top, especially at the very top, go a long way toward explaining how Volkswagen lost its way.

To be clear, some of Piech's ambitions were realized. During his ten-year tenure Volkswagen averted the disaster that some had predicted when he took over. The number of cars that Volkswagen produced rose dramatically, sales doubled, and its workforce expanded significantly. This explains in part why, even after Piech was no longer CEO, he continued to exercise power and influence in his new role as chair of Volkswagen's supervisory board.

Piech handpicked his successor, Bernd Pischetsrieder. But as soon as the new CEO tried to distance himself from the old CEO, specifically by ditching his tyrannical style of leadership, the new CEO ran into trouble. Pischetsrieder was blocked by the man who had selected him, Piech, who apparently felt "threatened by Pischetsreider's increasing independence and his obvious efforts to remake Volkswagen's culture along less authoritarian lines."[7] The result: at the end of his first and only five-year contract, Pischetsreider was terminated.

Enter Martin Winterkorn. When Winterkorn was appointed Volkswagen's CEO in 2007, Piech was once again a dominant figure, maybe even *the* dominant figure, at the company. Nevertheless, Winterkorn (who previously had been head of Audi) had, so far as Piech was concerned, three traits in his favor. First, he was someone Piech could control. Second, his leadership style was like Piech's—he ruled with an iron fist. And third, his ambition mirrored Piech's—it was unbridled. Whatever it took to get ahead of the pack, Winterkorn was ready, willing, even eager to do.

At the helm of Volkswagen, Winterkorn stood out for his drive to succeed. His lust for success was as bottomless as it was relentless.[8] Not only did he want and need success, but when he achieved it, he was only temporarily satisfied. Almost immediately his thirst for success would return, never entirely slaked.

Soon after he was named CEO of Volkswagen, Winterkorn announced his intention to make it the largest and most successful car company in the world. His overweening ambition was codified in a document known inside the company as "Strategy 2018." It was a ten-year plan that specifically targeted Toyota. Winterkorn wanted to best Toyota in units sold, in profitability, in innovation, in customer satisfaction—in everything. All this was announced in 2007, when Volkswagen was the number three carmaker in the world, Toyota was number two, and General Motors still ruled at number one.

At first, Winterkorn's ambitions, intentions, and proclamations were dismissed as merely the "usual hubris of an incoming CEO, a suit who'd be busy collecting his pension by the time 2018 rolled around." But early on the naysayers were proved wrong.[9] By 2009 it was clear that Winterkorn's words were not just hot air.

His early years as CEO seemed to confirm the validity of his vaulting ambition. He was demonstrably successful. Some of the reasons Winterkorn succeeded had nothing directly to do with Volkswagen. They were related to the changing context, most obviously the collapse of the financial markets in the 2008–2009 financial crisis and the subsequent crisis in the American car market, when General Motors ran into major trouble. When it finally resurfaced, GM had been restructured and refashioned, becoming much smaller and less competitive.

But other reasons Winterkorn succeeded had everything to do with Volkswagen. Under his leadership, and with Piech at his back, the company did very, very well. Three years after Winterkorn became CEO, Volkswagen was being described as "uncharacteristically gutsy." Its main competitors had been weakened—Toyota, for example, was having problems related to quality control—while Volkswagen was on a roll. In 2010 the company reiterated the goal it had outlined in "Strategy 2018." It continued to be committed "to seeking global economic and environmental leadership in the automotive industry by 2018."[10] This reiteration was relentless. When he made an appearance at a new Volkswagen plant in Chattanooga, Tennessee, in 2009, Winterkorn's refrain was the same. "By 2018," he asserted to the assembled, who included two U.S. senators and the governor, "we want to take our group to the very top of the global car industry."[11]

Phase II: Followers Join In

The head of any major global company has followers who are wide-ranging and far-reaching. There is, however, one clear divide: followers within the company (most obviously, employees) and followers without. In this case, the followers without included people in the car industry more generally, such as Volkswagen's competitors, members of the automotive press, and government regulators at home and abroad who were responsible for monitoring the car industry. Additionally, of course, followers include clients and customers, and potential clients and customers—crucial for any carmaker. In Winterkorn's case, most if not all these players were, for nearly the entirety of his tenure, generally supportive of what he was doing—or, more precisely, of what they thought he was doing. Specifically, they believed him when he said Volkswagen was destined to be superior to and more successful than its competitors.

Within Volkswagen it was no great trick for Winterkorn to get compliance. For even into the twenty-first century the company culture was still one of obedience to authority. Superiors said to do this and do that, and subordinates did it, no questions asked. What happened, then, at Volkswagen was not only a consequence of the specifics of the emissions scandal. The problem was a more general one that was a consequence of the culture at Volkswagen, which was a throwback to a time when command-and-control leaders were in, and followers were expected to fall into line without a word of protest. Like his mentor and predecessor, Ferdinand Piech, Martin Winterkorn ruled by fear. Winterkorn, a former soccer player, was physically intimidating, "with a stocky build and a way of walking that thrust his chest forward. When he was unhappy about something, which was often, he conveyed his feelings loudly and sometimes physically."[12] At one meeting he became so angry he banged his fist on the table so hard he broke it.

Without exception Winterkorn was described as a dominant, even tyrannical leader. Former Volkswagen managers admitted later that most of them never even dared to approach Winterkorn. "There was always a distance, a fear, and a respect. . . . If he would come and visit or you had to go to him, your pulse would go up. If you presented bad news, those were the moments that it could become quite unpleasant and loud and quite demeaning." Even in public Winterkorn ordered senior staff around.[13] Invariably, Volkswagen's management culture was described as "domineering," "rigid," and "top-down." Anyone who failed to meet targets "feared reprisals." Everyone feared Winterkorn himself, which was why no one dared to speak their truth to his power. As one former Volkswagen management trainee remembered, "It was like North Korea without labor camps."[14]

Winterkorn's followers, then—specifically those working at Volkswagen who wanted to continue to work at Volkswagen—essentially had no choice but to do what he told them to do. Those who had a problem with him or with the company had no place to turn. As even Volkswagen's middle- and upper-level managers saw it, they had only one alternative to staying put and remaining mum, which was to quit. But quitting was not an appealing option for most. To the contrary. Volkswagen provided generous financial incentives to stay. It had an unusually good bonus system, one that benefited every employee, from assembly line workers straight up to the C-suite. Moreover, the company rewarded consensus, and thereby, if only by implication, was prepared to punish dissent. In short, uniformity and even unanimity were encouraged. Doubts and disagreements, not to speak of divisiveness and disputatiousness, were discouraged.

The fact that management—first Ferdinand Piech, then Martin Winterkorn in alliance with Piech—got away with being dictatorial even into the twenty-first century should not have come as a surprise. Volkswagen had a long history of autocratic leadership and management, a deeply entrenched corporate culture, and a complicated governance structure. Even Volkswagen's headquarters was part of the hothouse context, as it was located in a company town, Wolfsburg, within which most associated with Volkswagen not only worked but lived. In sum, virtually everything about the company was in keeping with its long tradition of conformity and obedience.

It's clear that underlings at Volkswagen had no power or authority and little influence. But what about others at Volkswagen who did have some power, authority, and influence—notably Volkswagen's supervisory board? They chose not to exercise that oversight. The board lacked expertise as well as diversity. Seventeen of its twenty members were either German or Austrian. It did have one independent voice (the CEO of a Swedish bank), but as a group the board was weak and ineffectual. It was "short of people with relevant experience and skills and—significantly—independence."[15] Similar weaknesses extended to Volkswagen's legal and compliance staff, which either did not know about the emissions cheating or did not have the fortitude to warn or even speak about the legal and financial risks of being caught doing something egregiously wrong, especially in the United States.[16]

The net effect could have been predicted—but it was not. Nobody other than Piech and Winterkorn seemed able, or perhaps willing, to say out loud what they were thinking or feeling. Nor were there any meaningful checks or balances at the top. So for the entirety of Winterkorn's eight-year tenure, he was the Sun King. With Piech protecting him, Winterkorn effectively had absolute power. His followers followed where he led. While some seemed to suffer occasional pangs of conscience, even they were silenced by the context and the circumstance.

As we will see, the defeat device that was at the heart of the scandal was not originally Martin Winterkorn's idea. Nor did he ever directly and overtly approve of its use. Nevertheless, he profited mightily from its use, and from the first day of his tenure at the top nearly to his last, he encouraged his underlings to continue to install the device and to keep their handiwork secret. To be sure, none of this appears to have been explicit. But it was implicit. As the title of an article in the *Harvard Business Review* put it when the scandal first broke, "VW's Problem Is Bad Management, Not Rogue Engineers."[17]

It is correct to say that bad management, bad leadership, was a problem. In fact, it was the major problem. But it was *not* the only problem. "Rogue engineers" and their immediate superiors were an additional and significant problem. In other words, it's impossible to understand the emissions scandal just by looking at the leader, at Winterkorn, and holding him alone accountable. In fact, this case confirms yet again the validity of looking at leadership as a *system* with three different parts, each of which is equally important: leaders, followers, and contexts.

This case confirms that people who worked at Volkswagen were consummate conformists. They did what their leader wanted when he wanted it, and if what he wanted was wrong, they went ahead and did it anyway. So far as cheating on emissions was concerned, then, there was complicity at Volkswagen. Not many were involved, either directly or indirectly, with the company's wrongdoing. But some in addition to Winterkorn—and, almost certainly, Piech—were. Even years later the complicity of others was still being confirmed and reconfirmed. For example, in 2023 Rupert Stadler, the former chief executive of Volkswagen's Audi division, accepted a plea deal in Germany related to the scandal. Stadler was the highest-ranking executive to plead guilty. To receive a suspended sentence and a fine, instead of going to jail, he made a full confession, admitting that he knew cars with illegal devices were continuing to be sold.

Winterkorn's followers without the company were similarly compliant— or gullible. In retrospect, it's curious that so few questions were asked by, for example, Volkswagen's competitors, suppliers, and regulators. Why did no one ask for so many years why this car company seemed to have a secret sauce that no other car company could replicate? Why did no one ask for so many years why this car company performed differently on emissions testing in the lab than it did on the road? Why did no one ask for so many years why this car company had a leader who went unchallenged even as his claim to fame was as outrageous as erroneous?

Let's be clear. Winterkorn was able to lead badly because he was good at compelling followers inside the company to do his bidding. And he was good at persuading followers outside the company that his product was unique. For eight years, between 2007 and 2015, where Winterkorn led, others followed.

Phase III: Leader Starts In

When Winterkorn took over as CEO of Volkswagen AG, the parent company of the Volkswagen Group (which includes Audi), his ambitions knew no bounds. His intention was to nearly double Volkswagen's sales and

dramatically improve its profit margins. This was to be accomplished primarily by selling diesel cars, which could rack up millions of dollars in sales in
the United States alone. There was a problem, however. To accomplish this
goal Volkswagen had to comply with the rules and regulations of American
president Barack Obama's new administration, which was toughening
U.S. standards on mileage and demanding that carmakers clean up their act,
literally, by reducing vehicle emissions. The company had to demonstrate
that its diesel engines not only provided better mileage but also were com-
paratively clean. Which is to say that as it pertained to emitting pollutants,
Volkswagen vehicles had to perform distinctly better than conventional
engines and better than their competitors.

Volkswagen's engineers had tried to solve the problem before Winterkorn
became CEO. They were aware of their mandate to produce cars superior to
those of their competitors; they were, after all, constantly being pressured by
Piech to excel. Specifically, they were charged by management to produce a
superior car so that Volkswagen could increase its market share in the United
States and become the biggest carmaker in the world.

Beginning in 2005 and 2006, Volkswagen's engineers worked tirelessly to
address the still vexing problem of how their diesel cars could meet America's
relatively strict emissions standards. But a solution to the problem remained
elusive, especially since whatever the technical solution was, it also had to
be cost-efficient. Volkswagen cars were, after all, the "people's cars." They
could not be priced beyond the reach of the average consumer. But for all
the hard work, and despite relentless pressure, by the end of 2006, just before Winterkorn took over, the company remained stuck. As auto journalist
Jack Ewing put it, "Its global ambitions had bumped up against the laws of
physics." In fact, years later Volkswagen finally admitted in court documents
that its engineers had been unable to reconcile the conflicting goals of fuel
economy and emissions "within the allocated time frame and budget."[18]

Technically, there were several solutions to the problem that Volkswagen
faced. But most were rejected as being too clumsy, too expensive, or too
something else that ultimately made them infeasible or undesirable. So
the company chose a different route. It chose to cheat. Shortly before
Winterkorn formally assumed the top job, a high-level executive meeting
within Volkswagen took place to discuss the discovery by Volkswagen's
engineers of a "defeat device." The defeat device was not actually a physical
device—it was a few lines of software code that ran inside the engine control
unit. The engineers had inadvertently discovered that this software had the

dubious distinction of defeating the purpose of emissions testing. It enabled Volkswagen's vehicles to pass U.S. emissions tests by *falsifying the results*.

Some fifteen Volkswagen executives attended the meeting at which the decision was made to proceed: to install the defeat device, which would enable their cars to meet the requisite standards while "the emissions police were watching." In other words, the defeat device, which was illegal both in the United States and in the European Union, was specifically approved for use by Volkswagen's leadership group.

Though the meeting at which this was decided was brief—it lasted less than an hour—it was contentious. Some participants expressed reservations about cheating on a regular basis, though in the end to no avail. Everyone in the group knew, in any case, that the company and its executives were about to take a major risk. Volkswagen would routinely install in its vehicles illegal software that would turn on maximum emissions controls only when the computer detected the car was being tested. Once the test was over, the controls were throttled back to protect the engine from excessive wear and tear. This meant the car's mileage and emissions were as advertised *only when it was being tested*. They were *not* as advertised when it was out on the road.[19]

Martin Winterkorn did not attend that all-important executive meeting. But just four weeks later he became Volkswagen's CEO. Moreover, even while he was formally still CEO of Audi and not yet formally CEO of Volkswagen, he was a member of Volkswagen's board of management. Inevitably, then, Winterkorn was not just *a* central player but *the* central player during the entire emissions saga. Whatever the answer to the question of what exactly he knew and when exactly he knew it, the fact is that from the time he took over as Volkswagen's CEO until the scandal broke eight years later, he presided over a company that was cheating in a big way. Some customers were hoodwinked into buying cars deliberately designed to mislead on emissions. Everyone was subjected to more pollutants than they knew or had any reason to suspect.

There is no evidence that Martin Winterkorn gave the initial order to install the defeat device. This made it possible for him, when the scandal first broke, to deny culpability or responsibility. What he said instead was that whatever the "irregularities," they were in consequence of mistakes made by "only a few." He added that he in any case was innocent—a victim of what happened not a perpetrator. He was a leader who was duped by his followers, Winterkorn maintained, stating for the record that he was unaware "of any wrongdoing on my part."[20]

The "only a few" to whom Winterkorn referred were, obviously, his subordinates, specifically Volkswagen's engineers and technicians and their immediate superiors. They were the experts who originally if inadvertently discovered the defeat device, and who subsequently agreed to install it, nearly all without a word of protest—first initially, then regularly and repeatedly, hundreds of thousands and then millions of times, from when their managers first approved its use in 2006–2007 to when the scandal broke in 2015.

When the scandal began to come to light, Winterkorn and Volkswagen more generally stuck to their story: they insisted that blame for the confidence game was limited to just a very few, mainly technicians. Michael Horn, chief executive of Volkswagen Group of America, told U.S. lawmakers in sworn testimony in October 2015 that there were only "a couple of software engineers who put this in, for whatever reason." Then he said that three engineers were involved. Then he admitted that he did not know the number of those who were culpable, but he went on to add, "To my understanding, this was not a corporate decision."[21] Horn maintained, in other words, that the initial decision to install the defeat device and the subsequent decision to continue to install it indefinitely were made not by those at the top of the organizational pyramid but by those in the middle.

Not long after the scandal broke, it became apparent that some of Volkswagen's many engineers and technicians, along with their immediate superiors, did in fact play key roles in the drama that soon became one of the biggest corporate ignominies of the early twenty-first century. There is modest evidence that during the eight years of Winterkorn's tenure some midlevel employees, including some engineers and technicians, tried to alert their superiors to the emissions rigging. But there is compelling evidence that they were ignored. Which is to say that in the end no one at Volkswagen ever broke ranks. No one went to the press or to any regulatory agency with a complaint. No one blew the whistle.

Clearly, then, where Winterkorn led many followed. Specifically, every Volkswagen employee familiar with the defeat device was complicit in the wrongdoing, either actively or passively. Either they were active—they in some way participated in installing and monitoring the misleading software. Or they were passive—they knew their employer was cheating on a regular basis but did nothing and said nothing. The numbers of those who fell into one or the other of the two groups remain unclear. What is clear is that within a few weeks of the announcement of Volkswagen's amnesty program—to encourage those who knew anything about the cheat device to come forward—about fifty employees admitted that they had had, in real time, some knowledge of the wrongdoing.

Even this number is an indicator: it indicates that many more people—many more followers—were in some way implicated. As an article in *Newsweek* that appeared when the scandal first broke put it, "The number of engineers, technicians and managers needed to coordinate the vehicle functions with emissions-cheating software would likely be substantial." The piece went on to quote the director of the Environmental Protection Agency's Office of Transportation and Air Quality, who said that "writing the code could, in theory, have been the work of one person, but making it work with other parts of the engine is a more complicated task that would likely have involved more people." This was confirmed again not much later when Volkswagen decided to suspend nine managers in connection with the case. Some were members of the company's various boards; others were quality control managers, plant managers, and engine designers.

In addition to those involved in the rigging scandal within Volkswagen, outsiders were implicated. An example is Bosch, a multinational German engineering and technology firm that supplied the carmaker with the software that could be altered to rig emissions. While it would have been difficult or even impossible for Volkswagen to modify the software without Bosch's at least tacit approval, to no one's surprise Bosch denied any wrongdoing. Instead, the company insisted that "how these components are calibrated and integrated into complete vehicle systems is the responsibility of each automaker."[22]

We know that when he came on board in January 2007, Winterkorn was aware that there was no easy or obvious solution to the emissions problem. We further know that it was approximately during his tenure that Volkswagen's engineers managed, as if by magic, to solve the problem. How do we know this? Because just over a year later, in April 2008, Volkswagen's newly revamped motor was far enough along for the company to unveil it at the Vienna Motor Symposium, an annual event that attracts automotive executives from across Europe. Winterkorn's presentation was all about "Volkswagen's new 2.0-liter TDI engine," which, he declared, would "fulfill the most stringent emissions standards." In fact, he seized the opportunity to hype his new product, boasting that Volkswagen would "set new benchmarks for high fuel economy and environmentally sound motoring." It was his objective, he piously promised, "to reconcile sustainability and mobility around the globe."[23]

To be clear: Winterkorn was not a neophyte who could easily be duped. Hardly. He had joined the Volkswagen Group in 1981 as a quality controller, a job for which he was extremely well qualified. He was a highly trained engineer who had studied metallurgy and physics at the University of Stuttgart, and later earned a doctorate in metal physics at one of the prestigious Max Planck Institutes. Additionally, he had worked alongside Ferdinand Piech for decades. It was said of the two men that their partnership was so productive because while Piech was responsible for developing new ideas, it was Winterkorn who was responsible for implementing them. Impossible, then, to think him an innocent, ignorant of what was happening right under his nose, year after year after year.

Phase IV: Bad to Worse

To repeat: It beggars belief that Winterkorn was totally unaware of the defeat device or of Volkswagen's decision to cheat on emissions. Not only did he take over the company within weeks after the decision was made, but he was a tyrannical boss who micromanaged everything and everyone. Finally, he was an extremely well-educated and highly trained engineer. He was deeply knowledgeable in precisely the specialized area in which the defeat device was developed and installed. (This similarly applies to Piech.) So when Winterkorn insisted after the scandal broke that he had done nothing wrong, that he had no idea of what had happened on his watch as it pertained to a device of the utmost consequence, he was engaging, or trying to engage, in "plausible deniability."

In response to the charges leveled against him, Winterkorn pleaded innocence on the grounds of ignorance, claiming that he had had no idea what his subordinates had been up to. Setting aside the fact that it is, after all, the job of a leader to know what his followers are doing, Winterkorn's defense in any case fails the smell test. What is plausible is that Winterkorn did what some or even many leaders do in such situations, especially when there is a clear chain of command: they deny knowledge of or responsibility for any actions committed by or on behalf of others members of their organizational hierarchy. They may do so because of a lack of evidence that can confirm their participation."[24] What these leaders do, in short, is to shift the blame for wrongdoing from their shoulders to those of their underlings. Obviously, the temptation to do this can be strong, especially when the leaders have good reason to believe that even those who disbelieve their claim to innocence will be unable to prove otherwise.

From day one of his tenure at the top, Martin Winterkorn's lust to succeed was what drove him and his minions. Late in 2007, when he had been in his post less than a year, he spoke again to the board of his vaulting ambition. Within the decade, he said, he planned to push sales of Volkswagen cars and trucks to more than 10 million a year, up from 6 million. Ewing notes that anyone familiar with the auto industry would understand the implications of Winterkorn's ten-year plan. To meet his sales target, Volkswagen would have to beat Toyota and General Motors at their own game. Volkswagen would have to become the biggest carmaker in the world.[25]

As is the case with leaders who lust, Winterkorn's drive for success did not abate with success. He thrived on what he was able to achieve and on how he was able to act in consequence—like a regent. By 2013 Volkswagen was selling 9.7 million vehicles a year, and Winterkorn was living and acting like a master of the universe. He was one of the highest-paid, most visibly successful, and most powerful corporate leaders in Europe.

The cheating continued until one day it stopped. It stopped not because the management team at Volkswagen made a tactical change or had a change of heart. Not because the man at the top, Martin Winterkorn, or his partner in crime, Ferdinand Piech, scaled back their ambitions. Nor was it because they woke up one morning and decided to do what was morally as well as legally right. No, it stopped because it was made to stop. It stopped because the wrongdoing was discovered by outsiders who finally brought it to an end.

When Winterkorn became CEO of the Volkswagen Group the decision had just been reached to cheat—to install the defeat device. Given that he did not immediately reverse the decision and given that he continued to run the company as it continued to cheat, his leadership was bad from the get-go. Moreover, it went from bad to worse through the eight years of his tenure. Why? Because he continued to allow and therefore to encourage wrongdoing. Because he continued to be enabled by those who surrounded him. Because he continued to become more dictatorial and baronial. Because he continued to dupe not only his customers but also the public at large. Because he continued a company culture that obliged others to be complicit in his wrongdoing.

The effect of Winterkorn's bad leadership was cumulative. The longer it lasted, the higher the cost to everyone adversely affected. Volkswagen's cheating was not a single, quickly aborted instance of wrongdoing, never to be repeated. It was the opposite. It went on for eight years, the price paid by the victims of Volkswagen's wrongdoing escalating with each passing day.

If Volkswagen's leader went from bad to worse between 2007 and 2015, the same can be said of some of his followers. Given that on the matter of the defeat device Winterkorn's subordinates did what they were disposed to do anyway, which was to go along to get along, they too are culpable. Which raises the question of how responsible or accountable subordinates are who do no more, and no less, than follow their superior's orders. The question is probably as old as human history. It is certainly as old as the Second World War, in the aftermath of which questions were asked about the guilt or innocence of ordinary people, specifically of Germans who were in some way complicit in Nazi war crimes, even if only as bystanders. Let me be clear: speaking truth to power usually is hard, often is risky, and sometimes even is very risky. At Volkswagen it was always difficult to the point of impossible to speak up or speak out, and the price paid for dissent could be high. Still, when no one is willing to question wrongdoing out loud, the wrongdoing persists. And, inevitably, it gets worse.

If my decades-long study of bad leadership has taught me anything, it is that, as in the case of Winterkorn, bad leaders do not surrender their leadership posts or perks voluntarily. On the contrary: they do not, will not give them up unless and until they are forced to do so—which is precisely where the importance of good followership comes in. Had one or more of Volkswagen's engineers, technicians, and managers who knew about the defeat device dared either to dissent within the company or to speak out beyond the company at any point between 2007 and 2015, history might have been different. Volkswagen and many of those associated with it might have been spared not only their legal and financial liabilities but their humiliations. But that didn't happen. Leadership and followership at Volkswagen went from bad to worse for the simple reason that no one either thought to or dared to stop it.

For years, the diesel defeat device enabled new VW models to pass the tough U.S. emissions tests with flying colors. Volkswagen's wrongdoing was discovered only when the International Council of Clean Transportation partnered with three graduate students from West Virginia University to investigate why Volkswagen vehicles had different emissions levels when the car was stationary—when it was being tested—than when it was out on the road. Once the disparity was conclusively proven, the results were reported to the Environmental Protection Agency (EPA). After some additional testing, the EPA finally identified the software that enabled the cheating.[26]

When they were first asked to explain the incriminating findings, Volkswagen's U.S. managers were "evasive." They tried to "discredit" them, insisting the West Virginia University study was calibrated in a way that was "off." The discrepancies had to do with the "conditions under which the test was done," Volkswagen officials insisted.[27] In short order, however, the company was caught red-handed. There was no longer any doubt: *somewhere between 10 and 11 million cars containing the culpable software had been sold worldwide.* (At least half a million of these had been sold in the United States.) Finally, the company had no choice. It had to admit to at least some "irregularities" (Winterkorn's word). Volkswagen's CEO resigned on September 22, 2015, not long after the company he led was obliged to acknowledge that at least some of its diesel cars sold in the United States came with software "built to fool emissions tests." Again, in his resignation statement Winterkorn insisted that he was not "aware" of "any wrongdoing on [his] part." This time, however, he added, "As C.E.O. I accept responsibility for the irregularities that have been found in diesel engines."[28]

The blame game went on for months and then years. Toward the end of 2015 Volkswagen claimed the emissions deceptions were the result of a "chain of mistakes" and of a "culture of tolerance" for rule-breaking that allowed the cheating to continue for almost a decade.[29] It even dragged in the name of Winterkorn's predecessor, Pischetsrieder, who promptly denied any knowledge of the fraud and offered to swear to that effect. Moreover, while Volkswagen's supervisory board initially issued a statement saying it did not believe that Winterkorn had any knowledge of the defeat device, by May 2016 the company had to admit he did know—or could have known, or should have known much earlier than he claimed.

Why? Because by May 2014 Winterkorn was in receipt of a memo written by one Bernd Gottweis, Volkswagen's head of product safety. In his memo Gottweis made clear that some Volkswagen cars were producing up to thirty-five times more nitrogen oxide emissions than was permitted by law. Additionally, he warned management at the highest level to assume "that the authorities [would] investigate."[30] To be sure, as Volkswagen pointed out, though it was proven that Winterkorn received the memo, it was not proven that he *read* the memo. It was hypothetically possible that he missed it. But, again, this excuse—that it was just another item in Winterkorn's "extensive weekend mail"—fails the credibility test.[31]

During Phase IV it emerged that Volkswagen not only was guilty of cheating but also was guilty of a cover-up. By 2017 the evidence was in: the company had deliberately tried to hide its culpability, especially toward the end, when management could sense the screws were tightening. "Volkswagen employees manipulated not only the engine software, but also generated reams of false or misleading data to hide the fact that millions of vehicles had been purposely engineered to deceive regulators and spew deadly gases into the air."[32] The cover-up further distinguishes Volkswagen from other carmakers, who when confronted with evidence of emissions violations acknowledged the problem. Other car companies made the decision not to fight the regulators. To the contrary, they cooperated with them. Volkswagen, though, chose a different path. It continued for at least another year, between 2014 and 2015, to obfuscate and conceal.

Ultimately the law caught up with the company, and with at least some who were guilty of wrongdoing. In the United States lawsuits were filed by regulators, shareholders, and customers, and criminal prosecutions were launched.[33] In 2018 Martin Winterkorn was indicted in the United States on charges of fraud and conspiracy. And in 2019 the U.S. Securities and Exchange Commission filed a complaint against him and Volkswagen, alleging they had defrauded investors by selling corporate bonds and asset-backed securities while knowingly making false and misleading statements to government regulators, underwriters, and consumers as to the quality of their automobiles.[34]

In 2019 Winterkorn was also charged in Germany on several different counts including fraud; in some cases the charges are still pending at the time of this writing. It is not clear that in Germany his case will ever be brought to trial. As far as the United States is concerned, as of 2023 Winterkorn remained a fugitive from American justice. He was wanted by the Environmental Protection Agency for conspiracy to defraud the United States, for committing wire fraud, and for violating the Clean Air Act. But so long as he does not set foot on American soil, he is unlikely ever to set foot in an American court.

Volkswagen did not get off so easily. By fall 2016 its stock price had dropped by nearly a third (though it later recovered). And by 2020 the scandal had cost the company €31.3 billion in fines, settlements, and legal fees. Volkswagen's legal costs alone were immense. To give a single indicator, within just a few weeks after the wrongdoing was revealed at the end of September 2015, Volkswagen was slapped with at least thirty-four class-action lawsuits.

Moreover, the saga seems never-ending. In May 2022 Volkswagen agreed to pay nearly $250 million to settle claims filed in England and Wales, while civil suits remained ongoing.[35]

Amid all the messiness and sordidness are exactly two people who (so far) have paid dearly and directly for their related crimes. (As of mid-2023 there were several other court cases besides Winterkorn's that remained unresolved: a few former Volkswagen managers were still standing trial in Germany.) Were they high-level executives who bore the brunt of the blame for what happened? No. The first was James Liang, an engineer at Volkswagen who helped develop the software that concealed the high levels of pollutants generated by Volkswagen's diesel engines. In 2017 he was sentenced in the United States to forty months in federal prison. The second was Oliver Schmidt, another engineer, who because he had the bad luck to be on American soil in January 2017 was arrested in a men's room in a Florida airport and charged with conspiracy to defraud the United States. Had Schmidt made it back to Germany, it's not clear that he ever would have been prosecuted. But as it happened, he was caught during a brief stopover in the United States and was ultimately sentenced by a federal judge to seven years in prison and fined $400,000.

A reporter who studied the Schmidt case concluded there was no doubt he was guilty of participating in the cover-up. But he was far from being any kind of mastermind. In fact, Schmidt heard about the defeat device only in 2015, when he was instructed by his superiors, including his über-boss, Martin Winterkorn, to try to persuade U.S. regulators to allow the sale of 2016 Volkswagen vehicles. According to Schmidt's sentencing memo, "Rather than advocate for the disclosure of the defeat device to U.S. regulators, VW executive management authorized its continued concealment." In other words, when Schmidt was sent on his U.S. mission he was specifically instructed "not to disclose the defeat device or any intentional cheating." For his dedication to the company and his wish to ingratiate himself with his superiors, Schmidt, who had only recently been promoted to midlevel management, paid a high price. In 2017 he started serving time in prison in Michigan. In 2020 he was transferred to a correctional center in Germany. Finally, in January 2021, he was released on parole.[36]

It is impossible to blame any single death solely on Volkswagen's cheat device. Nevertheless, several researchers tried to quantify the costs of the company's crimes. For example, an MIT professor estimated that the excess pollution released by Volkswagens in Europe would eventually result in twelve hundred premature deaths. Another study suggested that by 2016 Volkswagen would be responsible for sixty premature deaths in the United States (where diesel vehicles were much less common). More generally, the European Environmental Agency estimated that pollutants emanating from all diesel vehicles were the primary cause of premature deaths of some 75,000 Europeans every year.[37]

Meantime, Martin Winterkorn continued to avoid paying dearly for his crimes. Though in June 2021 Volkswagen revealed that he was finally obliged to compensate the company to the tune of almost $14 million for "breaches of due diligence," his wealth remained largely intact. To be clear, Winterkorn is forever disgraced. And technically he remains within reach of the law. In 2021 prosecutors in Berlin finally charged him with lying to the German parliament about what he knew and when he knew it. (As of this writing, the ultimate disposition of his case remained however uncertain.)

Winterkorn was in any case culpable. To assume that he did not know about the defeat device beginning in 2007 is, as indicated, to defy logic. Moreover, in the exceedingly remote event that he was not lying about not knowing—that is, if he had no idea until 2015 that there even was such a thing as a defeat device—he still was culpable. In the first event he was guilty outright. In the second he was responsible for having led a company that operated "on the basis of unspoken assumptions, unacknowledged pressures, and unwitting signals." As Professor Marianne Jennings observed about the case, "If the CEO knew, there are no excuses. If the CEO did not know, there are no excuses."[38]

Martin Winterkorn was a general who gave his troops a vision of the promised land—a land in which Toyota, General Motors, and every other carmaker in the world would lag while Volkswagen reigned supreme. But at the same time, he explicitly and implicitly sent his underlings a message: if they failed to comply with his demand for complete commitment to the cause as he defined it, they would be punished, or at least they would fail to be rewarded.

They, in turn, fell into line. Nearly all his followers followed his orders. And a number were complicit from start to finish, including in the cover-up. What happened at Volkswagen was then a consequence of bad leadership and bad followership. Both evolved over the years, and congealed over the years, from bad to worse.

Winterkorn was a callous leader—by every available account, he was uncaring and unkind to his followers. He was also corrupt. Corrupt leadership is, as noted in Chapter 3, when the leader and at least some followers, lie, cheat, or steal. To a degree that exceeds the norm, they put self-interest ahead of the public interest. If Winterkorn and at least some of his followers do not fit this description, it's hard to know who does.

6

Recep Tayyip Erdogan, President of Turkey

Recep Tayyip Erdogan was prime minister of Turkey from 2003 to 2014. Then he became Turkey's president. During this twenty-year period, he started out as a democrat and became an autocrat. For as it turned out, Erdogan had a lust for power. It's why for more than two decades he did what he could not to give it up. It's why after two decades in power he ran for president again in May 2023, and won.

Turkey is part of Europe, and also part of Asia. In the modern era it has sometimes been a democracy, other times an autocracy. Nearly all Turks are Muslims, though since the establishment of the Turkish republic in 1923 under the legendary leadership of its first president, Mustafa Kemal Ataturk, Turkey formally, constitutionally, has been secular. It is an ally of the United States and a longtime member of the North Atlantic Treaty Organization (NATO). But Turkey is not always a reliable friend, certainly not under Erdogan.

During the decades between the presidencies of Ataturk and Erdogan it was assumed the ideas, ideologies, and institutions that Ataturk established would remain fixed. Not that they would remain impervious to change entirely, but that they would change slowly and gradually, not rapidly. It was further assumed that religion and politics would remain largely separate and that Turkey would continue to lean, socially and culturally as well as politically and economically, more toward Europe than Asia. To be sure, these generalities applied more to certain parts of Turkey than to others—more to cities in the country's west, for example, than to rural areas in the east. Still, for more than three-quarters of a century Turkey remained as Ataturk had created it: a secular democracy disposed to Western values. Only since Erdogan has this stance been thrown seriously into question.

Born in Istanbul to a pious, working-class family, Erdogan seemed an unlikely leader for a country that is one of the most important in the world, in good part because of its strategic location at the crossroads of Europe and Asia. Despite his modest origins, he made his mark on Turkish politics at an early age. Moreover, he became in time the prototype of a certain type of successful politician not only within Turkey but elsewhere as well. In Europe and in the United States, Erdogan's type of nativist, populist, authoritarian politics has come to provide stiff competition to traditional liberal democrats.

Turkey has never been either as liberal or as prosperous as Western European countries such as Germany and France. Nor, notwithstanding Ataturk's secularism and constitutionalism, does Turkey have a long or strong democratic tradition. To the contrary. Authoritarian tendencies and legacies have shaped the modern Turkish state, including that of the Ottoman Empire and Ataturk himself, who held power from when he founded the republic in 1923 to his death in 1938. In this sense, then, the political and ideological changes instigated by Erdogan are in keeping with Turkey's history and political culture. Moreover, given the worldwide shift in recent years from a smaller number of democratic leaders to a larger number of autocratic leaders, the early twenty-first century provided fertile soil for a nascent autocrat such as Erdogan. An autocrat who, though he appeared to come out of left field, turned out to be hell-bent on spreading not only his politics but also his personality, his ideology, and his own personal blend of autocracy and theocracy.

Erdogan remains less well known in the United States than some other recent leaders of NATO countries, such as Germany's Angela Merkel and France's Emmanuel Macron. Nevertheless, Erdogan has had a major impact both on his country and on the wider geopolitical landscape, especially in Europe and the Middle East. In 2019 he became the longest-serving Turkish leader in modern history.[1] And if his tenure in office continues unimpeded, he will remain president until May 2028, at least.

Of course, whether he will ultimately be deemed a good leader or a bad one will be determined not only by the judgment of history but also by who is doing the judging. Again, I write as a liberal democrat, so my assessment of him is from this perspective. And from this perspective he was bad, in that over time he pushed and pulled his country from fitful democracy to entrenched autocracy.

Phase I: Onward and Upward

To trace Recep Tayyip Erdogan's rise to power, start with his boyhood in the 1950s and '60s, when Turkey's politics were still strongly secular and hostile toward piousness. Specifically, piousness as practiced by Muslims who "wore their religion on their sleeve" and who were often made to feel not only unwelcome but unequal among members of the establishment. The implications of this were considerable for a boy such as Erdogan who, at age eleven, was placed by his father in a religious school at a time when such schools were considered second-class. Generally, these were vocational schools whose graduates were limited to attending university only to study theology. In a 2012 interview, Erdogan remembered how he and his peers felt "othered" during their years in school, emphasizing how they were repeatedly told their education would disqualify them from any profession other than the clergy.[2]

It's not hard to imagine the impact of this stigma on Erdogan, just as it's not hard to imagine it was precisely this exclusion that fueled his ambition. That made him more rather than less determined to succeed in politics while at the same time loudly and clearly championing his cause. What, specifically, was his cause? To raise Muslims to what he and millions of other Turks deeply believed was their rightful place in Turkish society. Though at first Erdogan sought to sidestep his commitment to political Islam—early in his career he said, "Before anything else I am a Muslim. . . . But I try now very much to keep this away from my political life, to keep it private"—over time it became the platform on which he stood for the rest of his political life.[3]

From an early age Erdogan aspired to a career in politics. So for his last year of high school he transferred to a public school with a secular curriculum. He apparently understood that at least a modest secular education was important to someone like him for practical, professional reasons and for his intellectual development. At the time, political debates in Turkey and in the wider Middle East were not only about secularism versus Islam but also about communism versus nationalism and the left versus the right.

In his early twenties Erdogan became involved in politics. First, he joined the National Turkish Student Union, an anticommunist action group. Then he became head of a youth group that was part of an Islamist party. A decade later, he became a member of the Islamist Welfare Party, and not long after chair of its Istanbul branch. By the age of forty Erdogan had established himself as a successful professional politician: he had been elected mayor of Istanbul despite being a "dark horse candidate who had been mocked by the mainstream media and treated as a country bumpkin by his opponents."[4]

Though Erdogan's mayoralty was generally judged successful—early on he developed a reputation for being competent as well as pragmatic—he quickly ran into trouble. Turkey's politics were growing increasingly fractious, so when he read a poem in public that ostensibly extolled the virtues of Islam, he was promptly arrested for inciting violence and religious hatred. Erdogan was sentenced to ten months in prison—he served four—and forced to surrender his post as mayor. Predictably, perhaps, the experience hardened him, especially his pro-Islam position. It made him more determined, not less, to raise the status of Islam in Turkish politics, in Turkish society, and in Turkish culture.

The political parties to which Erdogan belonged early in his political career ended up being mostly banned, either by the army or by the courts. So in 2001 he formed another party, this one in his own image. Named the Justice and Development Party (AKP), since its inception it has been the "primary vehicle for change under Erdogan."[5] Though the AKP benefited from comparison with the corruption and incompetence that had characterized Turkey's previous ruling parties (all of which were secular and center-right), especially in the 1990s, it was the AKP's primary identity as an Islamist party that stood out from the start. Initially it was advantaged by the context in which it was situated: the AKP profited, for example, from an economic crisis in 2000 and 2001, for which blame fell squarely on the shoulders of the previous government. But by 2002 the AKP won its own solid majority in the legislature. It was this win, one of the president's biographers later wrote, that opened "the gates of unchecked, and lopsided, legislative power for Erdogan, who became prime minister the following year. In due course, the Turkish leader would ensure that he would not lose this power, with grave ramifications for Turkey's democracy."[6]

When Erdogan became prime minister, he correctly believed that many in the old Turkish establishment distrusted him, looked down on him, or both. They did not think him stupid or incompetent—he had already proven himself as mayor of Istanbul, where he adopted modern management practices and was adroit at promising and then delivering services. But they were suspicious of his commitment to the secular norms that had, since Ataturk, defined their country's politics and their society more generally.

This meant, of course, that many of the approximately 80 million Turks felt quite the contrary. Erdogan proudly presented himself as authentic, declaring at one point that he was the "imam" of Istanbul. He relished making his Muslim identity clear, declaring, "In this country, there is a segregation of Black Turks and White Turks. Your brother Tayyip belongs to the Black Turks." (White Turks were considered urban and secular, people who thrived on and benefited from Turkey's modernization. Black Turks, in contrast,

were generally viewed as conservative, Islamic, more rural, and less privileged.)[7] Erdogan was, predictably, rewarded for his strong allegiance to the
masses by their strong allegiance to him, especially by those who were pious.
As one Turk, a barber, put it early in the prime minister's tenure, "He was
raised in a place like this. He doesn't come from a palace. When he shops, he
carries the bags himself."[8]

During his early years as prime minister Erdogan engaged in a constant
balancing act. On the one hand, he worked at appealing to his natural constituency, his Islamist base. On the other hand, he sought not to alienate
the millions of secularists, especially members of the political elite and the
military. So even as he proudly and repeatedly identified himself as a "Black
Turk," he also went to considerable lengths to assure White Turks that he
remained committed to their democratic, pro-Western values. Hence his
reputation as a leader who in the early aughts was, as *The Economist* put it,
"mildly Islamist."

Still, what is most striking about Erdogan's early years as a politician at
the national level was the strength of his appeal to Turks who throughout
Turkey's recent history had felt themselves to be second-class citizens. No
matter it drove members of the old Turkish establishment crazy. Erdogan
promised a new Turkey in which the millions of recent migrants from rural
to urban areas, most of whom were demonstrably pious, would successfully be integrated into a society previously dominated by cosmopolitans.
Erdogan's strategy was to chip away slowly but surely at the economic and
political power of the secular elite, especially that of his most formidable
opponent, the Turkish military. Still, for years he was careful not to antago-
nize members of the military, for Turkey's powerful generals continued long
after Erdogan became prime minister to see themselves as "the guardians of
Kemal Ataturk's secularist legacy." They called themselves "guardians" for
good reason: in their self-appointed role they had since 1980 successfully
overthrown no fewer than four governments.[9]

This balancing act—most obvious during the early years, the years during
which Erdogan tried, with a measure of success, to please most of the people
most of the time—was later referred to by an expert on Turkey, Dimitar Bechev,
as the "Golden Years."[10] They were the years that constituted Phase I, when, as
mayor of Istanbul, Erdogan thought of politics "as non-ideological but instrumental for solving the daily problems of people." Politics as "problem solving,
not as a means to build an ideologically oriented Islamic community."[11] During
the Golden Years it was possible to imagine Erdogan not as an ideological

leader but as a pragmatic one. One who might unite the two groups of Turks, who up to then had been separate and distinct, if not in conflict. But they were also the years during which the prime minister continued to strengthen his base, to appeal even more than before to his natural constituents, Islamists.

Phase II: Followers Join In

For all his initial ostensible enthusiasm for embracing secular and Islamic Turks alike, the fact is that from day one Erdogan had a natural constituency: millions of Islamic followers he could count on even as the charges that he was a power-hungry autocrat began to mount. Though he was always a polarizing figure, and more so as time went on, what was described as his "preternatural prowess at the polls" explains not just his remarkable political success but also his growing conviction that he could do whatever he wanted. Turkey had not managed to field a viable opponent to Erdogan, or a viable opposition to the AKP, since Erdogan and his party first came to power in the early aughts. Over time, together, they "gradually elbowed aside the secular elites that had run Turkey for 80 years."[12]

The strong, enduring support bestowed on Erdogan by large swaths of the Turkish people can be explained in three ways: by who *they* were, by who *he* was, and by the *relationship between them*. First, who they were: those among Erdogan's followers who constituted his strongest and most enduring base of political support. Most obviously they were like Erdogan, Islamists who all their lives had felt diminished if not excluded by Turkish secularists. In the 2023 presidential election this applied especially to devout, conservative women who not only voted for Erdogan in large numbers but also urged their friends and relatives to do the same. Typically, Erdogan's supporters were strongly and visibly attached to their faith—it was the primary reason they were estranged from the Turkish establishment. And because they felt demeaned and disenfranchised by Ataturk and then his successors, they experienced life as an "uphill battle." The fact that establishment Turks had long been oriented toward Europe, not Asia, also played a role. When Erdogan's early (and, as it turned out, brief) romance with the European Union (EU) soured, and when in response Erdogan pivoted from the West to the East especially the Middle East—though after the 2023 election he again shifted, for economic reasons, from the East back to the West, at least slightly—not only he but his base found the terrain considerably more congenial.

Turkey's brief romance with the EU was of consequence. Though Turkey had been a member of NATO for years and had originally applied to join the EU in the late 1980s, it was being leapfrogged for membership by Eastern European, postcommunist countries with a much shorter record of both multiparty politics and market economies. This deepened Erdogan's "suspicion that what formed EU choices was religious and cultural bias" and further fed into his jaundiced view of the West.[13]

From his earliest days in politics Erdogan made it a point strongly to align himself with his most faithful followers—his base—by adhering to their religious values and cultural norms. He would visit people in need, remove his footwear before entering their homes, sit on the floor when meeting families too poor to have much furniture, and kiss the hands of elderly family members.[14] It was a role to which he naturally gravitated. After all, to identify with ordinary people, he had deliberately cast himself as a "poor pious man from the other side of the tracks." It was this identity that allowed him to unambiguously, if initially cautiously, suffuse Turkey with politics and policies that reflected conservative beliefs and traditional habits. For example, Erdogan's wife, Emine, was never seen in public without a head scarf.

Erdogan's persona and politics were as rooted in history as in Islam. Another expert on Turkey, Soner Cagaptay, writes that "Turkey's salvation had to derive from the stock of traditions and ideas that had made the Turks great in past centuries. . . . Turkey could become a great power again, returning to Ottoman glory, by breaking away from the West and the Jews, two adversaries who [were] constantly scheming to destabilise Turkey."[15] It was the right message at the right time. Because of erratic economies and misguided policies—presided over by elites who by then were better known for being corrupt than for being competent—Erdogan and the AKP appealed strongly to the legions of Turks who historically had felt politically excluded and who in the present day felt economically insecure.

Erdogan's political success can be further explained by who he was—by the man himself, gifted as both a leader and a manager. We saw that he was considered a highly competent mayor of Istanbul, and that he was credited with transforming Turkey in the early aughts from bust economy to boom economy. He also "revolutionized" Turkish politics by, among other things, flooding the country's political and educational systems with Islam. Further, he embraced Islam not only at home but abroad. His supporters resonated with his foreign policies as they did with his domestic ones. Erdogan's pivot to the East provided his base with an identity that conferred on them respect and self-esteem, while further dispelling their feelings of inferiority and marginalization. After many years, it seemed to Erdogan's supporters that Turkey's proper place on the world stage was finally being restored.[16]

As did Ataturk before him, Erdogan capitalized on another tradition in Turkish culture, going back to the Ottoman era: that of the "Bigman." The Bigman's leadership status is not inherited. Instead, it is acquired by virtue of his prowess at provisioning and protecting his followers. A Bigman leads by "skilled persuasion and a reputation for wisdom." The legitimacy of his leadership depends on networks of followers who support him and whom he, in turn, supports through his access to resources and networks of connections.[17]

Put another way, especially during his first decade in power, Erdogan profited personally and politically from having the will and skill to tap into a Turkish leadership archetype. He was skilled at accomplishing some of the country's most important leadership tasks. He was skilled at connecting with his constituents. He was skilled at changing with the times. And he was skilled at drawing on Turkey's Ottoman past when it suited him. As one observer put it, he "sees himself as equivalent to an Ottoman sultan and . . . is desirous of developing a similarly legendary image."[18] To this end Erdogan's government built new bridges, tunnels, and highways named after various Ottoman sultans. And it built a new mosque, Turkey's largest, intended to evoke the country's glorious past, when great men ruled its expansive world.

Finally, Recep Tayyip Erdogan has been described as a charismatic leader who exudes confidence and a sense of purpose. He was able, partly through his extensive use of symbols, to imbue himself with moral authority and appeal to the emotions of his most dedicated followers. He inspired them.[19] But Erdogan did not rely only on how his followers felt; he knew enough to benefit them in other ways as well. When the AKP first came to power it established a centralized system of rewards (and punishments) that was targeted especially at its supporters. This partisan allocation of resources—including public properties and state monopolies—led over time to the growth and expansion of a pro-AKP (that is, pro-Erdogan) business class, which in turn bestowed on him financial as well as political support. It was this group of merchants, entrepreneurs, and other businessmen that financed a substantial part of the AKP's political campaigns as well as the pro-government media.[20] In other words, Erdogan had his bases covered. He and his followers gave each other what they needed and wanted.

Phase III: Leader Starts In

We saw that during the early years of Erdogan's political career he tried with considerable success to please most of the people most of the time. These were the Golden Years, the "onward and upward" years when, Erdogan conceived of politics as non-ideological but instrumental.[21] Politics as problem solving.[22] Of course, this was also the period during which Erdogan continued to strengthen his base, to appeal even more than before to his natural constituents, Islamists.

It gradually became clear, though, that the Golden Years were finite. That a future in which White Turks and Black Turks joined hands to cooperate and collaborate was largely illusory. Though early in his tenure as prime minister Erdogan could arguably be seen as a role model, an Islamist politician able to reconcile his religious faith with political pluralism, within a few years he revealed where his true sympathies and political priorities lay. At home he managed to neuter the secularist military, eliminating it as a major personal and political threat. And abroad, especially on the heels of the Arab Spring in 2011, he began to play a notably greater role in regional affairs, again, especially in the Middle East, repeatedly aligning himself and his government with Islamic movements, including in Egypt with the conservative Muslim Brotherhood. In short, as time went on Turkey's prime minister turned to the East more and to the West less. Not only did he seem to care much more about his identity as an Islamist but also he seemed to care much less about his identity as a democrat.

The challenge Erdogan faced first in establishing and then in sustaining his leadership role had all along been personified by the military. It was suspicious of him from the start. Though Erdogan and the AKP had repeatedly pledged their commitment to secularism—and, pointedly, to the memory of Kemal Ataturk—the military remained uneasy at best. Over time, however, there was little the generals could do. Removing the prime minister from power was not a viable option—among other reasons was that there was no effective opposition, no individual or group capable of forming a new government. The military was additionally constrained by the fact that in the early years of the twenty-first century Turkey was still hoping to accede to European Union membership, for which civilian control of the military was a prerequisite.

The years 2002–2004 were a standoff, with the generals continuing to resist Erdogan and the prime minister continuing to resist the generals. Though the tension between them was never fully or formally resolved, as the years went by Erdogan felt increasingly secure in his leadership and comfortable with the idea that between him and the Turkish establishment was an irreconcilable difference. At the same time, the prime minister had his own supporters to contend with, especially hardliners in the AKP and militants at the grassroots. Though some Turks had voted for Erdogan as a reaction to the corruption and incompetence of previous administrations, many more did so because they expected that once he held the reins of power firmly in his grip, he would "ease restrictions on the expression of Islamic piety in the public sphere."[23] At some point, then, if Erdogan and his party wanted to remain in power they would have to deliver.

Which in time they did. They delivered twice over: practically and ideologically. In the first decade of the twenty-first century Turkish living standards improved dramatically. For the first time in its history Turkey had a majority middle-class society, in considerable part as a result of turning to the Middle East for new products and growing markets. As Cagaptay pointed out, under Erdogan's leadership Turkey's influence in the Middle East and Asia was not only political and economic but cultural as well. Erdogan exercised both hard power and soft power. First, a slew of Turkish products, from heavy-duty trucks to canned tomatoes, were exported to "happy consumers across the Middle East." Second, cultural exports such as Turkish soap operas, once obscure productions limited only to domestic audiences, were increasingly beamed into living rooms across the region, from Aden to Casablanca.[24] By 2017 viewers in nearly a hundred countries were watching Turkish TV dramas, Turkey ranking second only to the United States in such soft-power exports.

Several years after Erdogan became prime minister it became clear that most of the old tensions were persisting and getting more corrosive, while new ones were surfacing. It was women who most visibly symbolized the most persistent of the many splits: on the one side Islamic traditionalists who wore head scarves, on the other side establishment secularists who did not. Meantime, though secularists still controlled the military, the judiciary, the bureaucracy, and the presidency, the AKP was making significant headway, with Erdogan the primary beneficiary of a thriving economy. Though 2007 was a tumultuous political year—hundreds of thousands of people repeatedly took to the streets to protest the prime minister's possible presidential candidacy—when the election was held in July Erdogan and the AKP scored important and impressive victories. They racked up nearly 47 percent of the vote, making it only the second time in Turkish history that the governing party won an election by increasing its share of the popular vote.

Erdogan's winning streak continued. Four years later the AKP was even more successful at the ballot box, with almost 50 percent of voters casting their ballot in support of Erdogan's party. This made him the only Turkish prime minister to win three consecutive general elections, each time with more votes than the cycle before.[25] Clearly, Erdogan was doing something—many things—right. He was continuing to increase Turkey's prosperity at home and its status abroad. By 2011 Turkey had the world's seventeenth-largest economy. And it was a more important regional power than it had been in decades. Twenty-first-century Turkey was finally taking advantage of its singular strategic position in terms of both geopolitics and energy. Turkey is, to underscore the point, geographically situated close to nearly three-quarters of the world's proven oil and also gas reserves. One British journalist wrote that Turkey's influence in the Middle East had grown so far so fast, it threatened to "eclipse" that of the United States.[26]

It was, however, around this same time that serious concerns over Erdogan's high-handed ways began to surface more regularly. In 2011, British journalist Peter Beaumont wrote a piece in *The Guardian* titled "Recep Tayyip Erdogan: Is 'Papa' Still a Father Figure to Turks?" If Erdogan had a problem, Beaumont wrote, "it is not in alienating even further those . . . secularists who have always opposed him, regarding him as a kabadayi (a ruffian). Instead, it lies with an increasing number of liberal intellectuals who once supported him but now regard him as being too thin-skinned, overbearing and—they fear—increasingly authoritarian."

There was more. At the beginning of the year Erdogan announced the arrest of more than forty military officers for allegedly taking part in an attempted coup that had taken place seven years earlier. By the end of 2011 the number of military men in detention had swelled to two hundred, with five generals among them. Erdogan was starting to show signs of being more brazen in his exercise of power, above all by publicly taking on those who long had been his most obvious and dangerous enemies: members of the military. By 2012, the question was being asked: Is Erdogan an Islamic democrat? Or is he instead an "elected sultan"?[27] His proclivity to autocracy was becoming increasingly and indisputably clear.

The year 2012 was a turning point not just for Erdogan but for Turkey and the Turkish people. By then he had been prime minister for seven years. He had consolidated his power and boasted tirelessly about his considerable accomplishments. Turks had never had it so good, Erdogan insisted, eliciting in some circles unabashed admiration and in others growing fear and loathing. To his admirers he was dynamic, a modernizing force. To his detractors he was divisive and even threatening. "The AKP is not a party anymore," opined one of his opponents. "It is Erdogan's apparatus. There is huge polarization in this country." But on one subject there was no disagreement. For all the challenges he faced, Erdogan's grip on power had expanded to "encompass all of Turkey's institutions." By 2012 one of his political allies had been installed as president. The parties that opposed him had splintered. The once-hostile judiciary was now under his sway (or so his critics claimed). The media was either supportive or intimidated into silence (or so his critics claimed). And, in consequence of his increasing self-confidence, which translated into intimidating his opponents, the previously powerful military had been neutralized as a political force.

Moreover, Erdogan was by no means done. Though he was barred from seeking a fourth term as prime minister, he was not barred from seeking to become president. But the president's office was still largely ceremonial—which is why Erdogan began to make it unambiguously clear that if he was ever to run for president, the constitution would have to be changed and the president's powers greatly expanded.

Phase IV: Bad to Worse

In 2016 an article in *The Atlantic* posed this question: "It wasn't so long ago that [Erdogan] was seen as a model democrat in the Islamic world—what happened?"[28] For any but close observers, he seemed to have morphed in short order from democrat to autocrat. But as we have seen, in keeping with the point of this book, the change was *not* sudden but gradual. There had been clear hints of Erdogan's strongman ways for years. If Erdogan ever was a Muslim democrat, he had not been one in some time.

Beginning as far back as 2007 there were signs that despite Erdogan's initial posturing, Turkey's future as a liberal democracy was uncertain. By the second decade of the twenty-first century Erdogan had long since capitalized on his and his party's continuing popularity. He had already successfully taken on the Turkish military. And he had arranged for the new elections that his party then won handily, with a "broad coalition of pious and average Turks, Kurds, liberals, and big business." The so-called Ergenekon case, in which the police uncovered a supposed plot to overthrow the government, gave Erdogan an additional excuse further to consolidate his strength in ways that included punishing those he deemed his political enemies.

Steven Cook, who wrote the abovementioned article in *The Atlantic*, described what certainly in hindsight was a predictable sequence. Over time, Cook wrote, "Turkey's democratic reversal expanded and accelerated. Erdogan was emboldened by the decapitation of the military and imprisonment of other opponents, at the same time that he was unrestrained by the now-dim prospect of EU membership."[29]

Erdogan consolidated his power by arming civilian prosecutors with search warrants that allowed them entry into military bases; by holding trials in which large numbers of military officers were detained; by arresting, often on specious charges, journalists other than those who were favorably disposed to Erdogan; and by imposing massive fines on businesses whose owners had failed to support the AKP politically and financially. Of course, new media and old also came under government control, to the point where there was "a virtual ministry of information in the service of Erdogan and his party." Finally, there were the courts, which in the wake of a 2010 referendum increasingly had judges who not only were not impartial but were openly sympathetic to the prime minister and his governing party.

The first serious public display of resistance to Erdogan's growing power was in 2013 when a group of environmentalists peacefully protested the government's plans to replace a park in the center of Istanbul with a shopping mall. Erdogan would have none of it: he sent in the police to attack the protesters and evict them from the park. The government's aggressive, repressive response led to further protests and strikes across the country, the biggest in Turkey's modern history. Opposition to Erdogan became more wide-ranging and far-reaching; anger against his government became more explosive, touching on everything from freedom of the press to the erosion of secularism in public life. Some 3.5 million people took part in approximately five thousand protests, all starting with the opposition to the proposed destruction of Gezi Park. Ultimately, the government was held responsible for eleven deaths and eight thousand injuries.

Years later these protests, and the government's militant response, came to be seen as a turning point—or, more symbolically, as another nail in the coffin of both Turkish democracy and the government's alliance with liberal, pro-EU elements of Turkish society. While the most enduring legacy of the events at Gezi Park was the government's growing conviction that it could and should repress anyone and everyone who opposed it, it is likely no coincidence that those events occurred close in time to the stillborn Arab Spring and the start of the murderous civil war in Syria. Which is why the "vaunted Turkish model"—democracy and capitalism wedded to moderate Islam—was viewed as having suffered a "car crash."[30]

By 2014 the prime minister made clear that though he had already held power in Turkey for over a decade, he was by no means ready to stop playing a pivotal leadership role in Turkey going forward. Quite the contrary. Erdogan was preparing to begin a new chapter. Though, as we have seen, the post of Turkish president was traditionally and constitutionally less powerful than the post of prime minister, Erdogan made clear he intended to change what had long been the existing system. He would run for president, *and* he would change the constitution to make Turkey's presidency the country's most powerful political office by far.

Notwithstanding his extreme ambition—and arguably because of it—Erdogan cruised to victory. In the 2014 presidential election, he won 52 percent of the vote, which despite the ongoing investigations of him and some associates for corruption, and despite the tumultuous year preceding the election, was the biggest win of his political career. As always, after his victory he promised the moon and the stars. "I want us to build a new future," he declared, "while considering our differences as a richness and bringing forward our common values."

But the divisions in Turkey were real and they were considerable. On one side were those who believed that the country needed a "fierce president" and that "no one other than Erdogan is capable for the job." And on the other side were those who believed that Erdogan was "power happy and arrogant, serving only half of the population that supports him, while the other half he deems irrelevant."[31]

In July 2016 there was a significant, if ultimately chaotic and failed, coup attempt. The bid to forcibly strip President Recep Tayyip Erdogan and his government of their power was led by a faction of the Turkish military—even though Erdogan blamed what happened on a man he considered his archenemy, a Muslim cleric by the name of Fethullah Gulen who had long been living in exile in Pennsylvania. While the attempt to oust Erdogan had failed, it was nevertheless a body blow not only to the president but to Turkey's political system. Buildings were bombed, including the Turkish Parliament and the Presidential Palace. And more than three hundred people were killed, with another twenty-one hundred injured.

Erdogan himself was not in either Istanbul or Ankara when the coup attempt took place, and for hours thereafter he was missing in action. But within a day he was back in control, thundering against his enemies and threatening them with revenge and retaliation. "The army is ours," he declared. "I am the chief commander."[32]

In the wake of the failed coup Erdogan received support not only from his usual allies but also from his usual opponents. Few anywhere across the political spectrum had any appetite either for putting the military in power or for any sort of illegal seizure of power. Still, what happened next was both depressing and predictable. In the wake of the attack Erdogan warned his opponents they would pay a "heavy price" for their transgressions—which they did.

Within days it became apparent the government had previously prepared an enemies list, something that could be presented at a moment's notice. The list contained thousands of names, specifically of those slated to be purged from "government ministries, schools, courts, universities, nongovernmental organizations, police departments, military battalions, hospitals and banks."[33] The numbers were astonishing. In the immediate wake of the coup, some 45,000 military officials, police officers, judges, governors, and civil servants were either arrested or suspended, including nearly 3,000 judges, 15,000 teachers, and every university dean in the country. It was, as one publication put it, Erdogan's personal and political "counter-coup." (A year later these figures were bumped up to about 130,000 people fired or suspended and another 45,000 arrested.)

The attack on him and his government had traumatized Erdogan, and it further cemented his opinions and dispositions. First, Islam became even more important to his worldview. Second, he became even more authoritarian than he had been previously. And third, his pivot from West to East took on a harder edge. Before the coup Erdogan had continued to make modest efforts to maintain Turkey's traditionally strong ties to the West. After the coup these ties became more strained. He became visibly more anti-European and anti-American, and he aligned himself still more closely with countries in the Middle East.

From this point on the progression from a high degree of presidential control to an even higher degree of presidential control continued unabated. How could this have happened? It happened because the opposition was insufficiently organized and mobilized to step in and stop the Bigman. In 2017 Erdogan called for a referendum on the powers of the Turkish presidency, so that he would be politically positioned to expand them further. His proposal passed by a slim majority, enabling him to assume the sweeping powers that he badly wanted and persuaded himself he badly needed.

Given the office of the presidency was being transformed, it is no surprise that Erdogan's opponents viewed this period (2017–2018) as a turning point. Turkey's authoritarian rule was being set in stone—at least so long as Erdogan held power. Turkey's parliamentary system was being phased out and an all-powerful president was being phased in. The executive was given power to issue decrees and appoint many if not most of the judges and officials who were responsible for scrutinizing his decisions. Further, instead of being limited to serving two terms of five years, the president now had the option to run for a third. Finally, the president was now allowed to order disciplinary inquiries into any of Turkey's approximately 3.5 million civil servants.[34]

In 2018 Erdogan called for another presidential election, almost a year and a half early, primarily to consolidate his power still further, which upon winning the election is precisely what he did. Even before he was inaugurated, the government had published a 143-page decree that changed the way almost every government department and public body in the country operated. The prime minister's office was formally and permanently abolished; the military was brought under still stricter civilian control; the president was empowered to draft the budget, choose judges and many top officials, dismiss the parliament, call new elections at will, and to appoint nearly all of the country's top officials, virtually none of whom required any sort of confirmation by any other individual or institution.[35]

By every measure, then, Turkey had been transformed into what some experts refer to as an illiberal democracy—a country in which elections are held but they are neither free nor open. Turkey was now a nation in which civil liberties were curtailed, information was controlled, and corruption was rampant. Moreover, since the failed 2016 coup attempt, Turkey remained in a state of emergency that gave even more power to the police and further restricted the right of assembly.

By the end of 2018 President Erdogan had amassed what some were calling "sultanlike powers." Moreover, as obvious as his continuing political imprint was his continuing physical one. "From soaring bridges to a giant mosque to plans for the world's biggest airport," the *New York Times* reported, President Recep Tayyip Erdogan of Turkey was using gargantuan building projects as an engine of growth—and as a way of leaving a tangible mark on the country he had already led for nearly two decades. Projects like these were meant to symbolize his strength forevermore, to secure his "place in the pantheon of great Turkish leaders, from the Ottoman sultans to the founder of the republic, Kemal Ataturk."[36]

Erdogan was a strongman who lashed his skill to his will to impose himself on the Turkish people. He catered to them while simultaneously intimidating them. He dominated Turkey politically, economically, socially, and culturally. And he transformed its system of governance from a fragile democracy to a constitutional autocracy. Among Western experts there is no disagreement: Erdogan and his allies successfully emasculated elected bodies and weakened the bureaucracy, the judiciary, and the military. A 2021 German research paper titled "Turkey's Presidential System After Two and a Half Years" presents a graphic depiction of its political system showing the president at the center of power—the sun around which the other heavenly bodies pivot.[37] Erdogan has been the most consequential Turkish leader since Ataturk, no question. But over time he evolved from a putative democrat into a demonstrable autocrat who had no compunctions about compelling individuals and institutions to bend to his will.

And yet there is a distinction between an authoritarian leader and a totalitarian one. For all his escalating despotism, Erdogan has never been in complete control. Turkey has always had a political opposition. Turkey has always had a civil society. And when Turks are in some way deeply dissatisfied—for example, as they have been in recent years with the economy (in 2022 Turkey's inflation rate soared above 80 percent—they remain able to express their anger and frustration in carefully circumscribed ways. Additionally, Erdogan has suffered several ignominious public defeats. For example, in 2019 his candidate lost the race for mayor of Istanbul. And in 2020 he endured a family drama in which the second-most-powerful man in Turkey and Erdogan's likely successor, who happened also to be his son-in-law, abruptly resigned.

In 2021 the *Financial Times* published an article headlined "Erdogan's Strongman Rule Is Beginning to Fray." While acknowledging the president's proclivity for "one-man rule," the piece reported that he had not entirely crushed that half of the Turkish population that was opposed to his "intrusion into their personal and political space" and to his "amalgam" of nationalism, populism, and neo-Islam.[38] Erdogan's talent might be "ebbing," the article concluded, and "his luck may be running out." Around the same time a story in the *New York Times* described Erdogan as having "brazenly" stamped out the domestic opposition but then added that thanks to the pandemic and to his mishandling of the economy he now faced "severe domestic strains."[39]

After Russia invaded Ukraine, Erdogan found yet another political part to play—that of would-be peacemaker. He tried repeatedly to get the two parties to the conflict to negotiate, attempting to portray himself as a leader able to straddle both sides and thereby in a position to accomplish what other leaders could not. He persisted in this role into 2023, though by then his calls on Russian president Vladimir Putin to cease hostilities seemed more performative than anything else. At the same time, he remained a large thorn in NATO's side, refusing for months to approve the membership applications of Sweden and Finland. It took until July 2023 for Erdogan finally to agree to admit both countries—an agreement that was procured only after the West granted Turkey economic and military concessions. Recep Tayyip Erdogan has a demonstrable lust for power, evidenced by his behavior at home and abroad.[40] Moreover, like all leaders who lust, even after he got what he wanted, and then got more of what he wanted, he did what he could to get still more. But because enough is never enough, this bad leader, along with his followers, will give up the ghost only when he is forced to. Hence the trepidations preceding the presidential elections scheduled for May 2023. The fear was that Erdogan would do everything he could to hamstring if not silence the opposition, which is precisely why *The Economist* warned several months before the Turkish electorate was slated to go to the polls that under his "increasingly erratic" rule, Turkey could be "on the brink of disaster." It could be "pushed over the edge into a full-blown dictatorship."[41]

And then it happened. In an instant the context—that third critical element of the leadership system—changed. Radically, dramatically, tragically. On February 20, 2023, significant parts of Turkey were devastated (as were areas of Syria) by a massive earthquake. Some fifty thousand Turks died, and countless families were left homeless. The World Bank estimated that the catastrophe inflicted $3.2 billion in physical damage in Turkey alone, or roughly 4 percent of the country's entire GDP.[42]

The immediate impact on the Turkish government, and on Erdogan's political fortunes, appeared to be enormous—and awful. Among the slew of criticisms, arguably the most damaging was that the president and his government for years had turned a blind eye to shoddy and corrupt construction, including large blocks of apartments that were woefully ill-equipped to withstand the earthquakes to which Turkey historically has been vulnerable.

In fact, for his own political purposes and to his own political ends, in 2018 Erdogan had extended a "zoning amnesty" to buildings that had failed to meet proper zoning and construction requirements.

Given that even before the disaster Erdogan was looking more personally and politically vulnerable than he had in many years, it is no surprise that thereafter he seemed to hemorrhage support. Notwithstanding his preternatural political skills and his high degree of control over everything and everyone in Turkey—including the government and its many administrative agencies, the legal system, the political system, and the media—in the immediate aftermath of the earthquake it was uncertain whether he would be able to survive the disaster politically.

The uncertainty was fueled by polls—which, as it turned out, were wrong to prognosticate the political demise of the longtime Bigman. Erdogan handily beat his main challenger, Kemal Kilicdaroglu, getting another five-year term as president and giving him and his party a solid majority in the legislature. As Cagaptay put it, this most recent of his many election victories all but anointed Erdogan as "Turkey's indisputable sultan." Cagaptay went so far as to compare Erdogan to President Vladimir Putin. Like Putin, Erdogan silenced opposition leaders and civil society activists—sometimes by arresting them. And he demeaned, denigrated, and demonized opposing candidates and their parties. Additionally, like Russia's leader, Turkey's leader played the culture card—at one point during the campaign referencing homophobia by saying, "The opposition are all LGBTQ."[43]

After the 2023 presidential election Turkey was in many ways a country depleted. It had yet to recover from the recent earthquakes, its currency had plunged, it was experiencing runaway inflation, it was heavily in debt, and its economy generally was battered. Additionally, its politics were fractured. While approximately half of Turkey's population was gratified by yet another Erdogan win, the other half, the half that believed in and supported democracy and the rule of law, was demoralized and depressed. The likelihood that Erdogan would return to being more of a democrat than an autocrat was slim to none. His lust for power had—as is typical in such cases—proved unslakable. He had become *intemperate*, which, as laid out in Chapter 3, designates a leader who lacks self-control and is aided and abetted by followers who are unwilling or unable to intervene effectively.

During his early years in power Erdogan presented himself as both an Islamist and a democrat. He promised to be something new and different, oriented to the West but also simultaneously to the East. Had he stayed on this path, he might have played the part of bridge-builder. Given his considerable political and managerial skills, he might have been an exceptionally good leader. But Erdogan was unwilling or unable to harness his lust. And so, absent limits imposed by others, he was free to metamorphose during his many years in power from a leader who was in most ways a democrat to a leader who was in every way an autocrat.

7

Elizabeth Holmes, CEO of Theranos

Both founders and CEOs have been known to go down in flames. But in the first decades of the twenty-first century arguably no downfall was as spectacular as that of Elizabeth Holmes. There are competitors; for example, Adam Neumann, the "messianic" cofounder of WeWork, whose powers of persuasion were so great that he sold very many people for a very long time on the idea that his "unoriginal, lossmaking start-up could change the world—and the laws of corporate valuation."[1] Neumann was so convincing an operator and seemed so clever a leader, he was able to raise more than $10 billion for WeWork based on the dubious assumption that freelancers would be willing to pay indefinitely for the privilege of leasing a tiny workspace in a collective setting. Still, one could reasonably claim that Elizabeth Holmes is in a category of her own. Her story is so singular—her persona so captivating, her rise to fame so striking, and her subsequent descent so precipitous—that she is the monarch of leaders who fell from grace.

Holmes stood out from the get-go. She was, highly atypically, a woman who was leader in the field of technology, and she was very young. She started her blood-testing company, Theranos, when she was just nineteen years old. Additionally, she was preternaturally poised and persuasive. She was vocal and articulate. She was classy, well dressed, and good-looking—a tall, willowy blond, usually clad all in black, frequently a black turtleneck to emulate and evoke her idol, Apple guru, Steve Jobs. Holmes had a special talent for pulling into her orbit people who were rich and powerful, especially older men. Finally, in short order, she became exceedingly wealthy, at least on paper. Theranos had become a "unicorn"—a privately held start-up company valued at over $1 billion. In fact, by 2015 Theranos was worth $9 billion. And Holmes was, at age thirty, regularly described as the world's youngest female self-made billionaire.

But the story of the rise and fall of Elizabeth Holmes transcends her persona. It includes a large cast of characters that includes the rich and powerful in business, government, and academia; Holmes's longtime partner and lover, Sunny Balwani; members of the press, nearly all of whom were in her thrall; and her many other followers, most of whom gladly or at least willingly followed where she led, though a small number did not—and finally blew the lid off what became a sensational corporate scandal.

Holmes's story takes place in a particular context at a particular time: Silicon Valley, in the early aughts, when it was an exceptionally exciting locus of activity in technology in which rapid, uninterrupted growth was the mantra, especially for founders who led start-ups and whose ambitions were boundless. Start-ups such as Theranos and, yes, WeWork, were enormously eager to attract private investors, who made it possible for fledgling companies to circumvent the constraints of public markets. Typically, these private investors were sitting on large piles of cash, looking to make money on their money, especially in what then was a low-interest-rate environment. Moreover, their zeal for investing tended to grow exponentially if their Big Money was in support of a Big Dream. Which is why, especially early in the twenty-first century, many young entrepreneurs sold not just the idea of making big money but also the idea of making the world a better place. Adam Neumann spoke of "elevating the world's consciousness." Mark Zuckerberg promised that Facebook would "give people the power to share and make the world more open and connected." Google cofounder Larry Paige declared that if he and his cofounder Sergey Brin had been motivated only by money, they would have "sold the company a long time ago and ended up on a beach."[2]

Elizabeth Holmes was in this mold. She promised her investors they would make a lot of money. She also promised them they would revolutionize modern medicine. Holmes pitched a game-changer: a device that would allow people to have their blood tested by drawing just a few drops of blood with a single finger prick. Here is how a Harvard Business School case study summarized her pitch: "Drug makers running clinical trials could catch adverse reactions before they caused harm. Blood-based tumor markers could be used to diagnose cancer months before patients became symptomatic. Uninsured Americans without access to life-saving blood tests could access them for pennies on the dollar."[3] Theranos was, in other words, promising a product that would not only revolutionize but democratize American medicine.

Phase I: Onward and Upward

Holmes was born in 1984, in Washington, D.C. It has been said, by her among others, that she was different from other girls, that from a very young age she wanted to be a successful entrepreneur. John Carreyrou, the Pulitzer Prize–winning reporter for the *Wall Street Journal* who was the first to expose Theranos's shady, even fraudulent practices and who later wrote an authoritative book on the subject, reported that when Elizabeth was nine or ten, one of her relatives asked her what she wanted to be when she grew up. Without skipping a beat, she replied, "I want to be a billionaire."[4]

Holmes came by her ambition honestly: it was nurtured by her parents and a family with a distinguished record in business, medicine, and public service. On her father's side, for example, she was descended from Charles Louis Fleischmann, who had made a fortune in the yeast business. Holmes later remembered that as a child she heard "stories about greatness." She similarly recalled the stories carried a message: do something meaningful with your life or you'll squander it.[5]

As a girl Holmes was extremely competitive and not particularly popular, especially not in high school. She had few if any good friends; instead, she stayed up late to study and struggled with an eating disorder. In 2014 she told an interviewer that as a child she was a happy loner who enjoyed collecting insects and fishing with her father. "I was probably, definitely, not normal," she said. "I was reading 'Moby-Dick' from start to finish when I was about nine. I read a ton of books. I still have a notebook with a complete design for a time machine that I designed when I must have been like, seven."[6]

Her exceptional drive was in evidence by the time she was an adolescent. Among her courses in high school, for example, was one in Mandarin. Not content to confine her study of the language to the ordinary, Holmes determined she would be extraordinary. While still a high school sophomore she applied to study Mandarin at Stanford University, repeatedly calling the admissions office, which repeatedly told her no, the program was for Stanford students only. One day the head of the program became so annoyed with her persistence that he asked her questions on the spot—in Mandarin. When she answered fluently, also in Mandarin, he accepted her into the summer program, which is how Holmes completed three years of advanced Mandarin while she was still in high school.

She enrolled at Stanford University as an undergraduate in 2002. Years later her abortive, out-of-the-ordinary college career became a subject of scrutiny. In her freshman year she attracted the attention of a dean who was a celebrated member of the faculty, an engineering professor by the name of Channing Robertson. She took his course and begged him for a research position, which explains how she secured a position as an assistant to a doctoral student in only her first year of college. Second, during the summer between her freshman and sophomore years she completed an internship at the Genome Institute, in Singapore. Third, early in her sophomore year she wrote a patent application that was a precursor to Theranos. It was based on the idea that multiple measurements could be made with just a few drops of blood. Though another faculty member dismissed Holmes's idea as implausible, Professor Robertson, who by then had become a mentor, was encouraging. As the story first was told, and for many years thereafter, Holmes soon became consumed by the idea that what she wanted was not to continue college but to drop out of school to start a company.

In her sophomore year she left Stanford—with her parents' blessing and their financial support. They gave her the money they had put away for her tuition, which made it possible for her to start her new company. One month after dropping out of Stanford she launched Real-Time Cures, quickly renamed Theranos. In remarkably short order, Holmes had managed to secure her new company, hire her first employee, and recruit her first board member, none other than Professor Robertson. Years later Robertson recalled how impressed he was by Holmes's preternatural energy and creativity: "I never encountered a student like this before of the then thousands of students that I had talked to. I encouraged her to go out and pursue her dream."[7]

Much later, Holmes's version of what happened during this period changed. For decades her story had been that she dropped out of Stanford to start her own company. However, in November 2021, when she was on trial in California for fraud, she told a different tale. On the witness stand Holmes testified that while she was a student at Stanford, she was sexually assaulted. She further testified that it was the trauma of the assault that convinced her to drop out of school and devote herself to her start-up. "I was raped when I was at Stanford," she said tearfully in court, "and I decided to put myself into building Theranos. I wasn't going to class, and I was questioning how I was going to process that experience. And I decided that I was going to build a life by building this company."[8]

At age nineteen Elizabeth Holmes proved a powerhouse. Among her other talents, she was remarkably good at executing one of the most important tasks associated with any start-up: raising money. In this case, it involved getting investors to buy into the idea that she was on to something genuinely new, different, and important. Holmes's initial foray into fund-raising utilized a time-honored strategy: she leveraged her family connections. Still, her early supporters were obviously impressed with her boundless vision and unflagging determination. In a twenty-six-page document she used to pitch early investors, Holmes "described an adhesive patch that would draw blood painlessly through the skin using microneedles . . . and communicate its readings wirelessly to a patient's doctor."[9] At a tender age, then, she managed to marry her scant scientific skills to her superb sales skills to raise the funds necessary to launch her company. By the end of 2004, Holmes had received some $6 million from what Carreyrou described as a "grab bag of investors."[10] A year later her company had twenty-five full-time employees.

Around that same time a tech magazine, *Red Herring*, called Theranos one of the "hottest startups in the Valley." The endorsement enabled Holmes to raise still more money. She persuaded Silicon Valley billionaire investor Don Lucas and his protégé, Oracle founder Larry Ellison, to invest $9 million. And in another round of fund-raising, this one in 2006, when Holmes was still in her mid-twenties, she raised $30 million. It was this most recent tranche that catapulted Theranos into an entirely different category. It provided the company with the resources "to create a basic prototype, engage an all-star chemistry team to design blood tests, and hire Silicon Valley engineer Ed Ku to turn the prototype into a product."[11]

Phase II: Followers Join In

Where Elizabeth Holmes led, not everyone followed. For example, after a brief stint on the board of Theranos, Avie Tevanian, previously a high-level software engineer at Apple, became skeptical of Holmes as a leader and manager and stepped down. Somewhat similarly, two of her youngest and greenest employees, Erika Cheung and Tyler Shultz, both initially enthusiasts— Cheung said that at first she was "star-struck" by Holmes—started to see her very differently not long after they started working at Theranos (about a decade after it was launched). These three were the exceptions to the general rule that where Holmes led, others followed. In fact, most followed her to the bitter end, over the cliff.

Holmes was exceptionally talented at raising money and, relatedly, at obtaining followers who were ready, willing, and able to support her in other ways as well. Early on, Holmes recruited a select few who invested large sums of money in her and her company. Thereafter, she raised some $945 million from a set of additional investors. In the process of establishing herself, and her company, Holmes assembled a board that consisted almost entirely of all-stars; brought into her orbit well-placed members of the press, most of whom were persuaded that she was a singular leader destined for singular success; hired a considerable and respectable cadre of dedicated employees; recruited several star partners; and secured for herself a personal and professional partner, a man much older than she and much more experienced, who was willing if not eager to enlist in her crusade. His name was Sunny Balwani.

Holmes's major investors included some of the wealthiest and most financially experienced people in the country, such as famed venture capitalists Don Lucas, Tim Draper, and Dixon Doll; the fabulously rich heirs to the founders of Amway, Walmart, and Cox Communications; and wildly successful and powerful tech and media moguls such as Larry Ellison and Rupert Murdoch, both of whom invested big in Theranos early on. At Holmes's trial, it became painfully clear that nearly none of these world-class investors had done much if any due diligence—which made their willingness to invest in a fledgling company started by a young and inexperienced woman all the more baffling. At least on the surface.

An interesting but by no means unusual case in point is Dan Mosley, a lawyer and power broker who worked for some very wealthy families. In 2014 Mosley asked Holmes for her company's audited financial statements. She did not provide them either then or later. Did this stop Mosley from investing $6 million in the company anyway, or from writing Holmes a "gushing thank you email for the opportunity"? Hardly. As the *New York Times* later reported, the Holmes trial provided an especially vivid picture of the many ways in which even the most sophisticated investors were hoodwinked. They were "swept up in the hype of a hot start-up, ignoring red flags that look obvious in hindsight."[12]

Equally if not even more astonishing was Holmes's capacity to conjure for her company a star-studded board. A group of particularly prestigious people happy to near-blindly follow their leader. Theranos's board was replete with people—most of them older men—of outsized accomplishment. Only a few had even the slightest experience or expertise in either science or medicine—but, apparently, no matter. Their being on the board nevertheless bestowed on Theranos a certain status, a special place in the pantheon of start-ups, despite it not having much if anything to show for it. Here is a partial roster of board members—in addition to Holmes and Balwani—in 2015:

Garry Roughead, a retired U.S. Navy admiral

William Perry, a former U.S. secretary of defense

Sam Nunn, a former U.S. senator, once chair of the Senate Armed Services Committee

James Mattis, a retired U.S. Marine Corps general (and, later, President Trump's secretary of defense)

Richard Kovacevich, a former CEO of Wells Fargo

Henry Kissinger, a former U.S. secretary of state

George Shultz, a former U.S. secretary of state

William Frist, a former U.S. senator, and a licensed surgeon

William Foege, a former director of the Centers for Disease Control and Prevention

Riley Bechtel, the chair of the board of the Bechtel Group

Holmes had similarly high standards for her business partners, most of whom were top-notch. Three stood out. First was Walgreens, the second-largest drugstore chain in the United States, with eight thousand stores nationwide. The relationship between Walgreens and Theranos began in 2010 when Holmes reached out, claiming her company's technology "could perform any of 192 blood tests using only a few drops of blood." She said that if Theranos devices were installed in Walgreens stores, they "could help customers take control of their health and even promote the earlier detection of disease." Walgreens executives were immediately "intrigued."

However, one of the Walgreens scientists, Kevin Hunter, who had been hired by his company precisely to provide his expertise, was skeptical from the start. He warned his superiors that Holmes could be "overselling or overstating . . . where they are at scientifically." His repeated expressions of concern fell on deaf ears. Walgreens executives—blinded by their ambition and worried about the competition—decided anyway to go ahead and make a deal with Holmes. Given her intolerance for any hint of dissent, it's not surprising that in short order she specifically requested that Walgreens exclude Hunter from their conference calls. She claimed he created "too much tension," and in time Walgreens sidelined him altogether.

Another of Holmes's prominent partners was Safeway, the national supermarket chain, whose CEO, Steven Burd, thought a significant "wellness play" might help revive the fortunes of his sagging brand. It appears that Burd was hooked on a personal level as well as on a professional one. Apparently, again according to a Harvard Business School case study, he "was enamored of Holmes, bearing gifts for her each time he visited Theranos, including a model of a private jet." Before long Theranos and Safeway had a deal. The latter agreed to lend the former $30 million and to build wellness centers in eight hundred Safeway stores featuring Theranos's technology. By 2012 Safeway had invested a cool $350 million in building the centers.

Third was Elizabeth Holmes's unusual relationship with the U.S. Department of Defense (DOD). In 2010 she managed to meet General James Mattis, at the time leader of U.S. Central Command. He was yet another among the many men interested, or at least potentially interested, in buying what Holmes was selling—in this case, specifically the premise that her company would within reasonably short order be able to help save lives on the battlefield. While in subsequent years "Holmes would regularly cite her partnership with the DOD, to customers, investors, and the media . . . suggesting the technology was being used by the armed forces in combat zones," in fact this so-called partnership never materialized, at least not beyond the study phase.[13] Theranos's putative relationship with the DOD was among the more remarkable of her many fabrications. However, her capacity even to get in the door of the DOD was yet another example of what she excelled at.

Holmes had a similarly strong appeal to members of an overly credulous press. This was best exemplified by a case that became an embarrassment to all concerned—especially to the journalist most directly involved, Roger Parloff. Parloff was an experienced yet obviously somewhat gullible reporter—and lawyer—who worked for *Fortune* magazine. He had never previously heard of Theranos, but once he learned about the company and, more importantly, met Elizabeth Holmes, he was hooked.

Parloff's story, which appeared in *Fortune* in June 2014, amounted to "5,500 words of pure rapture about a Silicon Valley company few had ever heard of and its intriguing chief executive."[14] Moreover, it ran with a large, striking photo of Holmes dead center on the magazine cover. As Parloff later admitted, he was taken with, and taken in by, Holmes in every aspect, from her deep voice to her "smart and engaging" personality to, no doubt, though this was left unsaid, her youth and good looks. Parloff was further persuaded of her exceptional gifts by "character witnesses" who included George Shultz, Mattis, and Kissinger, each of whom Parloff interviewed.

When his story came out, it catapulted Elizabeth Holmes, age thirty, to "instant stardom." No wonder. That cover photo alone—of "an attractive young woman wearing a black turtleneck, dark mascara around her piercing blue eyes and bright red lipstick next to the catchy headline 'THIS CEO IS OUT FOR BLOOD' "—was riveting.[15]

But Parloff was by no means the only journalist susceptible to Holmes's charms. After the scandal broke, in 2016, an article in *Vanity Fair* went so far as to charge that the tech press was "the secret culprit in the Theranos mess." It had "embraced Holmes and her start-up with a surprising paucity of questions about the technology she had supposedly developed. They praised her as 'the next Steve Jobs,' over and over . . . until it was no longer a question but seemingly a fact."[16] Similarly, in 2021 a piece in *New York* magazine alleged that "journalists had in some sense created Theranos, splashing Holmes and her Jobsian black turtleneck on the covers of magazines like *Forbes*, *Fortune*, and the *Times*' *T*." The last featured a story that named Holmes one of "Five Visionary Tech Entrepreneurs Who Are Changing the World."[17]

At its peak, in 2015, Theranos employed some eight hundred people. Though when the company collapsed stories emerged about how unhappy many of them were, for about ten years (2003 to 2013) Holmes was the leader of a band of apparently dedicated followers. As mentioned, even those who later became whistleblowers, specifically Erika Cheung and Tyler Shultz—who, not incidentally, was George Shultz's grandson—initially were true believers. Early on they were persuaded that Holmes and her breakthrough company were using science and technology to make the world a better place. Cheung, for example, a recent college graduate, joined Theranos in 2013, when the company was creating "a buzz on campus." Later she recalled a Berkeley job fair at which the Theranos booth had "a line out the door of people waiting to talk to the recruiter."[18] Shultz similarly started his job at Theranos in 2013, convinced by his eminent grandfather, George Shultz, that the company had a great future and that working under Elizabeth Holmes would be a splendid opportunity for him to help transform public health.

Finally, and critically, among the large cast of Holmes's followers was Sunny Balwani. For years he was her partner in life and in work. Described in a 2014 article in the *New Yorker* as "key to the company's success," Balwani, two decades her senior, first met Holmes not long after she graduated from high school, in 2002.[19] At the time both were spending several weeks in Beijing, where they developed a relationship that appears to have been close nearly from the start. He, born and raised in Pakistan, had made millions of dollars in the United States during the height of the dot-com boom. She seems to have seen him as a friend and protector, and as a role model who had done what she hoped to do: make her mark as an exceptionally successful entrepreneur. Clearly, Balwani was eager to play her mentor for many years. Just as clearly, Holmes was eager to play his mentee for many years.

Balwani formally joined Theranos in 2009. Initially, no one seemed to have known that he and Holmes were romantically involved. (At her trial, in 2021, she alleged that he had abused her physically and psychologically.) People knew only that they were professionally close and that Balwani, whose formal titles were president and chief operating officer, was never far from Holmes's side. Notwithstanding his importance at Theranos, Balwani was not much liked, admired, or even respected by those who worked there. He flaunted his affluence. He knew nothing about either science or medicine. And he was dismissive, even offensive to those he considered beneath him.

What, then, did Balwani bring to the table? Hard to know exactly. What is clear in any case is that for more than a decade he gave Holmes what she wanted and needed when she wanted and needed it. He was a follower so completely dedicated to her and her cause that nothing else in his life seemed much to matter. (Tellingly, though Balwani invested some $15 million of his own money in the company, he never cashed out, not even after the value of his investment had soared to about $500 million.) She led the company; he managed it. She made the decisions; he executed them. Whatever the exact nature of their relationship, his dedication to her, to her fever dream, was all-consuming, which is why he remained for the duration, unwilling or unable to correct the errors of her ways. To the contrary. Balwani was a quintessential bad follower. He contributed mightily and for many years to the collapse of Elizabeth Holmes—and to that of her company.

Phase III: Leader Starts In

From the beginning, Elizabeth Holmes exhibited the leadership style that eventually did her in. She cultivated a corporate culture that all along should have raised red flags.

Of her several idiosyncrasies, three stand out. First was Holmes's extreme insistence on secrecy. Most founders are protective, eager for trade secrets not to be revealed or leaked to, or stolen by, the competition. However, some founders are more protective than others, and some, such as in this case, are obsessive. Under the thumb of Elizabeth Holmes, Theranos's insistence on secrecy was so exceptionally restrictive and punitive it was more than a culture of concealment—it was a *cult* of concealment.[20]

Going back to at least 2007, Holmes was known for being so inordinately protective of her product that she was, in effect, paranoid. She required "not just employees to sign nondisclosure agreements, but anyone else who entered Theranos's offices or did business with it." Moreover, within the company she kept "tight control over information" and created an atmosphere that was "oppressive."[21] The secrecy and repressiveness that were the inevitable result were pervasive. For example, Holmes insisted on erecting physical barriers to separate functional teams and on developing IT systems that prevented employees from sharing information, even to the point of barring instant messaging. Security and privacy were further enforced through intimidation. She "regularly threatened legal action against ex-employees who she often alleged had stolen intellectual property."[22]

Another red flag was Holmes's proclivity for punishing dissent. Differences of opinion, probing questions, and suggestions of skepticism not only were not encouraged but were discouraged, effectively forbidden. Employees with concerns quickly learned not to express them. "Holmes was volatile and could lash out at employees who expressed doubts" about Theranos, whether its product or its strategic plan. The company made clear that questioning it in any way was to risk being marginalized, ostracized, even terminated.

Examples of this abound. But some stand out, such as Tevanian, who was personally recruited by Holmes to join Theranos's board. Before long he had doubts about Holmes, among them her revenue projections, which he concluded were grossly exaggerated and based on deals not yet consummated. When Tevanian brought his concerns to another member of the board, Holmes's early supporter and financial backer Don Lucas, instead of getting a sympathetic ear he got the back of Lucas's hand. Without so much as a careful hearing, Lucas told Tevanian that, given how he felt, he should resign. In the end Tevanian faced legal threats and was essentially forced to waive his right to buy a company cofounder's shares. But he got the last word. In late 2007, Tevanian wrote Lucas a letter of departure that concluded as follows: "I do hope you will fully inform the rest of the Board as to what happened here. They deserve to know that by not going along 100% 'with the program,' they risk retribution from the Company/Elizabeth."[23]

Another egregious example of Holmes's zero tolerance for dissent was Ian Gibbons. He was the first experienced scientist Holmes hired, one of two men in charge of Theranos's chemistry laboratories between 2005 and 2010. The trouble was that Gibbons was a stickler for absolute accuracy in blood testing—and for the absolute truth. Neither endeared him to his higher-ups.

Gibbons, meantime, got frustrated to the point of being fed up. According to Carreyrou, "Ian had heard [Holmes] tell outright lies more than once and, after five years of working with her, he no longer trusted anything she said, especially when she made representations to employees or outsiders about the readiness of the company's technology."

Finally, Gibbons decided to share his feelings with Holmes's longtime mentor, Professor Robertson, who was also a longtime member of Theranos's board. The trouble was that Robertson turned right around and repeated to Holmes everything that Gibbons had said—whereupon she promptly fired him. Though a day later Gibbons was rehired, from that point on his position in the company was significantly diminished. He remained a technical consultant, but his leadership role was eliminated. Eighteen months later he was further humiliated when he lost his private office. After he was subpoenaed to testify in a lawsuit (brought by Theranos) involving misappropriation of a patent, Gibbons became disheartened and depressed. Not long after, he killed himself.

This is not to suggest that Elizabeth Holmes was responsible for Gibbons's suicide. He had other issues, including health problems that years earlier had entailed surgeries and chemotherapies. It is, however, to say that Gibbons was an example of a dissenter who was treated shabbily. His wife, Rochelle, never forgave Elizabeth Holmes. "She's a bully, she bullied him, she made him feel bad all the time," Rochelle Gibbons said of Holmes. "People like that should be in jail. They should not be allowed to destroy people's lives."[24]

Finally, another example of how dissent was squashed is Theranos's treatment of those two recent college graduates employed by the company who quickly became, in reaction to their frustration, whistleblowers. Erika Cheung and Tyler Shultz worked at the company only briefly. But after repeatedly witnessing what they saw as wrongdoing they expressed their concerns to their superiors. To no avail. After being stymied and stonewalled by Theranos's management, they decided to serve as a source for John Carreyrou, the reporter who broke the story that led to the scandal. According to Carreyrou, Cheung and Shultz were "appalled by the lack of scientific rigor that had gone into validating [Theranos] tests. . . . The company routinely ignored quality-control failures and test errors and showed a complete disregard for the well-being of patients."[25]

Erika Cheung expressed her doubts about quality control in late 2013 and early 2014 to two powerful players. The first was George Shultz, who long had been one of Elizabeth Holmes's mentors and a member of her board. Over dinner at Shultz's house, she and Tyler voiced their concerns and expressed not only their reservations but also their frustrations. George Shultz listened to what his grandson and Cheung had to say but did nothing.

The second prominent person to whom Cheung turned was Sunny Balwani. He was not exactly sympathetic. He told Cheung that she was not qualified to criticize Theranos, and that either she should do her job without objection or she should leave. At that point Cheung quit. She followed up by taking her concerns not only to Carreyrou but also to the Centers for Medicare and Medicaid Services, a federal agency that oversaw labs such as those at Theranos. For Cheung's troubles she was harassed and threatened by, among others, Theranos's legal team, whose famed litigator, David Boies, sent her a letter threatening legal action because she had the temerity to talk to a reporter.

The case of Tyler Shultz is more complicated and involves a family drama in which three generations ultimately become deeply and painfully embroiled. After he had worked at Theranos for eight months, Tyler was so concerned about what was happening at the company that he sent an email to Holmes complaining that Theranos had doctored research and ignored failed quality control checks. Holmes in turn forwarded Tyler's email to Balwani, who belittled Tyler's knowledge of science and suggested that he had secured his job only because of nepotism. "The only reason I have taken so much time away from work to address this personally is because you are Mr. Shultz's grandson," wrote Balwani to Tyler in an email. That same day Tyler Shultz quit his job, only to be told by his frantic mother that Holmes had called his grandfather to warn him that Tyler would "lose" if he challenged or questioned Theranos. But the younger Shultz was not deterred. Using an alias, he contacted New York State's public health lab and alleged that Theranos had manipulated its proficiency testing. In 2015 he spoke to John Carreyrou, for whom he, like Cheung, became an important source.[26]

At Elizabeth Holmes's trial, it came out that Theranos had spent $150,000 on private investigators whose sole job was to tail Erika Cheung and Tyler Shultz. Though Holmes did not invoke Shultz in the courtroom, of Cheung she said, "I sure as hell wish we had treated her differently and listened to her."[27]

Yet another red flag at Theranos was the one that finally got Elizabeth Holmes into trouble with the law: Holmes's habit of fudging, distorting, or outright lying. She was especially prone to exaggerating what Theranos had accomplished in the past and what it would deliver in the future.

To disrupt the $75 billion-a-year blood testing market by providing a highly attractive alternative to existing blood-testing procedures, the company developed a "mini lab." This lab was in a box that Theranos named "Edison." But during the seven years of research and development on Edison, Theranos made claims for the device that were false. All along the company had insisted that the device could perform somewhere between 240 and 1,000 different tests. But during the trial several former Theranos employees testified that Edison was able to perform only twelve. Any other tests that were performed were run on devices made by companies other than Theranos.[28]

The problem for Holmes and her company was the discrepancy between what was happening on the ground and what was happening in Holmes's head. These discrepancies did not diminish over time. To the contrary—they became endemic, until finally they were fatal. In 2015 *Forbes* estimated that Elizabeth Holmes was worth $4.5 billion. One year later *Forbes* estimated her net worth at zero.[29]

Phase IV: Bad to Worse

For about five years, from 2010 to 2015, Elizabeth Holmes sank deeper and deeper into a quagmire of her own making. She had been brilliant at selling her product—or, if you prefer, herself—but she got to the point of having to deliver on her promise and provide a product, which she was never able to do.

What happened at Walgreens is an example. Theranos had promised Walgreens the moon and the stars. A life-changing technology that would alter forever the way blood was drawn and tested and change the company's fortunes. Above all, it would enable Walgreens to vault ahead of its main competitor, CVS. In their zeal to grow and prosper, Walgreens executives ignored several red flags, deciding despite warnings to invest in Theranos and invest big.[30] A contract was signed in which Walgreens would purchase up to $50 million worth of cartridges from Theranos and loan it another $25 million. The commercial launch was slated for February 2013.

Two years later, however, it was clear there was a problem. There were growing doubts that Theranos could do what it said it could do. By then John Carreyrou was on the case, his investigative reporting having started in earnest. He was interviewing people both inside and outside the company, including patients and doctors who had used Theranos's technology at Walgreens testing centers in Phoenix. "The customers shared concerning experiences in which suspect Theranos tests results had led to false alarms and medical scares"—which encouraged Carreyrou to dig further. Before long federal prosecutors became involved, and by 2016 they had subpoenaed Walgreens (among others), requiring the company to provide information about its relationship with Theranos. A few months after that Walgreens closed all forty of its Theranos Wellness Centers.[31]

The year 2015 was the turning point. It was then it became clear that Elizabeth Holmes was a victim of her own success. She had excelled at selling but she had failed dismally at delivering. With every passing month the gap between promises made and promises kept became more apparent and acute. In April 2015 an article in *Yahoo Finance* carried this headline: "Scientists Are Skeptical About the Secret Blood Test That Has Made Elizabeth Holmes a Billionaire." Among the problems it described were Theranos's failure to publish a single scientific, peer-reviewed study that compared its blood tests to those already in use. Nor did the company allow independent experts access to its labs, using as an excuse the need to protect intellectual property.[32] By the end of the year the *New York Times* pointed out that though Theranos claimed to have conducted "millions of tests," it had not once permitted its technology to be objectively assessed.[33]

It was the *Wall Street Journal*'s Carreyrou who broke Theranos's back. Once he became involved in the story, his reporting was relentless. Even the first of his many related articles, which ran in October 2015, suggested his investigation would be devastating. In his subsequent book, *Bad Blood*, he described the essence of his initial piece: "In addition to revealing that Theranos ran all but a small fraction of its tests on conventional machines [as opposed to its own Edison], laying bare its proficiency-testing shenanigans and its dilution of finger-stick samples, it raised serious questions about the accuracy of its own devices."[34]

But Carreyrou focused on more than Theranos's science; he was interested as well in its organizational culture. For example, when employees showed Sunny Balwani some unsettling lab results or registered any other sort of significant complaint, instead of being open to new and potentially important information, he was furious, as had happened with Tyler Shultz. He wrote to Holmes that "samples should have never run on Edisons to begin with" and that he was "extremely irritated and frustrated by folks with no legal background taking legal positions and interpretations on these matters."[35] In March 2016 Carreyrou and a colleague wrote in the *Wall Street Journal* that according to a federal inspection report, "the blood-testing devices that Theranos Inc. touted as revolutionary often failed to meet the company's own accuracy requirements for a range of tests, including one to help detect cancer."[36]

The investigation led by Carreyrou was unstoppable, even though Holmes and her minions tried. Federal agencies started to smell blood, so to speak. Companies that had signed contracts with Theranos, including Safeway, voided those deals. Lawsuits were filed, such as with Walgreens, which sued for $140 million, alleging breach of contract. (That case was settled for an undisclosed amount.) Partnerships fell apart. Ordinary people who had had experiences with Theranos's testing, such as those doctors and patients from the Phoenix area mentioned previously, complained about everything from false advertising to mistaken testing. And in March 2018 the Securities and Exchange Commission accused Theranos of perpetrating an "elaborate, years-long fraud" against investigators, partners, and patients.

Three months later, Holmes and Balwani were indicted by a federal grand jury for wire fraud. Three months after that "Theranos, with just 25 employees remaining, went into credit default and closed its doors."[37]

Elizabeth Holmes's immediate response to the calamity was curious. Former employees later reported that throughout this final, dismal period she acted bizarrely, as if nothing were wrong. "The company is falling apart, there are countless indictments piling up, employees are leaving in droves, and Elizabeth is just weirdly chipper," reported one former senior executive.[38] While this would seem on the surface to be surprising, perhaps it is not. Perhaps it was simply in keeping with someone who, for the better part of two decades, initially had a dream and then chose to live in a dream world.

Whatever the legal culpability of Elizabeth Holmes, this much is clear. She fabricated and fantasized. She concealed and confabulated. She lied and denied. She looked like a Silicon Valley superstar. She posed like a Silicon Valley superstar. She promised like a Silicon Valley superstar. But she did not deliver like a Silicon Valley superstar. In the end, whatever her remarkable skills and talents, she was a hustler, a poser, a promoter, a trickster, a con artist, a fibber, a fabler, and a falsifier. Among her concealments, distortions, and falsifications were these: (1) the types of tests Theranos offered, (2) the number of tests Theranos offered, (3) the procedures involved in its tests, (4) the capabilities of Theranos devices, (5) the devices Theranos employed, (6) the company's medical and scientific readiness, (7) the company's financial stability, (8) the nature of the company's culture, (9) the nature of the company's partnerships, and (10) Theranos's capacity to deliver on its promise within the promised timeframe.

All of which raises the question of how for so long Elizabeth Holmes was able, was allowed, to go from being a bad leader to being a worse leader. There is no question that from 2010 to 2015 she and her company, and everyone associated with it, sank deeper and deeper into a quagmire that was of her own making. Similarly, there is no question that whatever the nature of her relationship with Sunny Balwani, at Theranos she was the leader, he the follower. She was the one to whom everyone was ultimately responsible and to whom everyone ultimately deferred.

To be sure, as with all cases of bad leadership, there is blame enough to go around. For example, the impact of the context is obvious. First, the story of Theranos took place in Silicon Valley, where the line between someone who is a visionary and someone who is a fraudster can be blurry. Holmes took a page right out of the Silicon Valley start-up playbook, which relied on "hype, exclusivity, and a 'fear of missing out' to win over investors. She embodied the start-up hustle culture by optimizing her life for the maximum amount of work." And, like most of her male peers, she "dismissed anything that interfered with her vision of a better world."[39]

This brings us, inevitably, to another aspect of leadership: the relationship between leaders and followers, which in this case involved both sexual attraction and sexism. I already implied that Elizabeth Holmes drew on her femininity—on what once would have been called her "feminine wiles"—to appeal to rich and powerful men, to reel them in as supporters, investors, and true believers. We now know that when it came to Holmes many of these men were not only feeble but feckless. Most tended to believe what she said without question, and to follow unquestioningly where she led.

Parloff was one of those who fell into this category, as did most of Theranos's board members. Garry Roughead later testified that even after concerns about the company became a matter of public record, he did not investigate, using as his excuse that he lacked the necessary information. Similarly, when he was asked if he ever questioned Holmes on the subject, he replied, "I did not ask her directly, no." Asked if he had ever raised questions with anyone else at the company, he admitted, "I did not." George Shultz testified similarly. He said he "didn't probe into" whether the firm's technology was what it claimed to be, adding, "It didn't occur to me. Since I didn't know I didn't have anything to look into."[40] Dick Kovacevich did not "remember disapproving" of anything that Holmes did. "Elizabeth made the decisions," he continued, while at the same time acknowledging that Theranos's board was "completely and totally different" from any other board with which he was familiar.[41]

As is often the case in such situations, the fact of Holmes being a woman was a double-edged sword. Ellen Pao, a woman with her own difficult history in the tech industry, argued that Holmes was put on trial for behaviors of which men had long been guilty. "Male chief executives and founders," Pao wrote, "just aren't held accountable in ways that would lead to reform . . . [a]nd even when they are made to answer for their actions, they find their way back into the fold very quickly."[42] (To Pao's point: in 2022 the thoroughly disgraced Adam Neumann was given a big, fat lifeline in the form of a big, fat check—about $350 million—from venture capital firm Andreesen Horowitz to support his next start-up.)

There is also the impact that Holmes had on other women, specifically on those who succeeded her, or tried to. In 2021 a *New York Times* reporter found that a "generation of female entrepreneurs—particularly those in life sciences, biotechnology and health care—is still operating in [her] shadow." Though Theranos collapsed in 2018, three years later its founder and leader still loomed "large across the start-up world because of the audacity of her story, which has permeated popular culture and left behind a seemingly indelible image of how female founders can push boundaries."[43]

In January 2022, after a long trial and deliberations that lasted for fifteen hours over seven days, a federal jury convicted Elizabeth Holmes on three counts of fraud and one of conspiracy. Eleven months later she was sentenced to serve eleven years and three months in federal prison. In March 2023 she was back in court to appeal the decision, but to no avail. On May 30 she reported to a minimum-security prison about a hundred miles outside of Houston to finally start serving her sentence.

In July 2022, in a separate trial, Sunny Balwani was found guilty on twelve counts of fraud. How it happened that Balwani was found more guilty of wrongdoing than Holmes is not self-evident. Perhaps it was because he had a different judge and jury. Perhaps her lawyers were better than his. Perhaps it was because he was older and more experienced. Perhaps it was because Holmes took the stand in her own defense and he did not. He also got a longer sentence. In December 2022 Sunny Balwani was sentenced to almost thirteen years behind bars. On April 20, 2023, his lawyer told CNN that Balwani had started serving his time in prison without incident.

Holmes's downfall is an exemplar. First, of the perils of bad leadership, specifically of *rigid* leadership. Rigid leadership, as noted in Chapter 3, is when the leader and at least some followers are stiff and unyielding. Although they may be competent, they are unable or unwilling to adapt to new ideas, new information, or changing times. Holmes was nothing if not a rigid leader—so rigid that she was effectively impervious to the growing mountain of doubt that her dream would be, could be, realized. Had she been able to hear the growing concerns, to grasp the hard, sad evidence that was piling up, it might have been possible for her to correct course and save herself and her company. But she could not.

Second, Holmes's downfall testifies yet again to how bad leadership gets worse over time unless and until something or someone intervenes—in this case, most importantly, John Carreyrou. It took years before the secrecy, the obstinacy, and the rigidity at Theranos hardened into fatal flaws.

8

Xi Jinping, President of China

In June 2022 the *New York Times* had a long piece, "How China Is Policing the Future: An Unseen Cage of Surveillance."[1] The word "cage" is evocative, as is the word "surveillance." Both suggest high levels of state-sponsored scrutiny, suffocating violations of privacy, and fear-inducing restraining that, because of new technologies, are unprecedented. They make George Orwell's "Big Brother Is Watching You" seem like child's play. They are also illustrative. The fact that by the third decade of the twenty-first century China's 1.4 billion people were constantly being monitored, recorded, censored, and controlled is indicative of the trajectory by which Xi Jinping evolved from an authoritarian leader to a totalitarian one.

Consumed by fears of instability and insecurity from the start of his time in power, Xi continually strengthened his personal control over everyone and his political control over everything—most notably over the Chinese Communist Party (CCP), which gradually asserted its authority over every aspect of Chinese life. This brings us to the word "totalitarian." Experts have never used it lightly, whether referring to a state or to a leader. The word first was used in fascist Italy, applied to Benito Mussolini. But it gained prominence in consequence of the experience of Nazi Germany and the Soviet Union, with Adolf Hitler and Joseph Stalin providing templates of what totalitarian leaders look like. As the word suggests, totalitarian states are those that have near-total control because everything they do not control is banned. A totalitarian regime thus has one political party, one dominant military, one educational system, one artistic creed, one unified media, one moral code, and usually though not always one centrally planned economy.[2] Totalitarian leaders, in turn, are those who have near-total control over totalitarian states. In a totalitarian state, nearly everything is under the thumb of the state. And under a totalitarian leader, nearly everyone is under the thumb of the leader—from those at the bottom to those close to the top.

Totalitarianism implies unswerving obedience to authority. It further implies that, absent the same, coercion can be and usually is considered justified by the state or party, as has been the case in China for at least the last few years. The overweening power of the state was captured in that *Times* article, which described in painful detail how the new Chinese technologies "further extend the boundaries of social and political controls and integrate them ever deeper into people's lives." And the overweening power of the CCP was captured in descriptions of the 20th Party Congress in October 2022, during which President Xi was effectively anointed leader for life. His comrades praised his speeches as if they were hallowed texts. They professed their loyalty with a fervor reminiscent of that previously reserved for the party's founder, Mao Zedong. And they engaged in repeated, regimented displays of limitless admiration and ostensible affection.[3]

What exactly is the purpose of total control? The answer to this question has not changed in seventy-five years. What is paramount to totalitarian states is political stability and national security. Any threat to this stability and security, even the slightest sign of internal disorder, disobedience, or resistance, must somehow be stopped, as must any external threat. What is paramount to totalitarian leaders—here President Xi Jinping—is sustaining their power. But, because enough is never enough, their power is not fixed or finite. In the book I coauthored with Todd Pittinsky, *Leaders Who Lust*, we wrote that leaders who lust for power—including, obviously, totalitarian leaders, though not limited to them—have a ceaseless craving to control.[4] They have a psychological drive that produces an intense want, even a desperate need for power, which, however, can be satisfied only temporarily. Leaders who lust for power have something akin to an addiction. The more power they get, the more they want. To repeat what Winston Churchill said of Adolf Hitler in 1938, "his appetite may grow with eating." As history testifies, it did.

Xi's lust for power is why, as this discussion will demonstrate, he went from bad to worse. This assumes that your definition of "worse" is like mine: in this case, a leader who went from being controlling to being very controlling, to being exceedingly controlling, to being controlling in the extreme. The lessons are always the same. First, over time leaders and their followers change. They do not stay the same. Second, over time bad leaders become worse leaders. Unless someone or something intervenes, this trajectory is inevitable. Third, over time the sequence from bad to worse is predictable. It consists of four phases that proceed from one to the next in a certain order, each indicating leadership more ineffective and/or more unethical than it was previously.

That President Xi changed during his first ten years in office is not in question. "During his decade as China's top leader, Xi Jinping has hardened and centralized the security state, unleashing techno-authoritarian policies to quell ethnic unrest . . . and enforce some of the world's most severe coronavirus lockdowns. The space for dissent, always limited, is rapidly disappearing."[5] Not all at once, but gradually, Xi came to exercise inordinate control over information and ideas, over institutions and individuals. The process was both pernicious and ubiquitous. Plus, as his domestic policies and priorities changed, so did his foreign policies and priorities. For decades, the Chinese government's primary focus was on what was happening within China. Under Xi this no longer applied. In time he wanted to exercise his power outside the country as well as within it.

A leader who inclines to totalitarianism cannot lead without followers who are willing, for various reasons, to go along. Sometimes, many times, they are forced to go along. They go along because effectively they have no choice, unless they are willing to pay a high or even the highest possible price. Other times, though, followers go along because they want to, willingly and maybe even eagerly playing the part of enablers—followers who allow or even encourage their leaders to engage in and then to persist in behaviors that are destructive.

To be sure, there are always some dissidents, some who refuse to follow. In this case, some Chinese who were (are) heroic, who resisted and even dared to protest under what typically were difficult and often dangerous circumstances. Under Xi, Nobel Peace Prize winner Liu Xiaobo, who died in 2017 of liver cancer while serving an eleven-year prison sentence purportedly for trying to overthrow the government, is perhaps the most famous example. Liu was a distinguished writer, philosopher, and human rights activist. Notwithstanding his eminence, Liu ran afoul of the government because of his political activities, which included calling for political reforms and, worse in the eyes of the regime, for ending one-party communist rule. For his troubles he was repeatedly detained and imprisoned, which is what happens to followers who resist totalitarian leaders. It's why most followers of most totalitarian leaders follow. They go along to get along. They go along because they are scared not to go along.

Phase I: Onward and Upward

In the beginning there was, as there usually is with someone new in a leadership role, hope. The promise of better things to come. Xi Jinping was no exception to this general rule. The Chinese people had every reason to expect good times ahead: stable and able leadership exercised by a stable and able man. Xi was well educated and highly experienced, the early years of his political career already having testified to his capacity to lead and manage. He was twenty-six years old when he began his steady climb through the ranks of the government and the CCP. By the time he was in his early fifties he was leader of the powerful Communist Party of Shanghai. Another ten years on, in 2012, he became general secretary of the CCP, and one year after that he became president of China.

President Xi Jinping's initial initiative was to clean up both the government and the party. To end the corruption and scandal that threatened the legitimacy of both, he went after high-ranking officials thought guilty of graft, illicit sex, or being involved with drugs, money laundering, and even murder. In 2013 the Central Commission for Discipline Inspection along with the Ministry of Supervision handled 172,000 corruption cases and investigated 182,000 officials, the highest number in thirty years. By 2016 the government had purged hundreds of high-level bureaucrats, thereby confirming that Xi could be trusted to do what he said he would do. Under his leadership the party and the state would be pure as the driven snow.[6]

The president's second major initiative was to restructure and strengthen the People's Liberation Army. This was similarly certain to appeal to the Chinese people, for it was widely known that China's military was "markedly unprepared for modern warfare." Though it would take several years to finish the job, within two years of taking power Xi was able to claim major upgrades to the army, the navy, and the air force. As one expert on China put it, Xi's reforms "all contributed to a strategic shift away from a Soviet-style, army-centric system and toward what analysts call a Western-style joint command."[7]

Xi's third major promise to the Chinese people was arguably his most important: to reform and revitalize China's lagging economy. His goal was to provide every Chinese citizen with a middle-class lifestyle. Ironically, given the subsequent deterioration in relations between China and the West, especially the United States, Xi's initial intention was to shift from a socialized economy to one that was more market-oriented. It was the private sector, not the public sector, that was expected to drive China forward. "With a road map for financial liberalization, service-sector development, and a new state of environmentally friendly urbanization," the still relatively newly minted president of China, Xi Jinping, set a bold agenda for economic change.[8]

In November 2013, the Communist Party plenum published an economic blueprint that convinced many both within China and without that Xi's government would undertake significant economic reforms. Moreover, it was widely assumed these reforms would increasingly be in keeping with market capitalism and with the accelerating trend to globalization. To be sure, the blueprint, formally titled "The Third Plenum Communique," was somewhat vague. Nevertheless, it declared in no uncertain terms that the government "must unswervingly encourage, support, and lead the development of the non-public sector economy."[9]

Finally, Xi started to make clear that he intended to focus not only on what was happening at home but also on what was happening abroad. Within a year of becoming president Xi signed a thirty-year gas deal with Russian president Vladimir Putin, reached out to South Korea, and made it a point to assert that China had a right to exert its influence across large swaths of Asia. He also initiated what was later described as his "signature foreign policy undertaking," the world's largest infrastructure program, the Belt and Road Initiative (BRI).[10]

The BRI—which by 2023 was plagued by construction flaws and spiraling bad loans—was initially designed to connect China's coastal cities to its underdeveloped interior, as well as to several of its Asian neighbors.[11] But the BRI quickly grew exponentially, to where ten years after it was launched it was credited with hundreds if not thousands of projects all over the world. In other words, soon after he came to power Xi began to build a land-based economic belt that was intended to extend from China to Central and South Asia, and from the Middle East to Europe. Later he added the 21st Century Maritime Silk Road to link China to Southeast Asia, the Middle East, Africa, and Europe through major sea lanes—again, to "advance an array of Chinese economic, political, and geopolitical interests."[12]

President Xi Jinping's soaring ambitions at home and abroad distinguished him from his predecessors. Moreover, they paid off, providing him with the successes he needed to accomplish what all along were his priorities: first to consolidate his power, and then to expand it. Early in his tenure it became apparent that what had been since the 1990s China's collective approach to the exercise of leadership was giving way to a different model. One in which power, authority, and influence would be exercised not by many or even by a few—but by one.

Phase II: Followers Join In

Several years into his first term as president, it was clear that no matter who his political opponents were, Xi was hell-bent on controlling them or eliminating them altogether. His hold over the Chinese people did not decrease, it increased. Party ideology was coming to pervade every aspect of Chinese life, which meant that different views, not to speak of opposing views, were crowded out completely. The internet was largely censored. Foreign television content was strictly limited. Schools were expected to be "strongholds of Party leadership," and professors were punished for using unapproved texts or for "defaming the rule of the Communist Party." The anticorruption purges also continued. In fact, they never stopped. Instead, they become more sophisticated and pervasive, to the point where in 2021 CCP "enforcers punished some 627,000 people for graft and other offenses," a number even larger than earlier in Xi's tenure.[13] In time the continuing anticorruption campaigns became even more obvious political tools, intended not only to clean up government but also to clean house, that is, to get rid of anyone Xi deemed a political threat.

It further became clear that Xi's status was being regularly and reliably enhanced both intellectually and ideologically. His main contribution to party theory, known as "Xi Jinping Thought on Socialism with Chinese Characteristics for a New Era," was drilled into Chinese politics and pedagogies. In 2019 China expert Elizabeth Economy identified more than one hundred institutes devoted to Xi's political thought, a phone app with mandatory quizzes for CCP members on Xi's ideas and activities, and college entrance exams that contained questions about what Xi said and did.[14] By 2022, kindergartens and high schools were hiring Marxism majors and issuing directives that required students as young as ten to study "Xi Jinping thought." Universities, such as one in Henan, were requiring modules on the "principle and methods of thought education," and eighteen hours of study of Xi's speeches.[15]

This system of control was buttressed not only by the threat of punishment but also by the promise of reward. People could be rewarded for behaviors that in the eyes of the state and the party were "good." For example, a social credit system was set up. It amounted to an experiment in social engineering intended to incentivize people to behave in ways that were in keeping with the preferences of state and party officials. As one scholar put it, the system is about "doing things that are right and incentivizing things that are right. But right is not something that people get to decide for themselves."[16] Rather, right required obedience to, and compliance with, what the state defined as good.

None of this is to suggest that President Xi Jinping was ever despised or even disliked by most of the Chinese people. He was not. According to relatively reliable polling, he has all along been generally admired and widely supported. While his popularity is in part nurtured, if not force-fed, by the state, it is also attributable to his significant successes. As we have seen, under Xi's leadership China's military went from second- or third-rate to first-rate. Similarly, for years the economy thrived, from which many millions of Chinese benefited and profited. National pride also swelled as China's standing around the world grew with every passing year. Objectively, under Xi China became in the main richer and, by virtually every measure, stronger. It's safe to say that generally, albeit with significant exceptions, Xi's most important followers, the Chinese people, approved of their leader not because they were forced to but because they genuinely believed that he was good for China. That he was a leader whose benefits outweighed his deficits.

Like every leader, Xi has different sorts of followers. Some, for example, are at a great remove, most obviously the public. Others are much closer in, including some who share with him varying degrees of intimacy. Xi's inner circle—of aides and assistants, puppets and protégés, lackeys and toadies, enablers and supporters, family and friends—has been crucial during his time in office. Members of his inner circle are especially important, given that they serve four purposes. First, they make it possible for him to sustain his power. Second, they help him implement his political, military, economic, social, cultural, and foreign policy agendas. Third, they provide him with personal as well as political and professional support. And fourth, they enable him to lead as a totalitarian. By the end of China's 20th Party Congress his choice of "wall-to-wall loyalists in his politburo standing committee" was, oddly, described as "shocking."[17] To anyone who had carefully watched him during his almost ten years as president, it was not.

Wang Qishan is an example of a member of Xi's inner circle. Their four-decade-long friendship is described as "arguably the most important factor in the consolidation of Xi's power and the implementation of his . . . policy initiatives." It was Wang who was put in charge of Xi's initial, critical anticorruption campaign. It was Wang who led the essential effort to write new rules governing the CCP. And it was Wang whose long and successful career in finance proved invaluable to Xi as he managed the economy. No great surprise then that in 2018, Wang, described as a "statesman with outstanding financial expertise," was named vice president of the People's Republic of China.[18]

Because his friendship with Xi goes back many years, and because he excels at what he does, Wang has stood out from the rest. But other members of Xi's inner circle have been similarly important to his ascension to power and, subsequently, to his transition from authoritarian to totalitarian. Dictatorships are never the handiwork of a single individual. They require cadres of followers who are willing not just to fall in line but to reliably and rigorously support leaders who lust for power.

Xi also has close relationships with family members, to the point where an expert on the Chinese president concluded that they constitute some of his most trusted confidants, especially his wife, mother, and daughter, and his siblings and their spouses.[19] Additionally, Xi has demonstrated a lifelong talent for maintaining good relations with friends, close supporters, and associates. Long before he became leader of China, he developed trusted relationships, personal and political, that have continued over the years to serve him well.

Xi's close followers fall into a few different groups. One is the so-called Shaanxi Gang. Shaanxi is the native province of Xi's father; it is also where Xi spent his formative years and launched his political career. Regional loyalties are strong in China, which partly explains why members of the Shaanxi Gang came to occupy a "significant portion of the top leadership [posts] in the party, government, and military."[20] In other words, on account of Xi's personal history, Shaanxi province became a significant power base for China's national leadership, if not the primary one.

Another group of supporters is the "princelings"—descendants of people who held prominent posts during the early years of the People's Republic of China. Xi Jinping is a princeling himself, his father having been a Chinese Communist revolutionary and after the revolution a prominent, though intermittently politically persecuted, public official. This likely explains why other princelings gravitated to Xi, giving him support at key moments in his political career.

Finally there are Xi's early but enduring ties to the Chinese military. In his late twenties he was an assistant to the minister of defense, who at the time played an important role in domestic as well as foreign policy. It was another occasion on which Xi developed personal and professional ties that over time proved politically advantageous. The bottom line is that Xi has excelled at networking, at being in the right place at the right time, and at aligning himself with men (all, or nearly all, were men) who were loyal. Among his tactics was mentoring subordinates whose careers he promoted and interests he protected. Many turned out to be helpful to Xi during what turned out to be his lifelong political career: just as he looked out for them when they were starting out, they looked out for him as his power grew, and then grew some more.

Xi's power and authority were, then, enhanced by two different but mutually reinforcing resources. The first was institutional, the second individual. At the institutional level were these policies and prompts, all intended to ensure that his followers would remain faithful:

- Party and state organs were instructed to collect every piece of information on everyone who possibly was politically relevant.
- Security services everywhere had the authority to strike down anyone engaging in activities deemed politically threatening.
- Courts were under state and party control.
- State and party officials were regularly assessed for performances based on merit—and for obedience to authority.
- More than 1.4 billion people were registered in a national data bank.
- Every adult was required to carry a photo identification.
- Personal files were maintained on all Chinese citizens.
- Censorship was everywhere—including self-censorship, internet censorship, media censorship, and academic censorship.
- All public discourse was monitored and controlled—for example, in universities students were rewarded for reporting to the authorities any instructor who strayed from the party line.[21]

At the individual level were these tactics and strategies, all intended to ensure that Xi's followers would remain faithful—and useful:

- Xi had a large web of reliably loyal family, friends, and close associates who together constituted his inner circle, providing him with unflagging personal and political support.

- Xi placed many longtime colleagues and associates in top leadership posts as rewards for their competence—and trustworthiness. Xi was not apparently afraid of criticism for nepotism, favoritism, or cronyism. "His actions seemed to echo the Chinese dictum, 'Appoint people based on their merits without omitting relatives or friends.'"[22]
- Xi also valued experience and expertise. From the beginning of his time in power he brought into his orbit experts in, for example, party organization and discipline, domestic and foreign policy, economics, and state security.
- Xi also seems to believe in the virtues of diversity. His confidants and protégés have differed markedly in their personalities, educations, occupations, worldviews, and policy preferences.

During Phase I, "Onward and Upward," Xi Jinping promised the Chinese people that he would make their country great again. During Phase II, "Followers Join In," Xi solidified his base of support. He seems to have understood from the start of his political career that to gain power and then to sustain it he would have to enlist enormous numbers of followers who either wanted to follow or were obliged to follow no matter their own personal or political preference.

Anne Applebaum has written with compassion about how in totalitarian regimes ordinary people, followers, "learn to cope." She was writing about Stalin in the mid- to late 1940s and early 1950s, when under his leadership, behind what then was the Iron Curtain (the Soviet Union and Eastern Europe), some people "collaborated, willingly or reluctantly," some joined the party and other state institutions, some resisted "actively or passively," and many were compelled to "make terrible choices that those of us in the West, nowadays, never have to face."[23]

Phase III: Leader Starts In

As President Xi Jinping was promising his people the moon and the stars and enlisting a vast and variegated cadre of followers, he was beginning to aggressively accumulate power. In fact, as soon as he became leader of the CCP he started making what experts have called "radical adjustments."[24] What exactly were these "radical adjustments"? First, he established several new governing bodies, each of which bestowed on him greater power.[25] Second, he shrank the size of several old governing bodies—notably the Politburo, the decision-making body of the CCP—which lessened the likelihood of opposition. Third, he became chair of each of the most important political committees. Fourth, he downgraded the other political committees. Fifth, he established new economic committees, each of which had him at the helm.

Together these changes were transformative. And together they succeeded in "uplifting Xi's position from being first among equals . . . to being an all-powerful leader with absolute authority in handling domestic and external affairs."[26] In short, Xi quite quickly came to have a degree of power that far exceeded that of his immediate predecessors, reversing the trend toward collective leadership that for decades had been the hallmark of China's governing class. Not only was he adroit at using the institutions of government to his political advantage, but he also excelled at using the party, which he of course chaired, to similar effect. Oxford professor Stein Ringen pointed out that several years into Xi's tenure the CCP was once again dominating political life in China. It was "present in every government agency, central and local, in every unit of the military, in every town and village and neighborhood, in every school, in every university and university department, and student residence, in every business, and in every officially registered social organization."[27]

Xi also gained total control over the People's Liberation Army (PLA). The PLA is the ultimate guarantor of the party, which means it is the ultimate guarantor of the state, which means it is prepared to intervene anywhere at any time, either at home or abroad, when party leaders determine the need arises.[28] As Elizabeth Economy pointed out, this across-the-board power grab meant that Xi was, apparently deliberately, following in the footsteps of Mao Zedong. In 2019 she wrote that, like Mao, Xi had "prioritized strengthening the party, inculcating collective, socialist values, and rooting out nonbelievers." And, like Mao, Xi had encouraged the development of a personality cult of which he was the single political beneficiary.[29]

For years Xi's putative popularity among the Chinese people was supported by a propaganda campaign that placed Xi at the center of the universe. In keeping with Chinese history and tradition (though not with China's recent practice of collective leadership), Xi capitalized on the adulation of ancient emperors once known as "sons of heaven." In 2017 a close observer noted, "For the first time since the death of Mao four decades ago, a leadership personality cult is emerging in China. You can see it in Beijing's streets, where

President Xi Jinping's face appears on posters at bus stops, next to those of revolutionary war heroes. Scarlet banners fly with bold white letters saying, "Continue Achieving the Success of Socialism . . . with Comrade Xi Jinping at the core." The city felt, the observer added, as if it were preparing for a "coronation."[30]

In 2016, only three years after Xi became president, Ringen published a book presciently titled *The Perfect Dictatorship: China in the 21st Century.* Under Xi, Ringen pointed out, China is a country in which citizens are granted a few liberties, but only a very few. Beyond these, the authorities feel free to intervene with whatever level of force they deem necessary to stop any sign of political dissent or resistance. In other words, political life in China was beginning to hang heavy with "the threat of punishment, harassment, detention, the loss of job or home, retribution against family and friends, violence, and ultimately death."[31]

Not long after Xi became president it became more dangerous to be an activist. Suppression began to increase "markedly not only against human rights activists but also against dissidents, underground churches, Falun Gong adherents, petitioners, activist netizens, and liberal scholars."[32] At the same time, access to information was becoming more limited and political thought was becoming more controlled. Every year the reins tightened further. First they tightened further on the mainland; then they tightened further in Hong Kong. Of course, all those rules and regulations were easier to enforce with new technologies. Which is why by the end of the second decade of the twenty-first century it got to the point where threatening the Chinese people was almost beside the point—it had become unnecessary. For by then they had gotten the message: Fall into line and you'll be fine. But if you do not, you will not.

Early on, then, Xi Jinping began changing policies and politics at an astonishing pace, all in the interest of expanding his power. By 2017 he had moved so far so fast that he felt safe making a very, *very* bold move. It had been assumed that the 19th Party Congress would be the occasion on which Xi would nominate someone to succeed him when his term as president expired, in five years. Instead, he astonished the assembled by abolishing the rule that limited presidents to two consecutive five-year terms, "effectively making himself leader in perpetuity."[33] It was a striking departure from his predecessors—Xi making it as clear as he could that he had not the slightest intention of relinquishing power within the usual timeframe. With this single stroke, any lingering doubts about the nature of his leadership were erased.

For there is no stronger signal that a leader can send about his intentions than declaring himself leader indefinitely.

Xi used the CCP as his cudgel—it was his ultimate guarantor. In the recent past the party had receded in importance. But under Xi things were different: the CCP's power and influence grew with every passing year. Moreover, like Mao before him, Xi's identity and ideology were enshrined in the CCP's constitution.[34] In fact, the party became more important than the state because unlike the state, the party exerted control not only over what people did but also over what they thought.

Phase IV: Bad to Worse

If there were lingering doubts about Xi's ambitions, intentions, and proclivity to dictatorship, his treatment of the Uyghurs, a Turkic Muslim minority living in China, would have or should have erased them. Not long after Xi came to power the government began incarcerating what eventually became more than 1 million Uyghurs in internment camps. The purpose was to rid them of their separate identity and to force them to adapt to and assimilate into mainstream Chinese society. Within a few years the campaign against the Uyghurs became so brutal—the period from 2017 to 2019 appears to have been the worst—it was described by outsiders as "ethnocide," or "cultural genocide," or simply "genocide." Many Western experts came to conclude that there was a "word for what is happening in the Xinjiang region of China: genocide."[35]

The evidence for genocide or ethnocide of Uyghurs was persuasive. Chinese authorities had clearly engaged in a campaign of persecution and cultural eradication. Former detainees and prisoners reported they had suffered torture, rape, forced labor, and involuntary abortion and sterilization in state-run facilities. At least 800,000 children were separated from their families. President Donald Trump's last secretary of state, Mike Pompeo, declared that China's actions against the Uyghurs constituted "genocide and crimes against humanity." In his confirmation hearing, his successor, Antony Blinken (President Joe Biden's secretary of state), concurred with Pompeo's assessment.[36]

Xi's lust for power would not be confined indefinitely to the Chinese mainland. A few years after taking office he began to distance himself from China's commitment to a low-profile foreign policy. Now, in addition to expanding the Belt and Road Initiative, the president was determined to export his country's political values, tempt corporations to play by China's rules by promising access to its huge domestic markets, engage in military adventurism (for example, in the South China Sea), build a military base in Cambodia, approve a hypersonic test, and to encroach slowly but certainly on Hong Kong's autonomy despite its promise to abide for fifty years by the rule of "one country, two systems."

When the history of Xi's reign is written, none of his decisions will so deftly depict the trajectory of his leadership from bad to worse as the move to rip Hong Kong from its moorings and jam it instead into his own iron fist. So far as Xi was concerned, the restiveness in Hong Kong was becoming increasingly untenable. The tensions between the people of Hong Kong and the authorities in Beijing began escalating in 2014, when the Chinese government issued an edict that made elections in Hong Kong more restrictive, and therefore more likely to be decided in China's favor. Predictably, this new imposition did not go over well in Hong Kong. Less predictably it led to the "Umbrella Revolution," peaceful protests in which large numbers of Hong Kongers, mostly young people, participated.

Though public demonstrations against the government in Beijing waxed and waned in subsequent years, and though public opinion in Hong Kong was mixed, the span between 2014 and 2019 was contemporaneously, and correctly, seen as one in which many if not most of the city's residents were increasingly straining against the growing intrusions of the Chinese government. This was happening even as China's president was becoming more intolerant of and impatient with a territory that was becoming rambunctious if not downright rebellious—and which, so far as he was concerned, was properly part of China.

Things came to a head in 2019 when a law strongly favoring Beijing was issued by the torn but in this case compliant Hong Kong government. The law—an extradition treaty that could and likely would abolish the existing separation between Hong Kong's legal system and that of mainland China—met with fierce public opposition. Hong Kongers feared it would further erode the principle of "one country, two systems," which already was under assault. Finally, on June 16 an enormous crowd poured into the streets to protest. Given the estimated 2 million demonstrators (out of a total population of less than 8 million), Xi's patience, his willingness to put up with the growing resistance in Hong Kong, was tested to the breaking point.

By spring 2020 he was fed up. Whatever China's original promise to Hong Kong, it was scuttled by the new national security law imposed by Beijing, which formally came into effect in June. For the president it was obviously a high-stakes power play—he was risking reigniting the protests that had roiled the city only a few months earlier. He was also testing Hong Kong's global reputation as a major, reliably stable financial center. Still, Xi was not to be deterred—he would have his way. The new law changed Hong Kong completely, and for the indefinite future. It gave Beijing the power to shape life in the city in every aspect, and to end all public displays of political resistance.[37]

Within six months the worst fears of Hong Kong's democratic activists were realized. Subject to arrest, they went underground, while the previously free press was threatened, neutered, or rendered mute. Case in point: the *Apple Daily*, a two-decade-old pro-democracy newspaper that in 2021 was obliged to shut down when the authorities froze its assets, raided its newsroom, and arrested several of its editors for violating the new law. Other, similar outlets moved their operations abroad, while Hong Kong's public broadcasting station was refashioned as a government mouthpiece.[38]

By 2022 it was clear that Xi had done what he set out to do in Hong Kong, *to* Hong Kong. Wrote one China watcher, "Today Hong Kong is where the CCP is perfecting its playbook for smothering free and open societies. What China does in Hong Kong today it hopes to do in Taiwan tomorrow and everywhere else it is able."[39] Other China watchers noted that Hong Kong had been changed in major ways indefinitely, if not permanently. Entrepreneurialism had been stifled, the tourist industry crushed, and the city's once vibrant culture stilled. Further, tens of thousands of people had left the city forever.[40] In July 2022 Xi Jinping used the occasion of the twenty-fifth anniversary of Hong Kong's return from Britain to China briefly to visit the city. It was his first trip outside the mainland since before the pandemic. His stay was brief and muted but, from his perspective, triumphant. He warned Hong Kong residents against challenging China's grip on their city. And he made clear that from then on Hong Kong would be governed "only by patriots" charged by Beijing with navigating a "new stage of development, from chaos to order."[41]

Xi proved as good as his word. In January 2023 the authorities arrested six Hong Kongers on charges of sedition for selling pro-democracy books, trinkets, and souvenirs. One month later forty-seven pro-democracy activists were put on trial for conspiracy to commit subversion, most of whom had already been imprisoned for two years. And by mid-2023 the authorities in Hong Kong had banned all public performances and on-line dissemination of "Glory to Hong Kong," the unofficial anthem of pro-democracy demonstrators.

For ten years the world watched with a mixture of fascination and con-sternation as Xi Jinping moved through the four phases of bad leadership to worse leadership, from being authoritarian to totalitarian. He came to seem effectively untouchable, a leader so adroit at manipulating the levers of power that he did what he wanted to do when and how he wanted to do it.

Xi made virtually all the decisions, from those that were relatively small to those of enormous consequence, such as reining in China's capital markets.[42] It was Xi who brought an end to what many in the West initially saw as a "bold economic reform agenda," turning instead to repression of upstart tycoons, foreign investors, IPOs, offshore listings, and unregulated tech companies.[43] He especially started to vent against the very rich. In 2021 he called for a "reg-ulation of high incomes," signaling his refusal to tolerate excessive private wealth at the expense of the general welfare.[44] By 2022, it was obvious the economy was increasingly state-driven, not market-driven; that millionaires and billionaires were being pressed either to toe the party line or to leave their posts, in some cases even quit the country; that China was prepared to pressure foreign firms in various ways; and that Xi's priorities had changed. National security had become of primary importance, economic growth of secondary importance.

Moreover, until the end of 2022 his draconian approach to COVID con-tinued unabated. Tens of millions of people were effectively locked in their homes for weeks and months on end, denied permission to leave for any reason. Before it was all over, the pandemic provided Xi with "a powerful case for deepening the Communist Party's reach into the lives of its over one billion citizens." Since officials first isolated the city of Wuhan during the in-itial pandemic lockdown, the government had "honed its powers to track and corral people, backed by upgraded technology, armies of neighborhood workers and broad public support."[45]

There was, in short, unmistakable evidence that not only had Xi changed—by Phase IV he was a totalitarian—but China had changed as well. "Broad public support" notwithstanding, people were being oppressed and re-pressed, and Maoist development theories had moved from background to foreground everywhere, including schools and banks, courts, and military bases.[46] "The entire party must unify its thinking, unify its will, and unify its actions," Xi told officials in spring 2023.[47] Former Australian prime minister

Kevin Rudd, an expert on China, described Xi's evolution from bad to worse this way: "He has brought the era of pragmatic, nonideological governance to a crashing halt. In its place, he has developed a new form of Marxist nationalism that now shapes the presentation and substance of China's politics, economics, and foreign policy. . . . Under Xi, ideology drives policy more than the other way around."[48]

Of course, for all of Xi's omnipresence and omnipotence, the past did not necessarily prognosticate the present. Totalitarian leaders are like other leaders: they are vulnerable to the winds of fate, to changes in circumstances they either did not foresee or did not properly plan for, to failures of foreign and domestic policies, and sometimes even to followers who have the temerity, the bravery, to resist. So we cannot know if Xi can continue indefinitely to hold total power—or how deeply entrenched the CCP really is in the hearts and minds of the Chinese people.[49]

What we can know is this: that though the "scale and intrusiveness" of the Chinese government's deployment into everyday life was "on a whole different level," more extreme than anyplace else of such consequence in the world, this did not entirely or indefinitely preclude resistance to authority.[50] Astonishingly, remarkably, in response to Xi's extreme policies to forestall the spread of COVID, in November 2022 people protested the regime. Some followers were finally fed up to the point that they risked everything publicly to have their say, participating in demonstrations that, while not large in size or number, were nevertheless the most widespread in China since the 1989 demonstrations in Tiananmen Square. By protesting the government's draconian approach to COVID, the protesters took on the party, the state, and the supreme leader.

Even more remarkably, in response to the public protests, Xi made a 180-degree turn. Effectively overnight Xi threw in the towel, gave up on the COVID restrictions, and reopened China. He did so in response to an increasingly frustrated and furious populace, to an economy that had been dragged down by COVID restrictions (leading indicators of the economic decline included high unemployment, declining exports and retail sales, dropping property values, and a brain drain), and to China's increasing isolation, especially from Europe since Russia's attack on Ukraine. It's likely—though we cannot know for certain—that Xi made the decision to reopen China on the strong advice of close aides.

Xi's pivot was highly unusual. Totalitarian leaders do not typically reverse themselves, and certainly not so publicly. Reversals are, after all, an unmistakable sign that something went wrong. So, we cannot foresee how this will all turn out in the long term. It's possible that Xi's backtracking will cost him. But what is clear even now is that China was entirely unprepared to deal with the sudden change in health policy, which led to COVID spreading like wildfire in a population with little immunity.[51] Moreover, health policy was not Xi's only course correction. So was economic policy, the president reversing some of his recent decisions in an effort to stimulate growth and restore the country's influence on the global stage.

Perhaps to distract from the various disasters related to COVID, hard on the heels of his course corrections Xi reasserted his power at home—and inserted himself abroad. In March 2023 he reveled in the legislature's unanimous vote to bestow on him a third term in office, thereby formalizing what had already been decided at the party congress the previous fall. He seized the occasion to give a rather fiery speech that focused on the economy and on China's increasingly fraught rivalry with the United States.

Not content to rest on his domestic laurels, Xi additionally took the unprecedented step of brokering a détente between Iran and Saudi Arabia, thereby establishing for China a first diplomatic beachhead in the Middle East. Finally, the Chinese president traveled to Moscow to bestow on the Russian president, Vladimir Putin—who by then had been charged by the International Criminal Court with war crimes—just what he wanted and needed: a brotherly hug backed up by a vow of ironclad Chinese–Russian solidarity.

For a decade Xi was on an uninterrupted trajectory. His leadership went from bad to worse, from being controlling to being all-controlling. The small but seemingly highly influential protests related to COVID threatened to interfere with what he came to see as his destiny—which was to run China without interference. In the wake of the protests some Western experts predicted that Xi's COVID-spurred U-turn would make it harder for him to govern.[52] That his shift in economic policy would embolden some of his opponents. And that popular anger would "continue to bubble over."[53] (Which was among the reasons the government had launched a campaign of intimidation against the COVID-related protests.)[54] What quickly became clear, however, is that Xi was intent on proving these experts wrong.

It's no use for the West to delude itself. Xi remains broadly popular with the Chinese people. Moreover, they have learned to adapt, as people living under totalitarian leaders are wont to do. To be acquiescent and obedient, to compromise and collaborate. Of course, some of the people—we cannot know how many—are true believers. Authentic allies or even acolytes of President Xi Jinping's who genuinely believe in his rightness and goodness; who consider his total control to be not only necessary but desirable; who have known Xi for years and are personally and politically reliably loyal.

Xi proceeded in any case to put COVID behind him and to continue down his chosen path. He quickly recovered from what could have been a prolonged fiasco to come back full force, his actions and words reminding anyone who needed reminding that he is not a leader to be tampered with.

Under Xi's leadership China has been transformed. Under Xi's leadership the world has been transformed. China is now everywhere seen as central to the international system. It is the world's largest trading power and its greatest source of global lending. It boasts the world's second-largest population and its largest military. And it has become a global center of innovation.[55] Given these enormous accomplishments, how is it possible for me to conclude that Xi's leadership went from bad to worse?

To this question I can only reply as I did before: that "bad" and "worse" are in the eye of the beholder. By my criteria, whatever Xi Jinping's accomplishments, they do not compensate for his totalitarian ways. For a liberal democrat the benefits of Xi's leadership are far outweighed by the costs—the costs of being forced into a lifetime of deference, subservience, and obedience.

Finally, a reminder of how I defined evil leadership in Chapter 3: The leader and at least some followers commit atrocities. They use pain as an instrument of power. The harm done to men, women, and children is severe rather than slight. The harm can be physical, psychological, or both. By this definition, it's impossible not to conclude that Xi Jinping's leadership has been, in some ways, *evil*. Specifically, he has been responsible for making and implementing policies that for years have inflicted pain, physical and psychological, on China's Uyghurs. And his longtime insistence on virtually total obedience to his virtually total authority has been, if not evil, then awful.

PART III
CLOSING IN

9

Phase I: Onward and Upward

Leaders Paint a Picture of a Future Boundlessly Better than the Past

When they take power, many leaders, probably most, assure their followers that things will get better. That their lives will somehow improve. After all, that's how leaders get to be leaders in the first place. By persuading their followers that they have some sort of secret sauce that will enable them to provide what other leaders could not or would not.

What, then, distinguishes leaders who start out bad from leaders who start out good? Again, questions like these are impossible to answer with precision. We are talking humans, not widgets, and humans don't lend themselves to criteria or measurements that are exact. But in general we can say that leaders who are good, as in both ethical and effective, tend from the get-go to be more reasonable and realistic than leaders who are bad, as in unethical, ineffective, or both. Good leaders avoid the spectacularly grandiose. They avoid the implication that they and they alone can save us from ourselves. Bad leaders, in contrast, present themselves as heroes or even saviors, capable of greatness, of transcendence.

Bad leaders promise their followers the moon and the stars, a future that is a dreamscape in which the "other" will go down in flames, while their own every need will be met and their own every wish will come true. They envision a transformation—a change in people's circumstances so great that their future will be completely different from their past and even from their present. Whereas good leaders remain anchored in the possible, bad leaders get carried away to the land of the impossible. This capacity to threaten hell and damnation, to promise heaven on earth, and to make it all seem real as opposed to unreal is, of course, what appeals to followers. Think of it as the ultimate sales pitch in which leaders offer their wares and followers end up buying what the leader selling.

It's easy to see why sometimes the sales pitch works. First, bad leaders claim that they, and they alone, can lead their followers to the promised land. They insist that only they have the will and skill to lead them to where they want to go, which implies obviously that unless the leader is in charge and free to do what they want when they want, the promised land will remain out of reach forever. Second, this pitch appeals especially to followers who are angry or alienated, who feel they have been dismissed or demeaned, excluded as opposed to included. It also appeals to followers who want tomorrow what they lack today. Finally, the pitch finds fertile soil in contexts that somehow are or at least feel deficient—damaged or deprived, unstable or insecure, frustrating or alienating, threatening or downright dangerous. Contexts that could and should be improved, contexts in which betterment is not just wanted but needed.

As we saw in Chapter 4, Adolf Hitler provides a vivid example of the sorts of things that bad leaders say in Phase I. His rhetoric both before he became chancellor of Nazi Germany and during the years that immediately followed was nothing if not replete with utopian fantasies, with promises that he insisted he alone could keep. Of course, the context and those who peopled it were ripe for such rhetoric. Germans had been traumatized both by their defeat in World War I and by the Great Depression. Many were near desperate for a Fuehrer who could and would with one hand persecute and prosecute those responsible for their misery, and with the other hand lead them out of their wretched past and desperate present to a future that was almost unimaginably better. Specifically, in this case, toward a Germany that was in every way richer, grander, stronger, and more successful—and oh, by the way, significantly larger.

Hitler's enemies list was easily compiled: Jews at the top, plus enemies of the Nazis at home, especially socialists and communists, and enemies of the Nazis abroad, especially in the United States and Soviet Union. Also easily identified was the promised land, the land of milk and honey. As Germans were the chosen people, so Germany, grown distinctly bigger and decidedly more powerful, was the chosen nation. Germany would triumph over its failed past and its feckless present to take its proper place in the world order.

It is not too much to say that Hitler's vision of Germany's future was mystical, quasi-religious. Similarly, it is not too much to say that Hitler's idea of himself as the leader in the passion play that was Germany's transmogrification was similarly mystical, quasi-religious. To wit, his words on April 9, 1938, when he celebrated the occasion of Germany's annexation of Austria: "I wish to thank Him who allowed me to return to my homeland [Hitler was born in Austria], so that I could return it to my German Reich. May every

German realize the importance of the hour, assess it, and then bow his head in reverence before the will of the Almighty who has wrought this miracle in all of us."[1]

Martin Winterkorn

When Martin Winterkorn took over as CEO at Volkswagen, he was obviously aware of the company's history, both infamous and famous. Infamous was the story of its origin, forever associated with Hitler and the Nazi regime. Famous was the story of the company's astonishing post–World War II recovery, which transformed it in remarkably short order from an ignominious, defeated corporate behemoth into one of the greatest car companies in the world.

But Volkswagen had stalled. It was stuck with a governance structure that was rigid and old-fashioned when other car companies, not just in America but in Japan, were nimbler and more modern, and providing stiff competition. Volkswagen was trying to get ahead of the pack at a moment when times were changing. Gone were the days when hippies ruled the world and thought the only car to own was the fabled Volkswagen Beetle or bus. Now were the days when new models of new cars proliferated like wildflowers, and when conceptions of what people would and should look for in a vehicle were rapidly changing.

Clearly, it seemed to those who selected him that Winterkorn was the right man for the job at the time. Not only was his leadership style in keeping with that for which Volkswagen was known—top-down, hierarchical, and autocratic—but he was a man of vaulting ambition as well. "Onward and upward" captures the man and the moment, for as soon as he took over the top job, Winterkorn set himself apart by establishing the most ambitious and audacious possible goals for both his company and himself. As we saw, nothing would suffice that was short of transforming Volkswagen into the largest, most successful car company of them all.

Winterkorn became Volkswagen's CEO in 2007. In short order he made the scope of his ambition unambiguously clear. He had what amounted to a ten-year plan: "The Volkswagen Group is seeking global economic and environmental leadership in the automotive industry by 2018." In this sentence the key modifier was not, of course, the word "economic." It was the word "environmental." For as it turned out, originally more by happenstance than by design, the promise of cleaner air was to be the key that would unlock the door to Volkswagen's great and glorious future. That would allow it to vault over the competition by delivering what people wanted—a reasonably priced car that would perform well while significantly cutting emissions. A car that would not do what other cars were doing—fouling up the air, making it dangerous even to breathe. This was, after all, the twenty-first century, when protection of the environment first became an important issue, and when car companies that distinguished themselves by being cleaner and purer were certain to enjoy a considerable competitive advantage. In the United States and Europe especially, customers who were looking to buy cleaner cars were Winterkorn's special targets. They were the followers he was trying hardest to lead.

One could argue that he got caught in the net of his own rhetoric. That though the cheat device was first installed shortly before Winterkorn set his lofty targets, it was only after he committed himself to beating the competition that he proceeded to promise what he was unlikely to be able to deliver without engaging in wrongdoing. To do otherwise—to do anything other at this point than to proceed along his chosen path, at the end of which was the brass ring—was to risk public humiliation. But no such fear during the early, heady days of Winterkorn's tenure, during Phase I. So successful was he at persuading people that he and his company were moving "onward and upward" that in 2009 he was named Man of the Year by a jury of thirty-eight representatives from France's most respected media. Under his leadership Volkswagen was hailed as the "only automaker to buck the economic crisis." And he personally was extolled for having the "perfect, far-sighted management style."[2]

Recep Tayyip Erdogan

From the start of his political career Erdogan was a man on a mission. Given that he was a practicing Muslim, and given that Turkey's elite was nearly entirely secular, for him to climb to the top of the greasy pole would require fierce ambition and relentless determination. It also meant that Erdogan had a natural constituency: Turks who identified as Muslims, especially those who defied the secular norm and wore their religion on their sleeve. Whatever Erdogan accomplished in Turkey was in consequence of his special, strong appeal to this group, which had long perceived itself as second-class. Not for nothing did Erdogan openly declare early in his political career, "Before any-thing else I am a Muslim."

The fact that Erdogan so publicly identified with Islam and was so unam-biguously determined to claim his cause was itself a rallying cry. This cry was obviously not directed at Turkey's secular ruling class. Rather, the utopian vision of promises fulfilled and dreams realized was targeted at those who, like Erdogan himself, perceived themselves as having been long denied a seat at Turkey's table, and who were only too eager, therefore, to hitch their wagon to his star.

Still, during the early years, the golden years, Erdogan was able to have it both ways. However popular he was among more religious and conservative Turks, his original appeal extended beyond his most obvious constituents. He was a favorite among Turkey's liberal intelligentsia, most of whom were fluent in Western languages. And he was also a favorite among politicians in the West. At the beginning of his tenure, as Prime Minister Erdogan ad-vanced a series of political reforms, he and his party were welcomed by both the European Union and the United States. At a speech delivered at Harvard University in 2004, the Turkish prime minister spoke extravagantly about how if Europe could be transformed from a "hotbed" of war into a "geog-raphy of peace," the same could happen in the Middle East, with Turkey leading the charge. Moreover, Erdogan specifically rejected the assertion that democracy was incompatible with Middle Eastern culture or religion.[3]

He was, in other words, painting an almost unbelievably rosy picture of an almost unbelievable rosy world, one that was entirely compatible with a leader in Phase I. In fact, so secure was Erdogan in his popularity among liberals at home and abroad, they hardly noticed when he began making changes not long after he came to power—changes that were harbingers of the authoritarianism that lay in Turkey's future.[4]

In 2006, Prime Minister Erdogan paid a visit to U.S. president George W. Bush. The occasion was marked by expansive expressions of good feeling, a rapprochement, if any were needed, between Turkey and the West. After their White House meeting Bush reported they had had an "extensive and important dialogue" about how the United States and Turkey would "work together to achieve peace." Erdogan responded in kind, telling his American counterpart what "a great honor and pleasure" it had been to meet him, "an ally," at his invitation.[5]

When Erdogan first came to power Turkey officially had been a secular state for decades. But Turks were still overwhelmingly (over 90 percent)

Muslim, so it's no surprise that by the 1980s religion was starting to become a social and political flashpoint. In time, Erdogan was able to capitalize on the newfound restiveness among those who had long felt they were being treated as less than equals, and who in consequence were primed for a leader who promised them a political transformation, one in which they, like he, would rise from the bottom of Turkish society to the middle and even to the top.

To be sure, in his early years in politics especially, Erdogan had to be careful not to overdo it, not to ignore or dismiss the secularists entirely, because he needed them, or at least some of them, to stick with him as he tried to change the balance of power in Turkish society. But those with an interest in how and why he changed from a democratic leader to an autocratic one should understand that his primary audience was never all-inclusive, except perhaps at the outset. His paramount pitch was intended to appeal to Turks who constituted the large Islamic majority, not to those among its secular minority.

Erdogan was a greatly gifted political leader whose timing, especially in the beginning of his political career, was from his vantage point perfect. Turks were at that moment restless and contentious. Dimitar Bechev put it this way: "The rise of a conservative entrepreneurial class coupled with the rapid pace of urbanization in the 1980s and 1990s not only blurred the social and geographic distinction between the center and periphery but also fomented strife."[6] This strife was especially strident as it pertained to the place of faith in public life.

Which is where Erdogan's strongest supporters came in. Given the tensions between the privileged secular minority and ordinary folk, it's easy to see how Erdogan's personal and political identification with Islam promised the sorts of once-in-a-lifetime changes that millions of Turks were looking for. It was precisely because he was so welcome in so many circles that Erdogan was given license to gradually, and then more quickly, metamorphose from democrat to autocrat.

Elizabeth Holmes

She was a dreamer who accomplished what was usually difficult if not downright impossible. She grafted her dream onto others. She persuaded others not only that her dream could be realized and that she alone could realize it but also that they could be part of it. That if they would support her, financially or in another way, they could join her. Together with her, they could and would change the world to make it a better place. Given that Elizabeth

Holmes was young when she began her transition from bad leadership to worse leadership, and with precious little experience or expertise in testing blood, her ability to persuade people that she was on the threshold of a revolution in science and medicine is, in retrospect, astonishing.

In Chapter 7 I raised the question of how Holmes was able to accomplish this astonishing feat. I came up with several answers, each of which is persuasive, and which together provide a good explanation for how events at Theranos came to pass as they did. Still, one could argue that what happened during this first phase of the four-phase process remains somewhat puzzling. Specifically, it was during Phase I that Holmes managed to get her foot in the door, selling her idea to a few key people and managing to get them to provide initial, essential capital.

In addition, then, to my earlier answers to the question of how Holmes was able to accomplish what she accomplished when Theranos was no more than a gleam in her eye, here are two more. The first is the novelty and extremity of her dream, its very outrageousness. It's not uncommon for tech entrepreneurs to be visionaries, of course. In fact, the greatest among them see possibilities where the rest of us do not. Still, Holmes was green. She was nearly entirely inexperienced, untried, and untested in precisely the arena within which she wanted to transform how medicine was practiced: blood testing. In retrospect the idea seems so crazy that, coupled with the passion with which she sold it, further explains how her dream, which turned out of course to be too good to be true, came originally to be shared by some of America's best and brightest.

The second additional explanation for what happened early in Holmes's trajectory from bad leader to worse leader is the so-called contagion effect. She sold the idea that she was on to something big first to her mentor at Stanford University and then, not long after, to several wealthy investors. Once she snagged one well-known name, persuading some prominent person that she was on the threshold of a discovery of world-shaking importance, that person would lead to another who was also ready and willing in some way to help—to put in a good word, to invest some money, or to serve on Theranos's board. Moreover, once Holmes raised some big bucks and launched her company, word spread. In 2006 *Inc.* magazine identified her as a possible "lifesaver," one who might someday "save hundreds of thousands of lives."[7] It was around that same time that the tech publication *Red Herring* ran a piece about Theranos that called it one of the "hottest startups in the Valley."

In this case, the term "contagion effect" refers to several beliefs—about Holmes, her company, and her product—that spread from one person to another relatively rapidly, starting in Phase I. These beliefs included, first, that Elizabeth Holmes was extraordinary, a singular entrepreneur and leader. Second, that the blood testing technology to which she laid claim was so promising as to plausibly change science and medicine forever. And third, that the company Holmes founded and now led, Theranos, was the perfect vehicle for delivering on her promise.

The superlatives that described her before she had anything concrete to show either for herself or her company are, in retrospect, remarkable. At the time, everyone who was anyone seemed to be intoxicated by her, and she was recognized for forming "the most illustrious board in U.S. corporate history." And as part of an interview for Medscape, she was praised by the eminent scientist and cardiologist Eric Topol for her phenomenal rebooting "of laboratory medicine."[8]

Xi Jinping

By the time Xi Jinping became president of China, he had already served for a year as leader of the Chinese Communist Party. He was therefore perfectly positioned to get a fast start as leader of the state. Predictably, he promised his people swift, sure action on issues they deemed of major importance. Moreover, he was keen to demonstrate as quickly as possible and in no uncertain terms that he was in charge, that no other Chinese person or institution was strong enough to compete with him for power. In this sense his Phase I was a double-edged sword. On the one hand, he promised to give the Chinese people what they wanted and needed. But on the other hand, from day one he made clear that what he expected in return was unflinching loyalty, unquestioning obedience to his authority and (almost as important) to the authority of the party.

I earlier referenced Xi's anticorruption campaigns, which began when he was party chair. As it turned out, no single theme pervaded his decades-long tenure more than anticorruption. His relentless focus on the wrongdoing of others—whether real or trumped up—served three important purposes. First, it enabled him to keep the government relatively clean. Second, it enabled him to rid the party and the government of officials he deemed in some way undesirable, especially if they were considered politically threatening. Third, it enabled Xi to gain power, retain it, and increase it.

From the start Xi insisted, with what at the time was good reason, that corruption was an existential threat that, if unchecked, would lead to the "collapse" of the Chinese Communist Party and the "downfall of the state." This gave Xi leeway and even a mandate to undertake a sweeping, highly publicized campaign against graft—and against his political enemies. Two years after he became president (in 2015), an article in *Foreign Affairs* reported that according to official statistics, "the party has punished some 270,000 of its cadres for corrupt activities, reaching into almost every part of the government and every level of China's vast bureaucracy." Yet despite this excess, or perhaps because of it, Xi's first anticorruption campaign was enormously popular. His ostensible zeal for clean government provided him with precisely the sort of political support and high level of enthusiasm that he wanted and needed. China did have a real problem with corruption, one that Xi sought to address. But let's be clear: from the beginning Xi used regular, repeated, anticorruption campaigns first to establish and then to solidify his authority. To make clear that he was determined indefinitely to remain "the paramount leader within a tightly controlled system."[9]

Five years after Xi's first anticorruption sweep, it was estimated that 1.5 million government officials had been found guilty on a variety of related charges. No one was exempt from being caught in Xi's net: not army generals, not members of the party's influential Central Committee, not senior government officials. Early targets also included Xi's main political rival, Bo Xilai.[10] In addition to being a longtime party player, Bo was ambitious and charismatic—which is, so far as we know, precisely why Xi quickly arranged for Bo to face three criminal charges: bribery, abuse of power, and embezzlement. Within months, Bo was put on trial, found guilty on all counts, stripped of his personal assets, and sentenced to life in jail.

The arrest and imprisonment of Bo were only one among several early indicators of where Xi was headed. Not long after he became president, critics were silenced, human rights lawyers were shut down or arrested, NGOs were either tightly controlled or eliminated altogether, and foreign textbooks were forced out of Chinese universities.[11] But early on, China's president took much greater pains than he did later to cloak his actions as being in the best interest of an increasingly prosperous Chinese people. And everything he did during this initial period was carefully presented as being in the best interest of an increasingly powerful Chinese Communist Party and Chinese state.

During Phase I, Xi's foreign policy was as ostensibly high-minded as his domestic policy, especially as it pertained to the United States. For instance, in September 2015 the Chinese president visited the American president, Barack Obama, in the White House. According to a Chinese government press release, on a day that was "refreshed by the breeze and permeated with charming autumn scenery," Xi and his wife were "warmly greeted" by Obama and his wife. Xi took the occasion to "convey the sincere greetings and best wishes to the US people from over 1.3 billion Chinese people."[12] He went on to say that he and Obama had an "in-depth, sincere, and candid discussion on the domestic and foreign policies of China and the United States" and that China was "firmly committed to the path of peaceful development . . . deepening reform and opening the country wider to the world." China would work hard, Xi promised, "to push forward the noble cause of peace and development for all mankind."[13]

Just a few years later, such civility, not to mention comity, between the presidents of China and the United States was difficult to imagine. American politics had changed. Chinese politics had changed. And Xi Jinping had changed.

Early Warnings

This book looks at how bad leadership and followership develop over time into worse leadership and followership. As I wrote in the Prologue, typically "bad" creeps in and then grows gradually, until it has wormed its way into the group or organization of which it is a part—which it then seeks to alter permanently and, in time, to devour. I went on to add that this book is not intended simply as a theoretical exercise. As importantly, more importantly, it is intended to have practical import. To serve as an early warning system. Precisely because the progression from bad leadership and followership to worse leadership and followership is an incremental process—one that tends to move from one phase to the next slowly—it is easier to stop that progression sooner, in Phase I, rather than later, during Phase III or IV, when it has become toxic.

This raises two questions. First, how can we recognize bad during Phase I, given that the start of any leader's tenure, good or bad, is typically marked by hope and promise? As I described, during the "onward and upward" phase the nascent bad leader paints a picture of a future boundlessly better than the past. But I further pointed out that most leaders tend at the start of their tenures to be optimistic, to depict a future that is light and sunny as opposed to dark and cloudy. What then, to repeat an earlier question, distinguishes leaders likely to be bad from leaders likely to be good? How to tell if a particular leader is at the start of a progression that will go from bad to worse, a progression to be dreaded and possibly feared?

There is no science to which we can turn, no expert to help us make the distinction. Which is why it requires more of a judgment call than anything else. Still, there are some telltale signs, some indicators that signal the leader's intentions and directions.

- *Indicator #1: Past is prologue.* What the leader did in the past suggests what the leader will do in the future.
- *Indicator #2: Words matter.* Listen to what the leader says and take seriously what is said.
- *Indicator #3: Get real.* Is the leader anchored in reality? Or does the leader's utopian vision smack of grandiosity—personal grandiosity, professional grandiosity, and, or political grandiosity—and even fantasy?
- *Indicator #4: Teams are important.* Who is on the leader's team? Specifically, who are the leader's closest aides and associates, and what do they suggest?
- *Indicator #5: Strong preferences suggest probable priorities.* What the leader most cares about likely will determine what the leader does.

We are not, in sum, devoid of information, even at the start. While I grant that knowing for certain early in a leader's tenure how they will be and what they will do down the road is impossible, we do nevertheless have some signposts—some indicators of whether they are bad and likely to get worse.

The second question follows logically from the first. If some number of people decide early on that a leader is bad and is bound to get worse, what to do? Who is going to stop a bad leader in Phase I (or, for that matter, in Phase II or even Phase III) from getting worse? Again, leaders themselves are unlikely to stop on their own. Once leaders are bad, once they are anywhere along the continuum from bad to worse, it is highly unlikely they will intercept their own progression. To expect otherwise, to expect bad leaders to self-correct, is almost always fruitless and foolish.

Where does this leave us? The answer is as obvious as it is unsatisfying. If leaders will not stop themselves from being bad, others must do the heavy lifting. Either another leader, which happens only rarely and usually belatedly. Or, somewhat more frequently, the leader's followers.

Who, broadly defined, are these followers? They include at least these three groups: (1) members of the leader's team, that is, their immediate entourage or inner circle; (2) members of the leader's tribe, that is, their most eager and enthusiastic supporters, either active or passive; and (3) members of the public broadly defined, that is, people who are outside the leader's sphere of influence but nevertheless follow their lead because it is the path of least resistance. They might simply be bystanders, ordinary people who are paying attention but refraining from getting involved. Still, such bystander followers matter. By doing nothing and saying nothing, they have an impact. They are supporting implicitly even if not explicitly whoever has power and authority.

The answer to the question of what to do when bad leadership happens is unsatisfying precisely because even followers who detest their bad leaders are unlikely to storm the castle. History testifies repeatedly to how followers of bad leaders are, typically, more incentivized to do nothing than to do something. To do nothing to get rid of the bad leader rather than to take the risk of fighting what they likely consider to be a lost cause. Or even to invest the time and energy involved in taking on a bad leader when the costs are likely to outweigh the benefits. It is why bad leadership proliferates. It is why even though we constantly rail against bad leadership, most of the time nothing and no one stops or even slows it. The truth is that mostly we are unlikely even to lift a finger to diminish what we despise.

This book challenges what is, for good reason, the conventional wisdom. *It suggests that if we better understood the progression of leadership from bad to worse, we might be more likely to intervene early on, when intervening is easier and has a greater chance of being successful.* Again, it's up to us. If we don't block bad leaders, they won't be blocked—or stopped.

Phase I of bad leadership is the rough equivalent of a blinking yellow light. It means that followers should proceed with caution. Whenever leaders paint a picture of a future almost unimaginably better than the past and the present, attention should be paid. And whenever leaders warn that without them to lead the charge the world will come to an end, attention should be paid. Finally, whenever leaders send the message that they and they alone ought to lead, that no one else can possibly take their place, attention should be paid. Thus, there is not just one reason for that blinking yellow light but three: the promise of utopia ahead, the threat of calamity ahead, and the admonition "stick with me or you're dead ahead."

I am not a Pollyanna. I get that none of this is easy. Nevertheless, I am arguing that those of us who are not in leadership roles have obligations.

These obligations fall under the general rubric of being "good followers"— as opposed to being bad or simply lazy or timorous ones. This book makes clear that there are no bad leaders without bad followers. This book makes clear that bad followers are every bit as contributory to bad outcomes as bad leaders.

Just because we are saddled with a bad leader does not mean we have to go along. We can choose not to go along—*not* to follow. To be sure, choosing not to follow is not always easy. Sometimes it is difficult, even very difficult, to the point of being dangerous personally, politically, or professionally, or maybe even all three. Still, being aware of our options, understanding that we have choices, especially early in the process, before bad leadership congeals, is important.

It was never clear how Volkswagen developed a device that drastically cut emissions when the competition had failed repeatedly to do so. It was never clear on what basis Martin Winterkorn was able to promise in relatively short order that by controlling emissions Volkswagen would dominate the global automotive industry.

It was never clear how Turkey could harmoniously, seamlessly, reconcile its recent secular past with its contemporary faith-based present. Nor was it clear how Recep Tayyip Erdogan could satisfy his lust for power by remaining a democrat, especially once the allure of becoming a strongman went from palpable to irresistible.

It was never clear that Elizabeth Holmes had either the experience or the expertise to credibly promise, not to mention deliver, a transformation in science and medicine. Best to think of Holmes in Phase I as something of a cult leader, a leader who was able based on precious little other than her own persona to persuade others to follow her lead, to become true believers.

Finally, it was never clear that president and party chair Xi Jinping could remake China in his own image without requiring total obedience to his authority. Xi never promised his followers a rose garden. In fact, he made clear early on that he would be demanding and controlling. What he did not make clear in Phase I was just how much more demanding and controlling he would become over time—so long as he was given a free pass.

10

Phase II: Followers Join In

Leaders Energize and Secure Their Base of Support

I have long been baffled by followers being so consistently and persistently omitted from the conversation about leadership. There is no leadership without followership, no leader without followers, and no bad leader without bad followers. The reason is simple: no single individual, no matter how powerful, can do the work alone. Usually, though admittedly not always, to lead is to do something as opposed to doing nothing. And to do something, to carry out any leadership task, often requires not just a *team* but a *tribe*. Not just a few people but many people.

Recall that leadership is a system with three equal parts, of which contexts are one, followers another, and leaders another. It is impossible, therefore, to understand what happened in Nazi Germany without understanding German history, especially but not exclusively in the early to the mid-twentieth century; the German people as they largely were from the late 1920s to the mid-1940s; and, of course, Adolf Hitler. To take an example of the importance of followers: so far as we know, Hitler never himself killed a single Jew. Some 6 million Jews died because others, Hitler's followers, were willing to do his dirty work for him.

By now we have also learned that there are important distinctions among followers. Some of Hitler's followers were bystanders, while others were isolates (those who in no way participate in the group or organization of which they are members) and yet others were activists. Some were weak supporters of Hitler, some were strong supporters of Hitler, and some were acolytes of Hitler. And some—not many, but some—resisted Hitler. The distinctions among followers are especially important as they pertain to bad leaders and followers. In my book *The Enablers: How Team Trump Flunked the Pandemic and Failed America*, I wrote about those who enabled President Donald Trump during the last year of his administration, 2020, which coincided with the first year of the pandemic. Enablers, I argued, contributed as much as did Trump himself not only to the administration's miserable mishandling of the coronavirus but also, to take another obvious, in this case dramatic example, what happened on January 6, 2021, with the attack on the U.S. Capitol.

In *The Enablers* I kept it simple. I placed followers into just two different groups: Trump's "tribe" and Trump's "team." His tribe was broadly equated with his base. It consisted of ordinary Americans who were his hardcore supporters. Of course, most members of President Trump's tribe never came close to the White House nor, obviously, were they directly involved in the president's management of the pandemic. They were, though, the rock-solid foundation on which Trump stood during his entire time in the White House. Members of Trump's team were different—they were directly involved in his management of the pandemic. They included members of Trump's family, of the media, of Congress, and of the cabinet; some senators and governors; and all Trump's senior advisors. In his recent book, *Leadership*, Henry Kissinger divided followers similarly. He called the leader's tribe the leader's "people." And he called the leader's team the leader's "immediate entourage." It is this entourage that is charged with translating what the leader wants into public policies that "bear on the practical issues of the day."[1]

Trump's team (or entourage) was a management team charged in this case with translating the president's thinking into his management of the pandemic. Because all team members were deeply involved in how the president responded, or did not respond, to the virus crisis, they were the clearest and most complicit of his enablers. As I wrote in *The Enablers*, Trump's team was almost as responsible as the president himself "for so many Americans dead, for so many Americans sick, for so many Americans out of a job, for so many American lives destroyed, displaced, disrupted."[2]

As earlier described, enablers are "followers who allow or even encourage their leaders to engage in, and then to persist in behaviors that are destructive."[3] Every enabler is, then, a bad follower. Which raises this question: Is every follower of every bad leader an enabler? Or, to put it somewhat differently, is every follower of every bad leader a bad follower? To which I would reply no. Some followers of bad leaders are largely or even entirely unwitting, following out of indifference, or ignorance as opposed to enthusiasm. Moreover, there are other followers of bad leaders who believe they have no choice but to follow, or who think it is their best option, perhaps because they are fearful or famished, unstable or insecure, lonely, angry, or unknowing. To be sure, sometimes followers are in denial, even willful denial. The point is that among followers of bad leaders are degrees of responsibility and culpability—if even any.

Again, bear in mind that we are dealing here not with widgets but with humans. It's usually impossible, therefore, to draw bright lines, lines that make clear without room for argument which followers are complicit in being bad and which are not. Which, for example, are knowingly involved and which are just going along passively as opposed to actively. Notwithstanding complexities and ambiguities such as these, we, collectively, are responsible for addressing these sorts of problems. For when a bad leader with considerable power, authority, and influence is being enabled by those I name enablers, or if you prefer accomplices, in any case by those who are in some way complicit, his or her enablement has implications and ramifications, negative ones, that can be far-reaching and consequential, to the point of deadly serious.

In each of the four stories told in this book followers were aggressively recruited and enlisted early on, during Phase I and especially during Phase II. Moreover, even as the progression from bad to worse continued uninterrupted, most stayed for the duration. Most followers did not bail when things got bad, or even when they went from bad to worse. Having made their commitment, by and large they kept their commitment, either unwilling or unable to switch horses midstream.

People are vulnerable to paying, sometimes dearly, for sticking to "sunk costs."[4] What is a sunk cost? It's an investment we make—with, say, time, money, or emotional energy—that likely is lost but that we think we can recover if we just hang in. For example when we buy a stock we're certain will go up, and then continue to hold even when it goes down—and then goes down still more. Though there is growing evidence that we might well have made a mistake, rather than cutting our losses, we continue to cling to our original decision to buy because we are unable or unwilling to admit even to ourselves that we made a mistake. We hate to lose, we hate to admit we were wrong, and we hate to change our ways. So, as we have seen in this book, we likely will stick with the leader with whom we were initially paired or whom we initially chose—even if that leader goes rogue or goes bad.

Martin Winterkorn

Volkswagen's CEO from 2007 to 2015 was not warm or fuzzy. Quite the contrary. Martin Winterkorn was a demanding and intimidating superior who did little or nothing to ingratiate himself with his subordinates. The record shows that, if anything, they feared him. He was imperious in the office and outside it, playing to the hilt the part of grand seigneur, CEO of one of the world's leading car companies—who, by the way, made boatloads of money and behaved accordingly.

Winterkorn's style of top-down leadership had long been in the German tradition. So Winterkorn's tyrannical tendencies, his arrogance, and his high-handed ways were not out of step with Volkswagen's rigid but long-standing corporate culture. Still, they were at odds with changing styles of leadership and management—with what generally in the West was a loosening of previously fixed corporate hierarchies. For by the second decade of the twenty-first century, certainly in the United States, the old command-and-control style of leadership was out and a more cooperative and collaborative style of leadership was in. Hierarchies were being flattened, employees were being empowered, and what previously had been a cavernous gap between those at the top and those in the middle and at the bottom had been closed at least somewhat.

For the purposes of this piece, Winterkorn's *tribe* consisted of everyone both inside and outside the company who was unaware that since early 2007 Volkswagen had been routinely and repeatedly installing a cheat device in vehicles it sold by the millions to unsuspecting customers. These countless members of Winterkorn's tribe gladly bought what he had to sell, both figuratively and literally. They included hundreds of thousands of Volkswagen's employees; most members of Volkswagen's management team, including members of the board; hundreds if not thousands of government regulators in Europe and in the United States; Volkswagen's competitors at home and abroad; people associated with the automotive industry in Germany and globally; and, of course, Volkswagen's countless customers. Given that Volkswagen's cars were advertised as sharply reducing dirty and deadly emissions, the public had good reason to believe that among car companies Volkswagen was a model corporate citizen. It turned out though that nearly all members of Winterkorn's tribe were duped. They were fooled, hoodwinked, into believing what he and his team claimed was the truth.

Members of Winterkorn's *team*, in contrast, were all-knowing and all-important. Why? Because he himself did not install the defeat device, not in a single Volkswagen vehicle. Like most bad leaders, Winterkorn had others do his dirty work for him. For that matter, Winterkorn did not even directly oversee or closely monitor the process. He was, in more ways than one, above it all. Rather, the nasty goings-on were executed by some indeterminate number of his subordinates within the corporate hierarchy. They were ex-ecuted by some managers, engineers, and technicians who knew that they were engaging in wrongdoing but went ahead and did it anyway.

By now we know something about why members of Winterkorn's team went along with a scheme that they knew was wrong. On an individual level, they had incentives to keep their heads down, to obey authority and just do as they were told. Most if not all considered that they had good jobs that made it possible for them to lead good lives—lives they typically did not in the least want to disrupt, not to speak of give up. In addition to their individual reasons for remaining on Winterkorn's team throughout his time at the top were group reasons. Or, perhaps more precisely, contex-tual reasons, reasons rooted in the situations in which these people found themselves.

Philip Zimbardo is the psychologist famous (or infamous) for the Stanford Prison Experiment, which was conducted in the early 1970s to examine the impact of the situation on individual behavior. Decades later Zimbardo wrote a book titled *The Lucifer Effect: Understanding How Good People Turn Evil*, which is as much about bad followership as bad leadership.[5] To further explain why members of Winterkorn's team went along with a leader who implicitly if not explicitly sanctioned wrongdoing, I draw on Zimbardo's work to make three key points.

First, again, is our proclivity to obey authority. This holds even though in corporate settings wayward followers are not punished physically. Still, the so-called administrative obedience paradigm makes it difficult, sometimes seemingly impossible, for subordinates in large organizations to stand up to their superiors.[6] To repeat what by now is familiar: speaking truth to power is hard.

Second is our need, our wish, to fit in with those around us, specifically our peers. All or at least most of us have a need to belong, to associate with and be accepted by others. In fact, so strong is this need for identity and community that the fear of rejection by people we work with can interfere with our initia-tive and constrain our autonomy.

Finally is the power of the group, which "can get us to do things we ordi-narily might not do on our own."[7] The influence of groups is usually indirect. In general, groups don't literally tell us what to do or how to do it. Rather, they model the behavior that we are expected to emulate, and therefore typ-ically do emulate. In other words, we are far more likely to conform to the group norm than to go against it or even rail against it.

Understanding these sorts of pressures, all of which prompt us to go along to get along, makes it possible for us to understand why members of a team such as Martin Winterkorn's followed his lead even though they knew they were behaving in ways that were bad—both immoral and illegal.

Recep Tayyip Erdogan

To understand President Erdogan's progression from bad to worse, from a leader who was a democrat to a leader who is an autocrat, requires of course that we understand not only him, the leader, but also his followers, his tribe and his team. We further need to understand the context within which the leader and his followers were situated—the historical, structural, and institutional forces that shaped Turkey's policies. As Dimitar Bechev observed about the context, Turkey's "illiberal features" go a long way toward explaining how Erdogan was able to transform it from a democracy to an autocracy. What were some of these illiberal features? A polarized society. Undemocratic institutional arrangements. And exclusionary nationalism. Put differently, Turkey did not have a long political history of democracy, an entrenched political ideology that encouraged democracy, or a clear, cogent, and cohesive political culture that was conducive to democracy.

Further, Erdogan's tribe, for whom political Islam was so powerful an attraction, was ready and willing to follow a strongman in the Turkish tradition. This was key to why he was able to get so much power and to keep it for so long.[8] It was Erdogan's base, his tribe, to whom he owed his political career.[9] This meant that as he changed over time, so did they. Originally Erdogan's followers supported a leader who was relatively liberal and democratic. Later, however, they supported a leader who was much more illiberal and much less democratic. They stuck with him even as he evolved from being one type of leader to being another type. This indicates that they were far more devoted to him personally than they were politically or ideologically.

The two events that testified most vividly to the enduring loyalty of Erdogan's tribe—no matter his evolution from democrat to autocrat—were in 2013 and 2016. The first was in the aftermath of the protests at Istanbul's Gezi Park, when, on account of Erdogan's ferocious and even vicious response to the widespread demonstrations—to quash the peaceful but potentially contagious outbursts he sent in riot police equipped with armored vehicles, pepper gas, and water cannons to forcibly clear the scene—it became clear that Turkish democracy was eroding. The second was hard on the heels of the attempted coup against Erdogan. His immediate response then was to declare a state of emergency—which ended up lasting two years. During this period, he ordered a series of unprecedented purges, including mass dismissals, detentions, and arrests. Ultimately, at Erdogan's direction, tens of thousands were charged with criminal offenses.

Notwithstanding his continuing suppression of the opposition and his changes to the constitution that obviously were to his benefit, Erdogan remained personally and politically popular. This is not, of course, to say that he will remain in power indefinitely. It is not written anywhere that Turkey is destined forever to be subject to his (or anyone else's) one-man rule. But so long as he remains healthy and still wants to be president, he will do what he can to shut up and shut down his political opponents.

Members of Erdogan's team—his immediate entourage—have been predictably, reliably loyal and unfailingly compliant. Without exception they are sycophants, close to the president but unable or unwilling to talk to him openly and honestly.[10] To speak their truth to his power. Nor are members of the political and economic elite any more willing or able to resist him. One high-ranking executive at a major Turkish conglomerate recalls being told by one of Erdogan's associates that he should "talk to the president, so he understands the situation." To which the executive responded, "But why should we? This is [the ministers'] job."[11] It's clear that Erdogan is rarely challenged by anyone, including members of his own cabinet. As one senior advisor put it, "The president doesn't like strong people around him. Everyone knows that. So, no one is willing to speak the truth."[12]

To be sure, in the wake of the 2023 earthquake and the severe economic downturn to which it further contributed, Erdogan has had no choice but to back down on some of his earlier policies. Specifically, while he long supported artificially low interest rates, he agreed in 2023 to reverse course, to support higher interest rates—though only because he was finally persuaded the situation as it currently existed was dire.

Erdogan's reluctance to speak openly and honestly extends to members of the Turkish press. Why? Because as Steven Cook noted, under Erdogan's leadership Turkey has become a "leading jailer of journalists in the world."[13]

Given his isolation and self-protection, it is difficult to know exactly how Erdogan operates from day to day or makes decisions. Cook admitted that while "we know that the president's inner circle is made up of sycophants and family members," we do not know much more. Which reduces us to speculating about Turkey's "court politics."

Finally, it should be noted that during most of his very long tenure, President Erdogan has had no obvious successor. At one point his son-in-law, Berat Albayrak, seemed the heir apparent. Erdogan put him in charge of a new ministry, Finance and Treasury, presumably to groom him for higher office. But Albayrak's time at the highest echelon of Turkish politics did not last long. Just a couple of years later, in 2020, he and the president had a bitter falling-out, in consequence of which Albayrak resigned his post, purportedly for reasons of health.

Turkey's democracy has been in steady decline because for so many years Erdogan's followers—his tribe and his team—fell into line and stayed in line, no matter what he said or did. To be sure, all along there has been a political opposition. But so long as Erdogan remains in office, it is not likely that large numbers of his followers will take a stand against him. Not publicly, not privately.

Elizabeth Holmes

Easy enough to identify Elizabeth Holmes's tribe. Given how driven and dedicated she was, how single-tracked and single-minded, even before Theranos was fully launched, her tribe consisted of people persuaded by what she had to say about testing blood. The list of those who belonged is impressive: her parents, who supported her financially and emotionally; venture capitalists who bestowed on her, on Theranos, large sums of money early on; members of Theranos's board, most of whom were rich or famous or both, and a number of whom came on board early; a few close advisors, some of whom remained by her side for years; members of the media, a few of whom quickly became acolytes; business partners, in some cases executives at the highest levels of corporate America; and employees, several of whom toiled at Theranos for the duration, convinced they were part of a company that would transform science and medicine by revolutionizing how blood was drawn and tested.

Every member of Holmes's tribe, especially those who came and remained among the faithful, was willing to play by her rules. Strict rules that were not to be violated lest the violator was prepared to incur her wrath. These included complete secrecy, total obedience without a hint of dissent, and ostracization of anyone who dared to differ.

How to explain the fact that though Elizabeth Holmes started early on to lead in ways that were or should have been suspect, her tribe by and large remained loyal? Remained loyal to her personally and professionally, and to the dream in which she appeared deeply to believe? After all, early on there were signs that Theranos might not be all that it was cracked up to be. And early on there were signs that Holmes's highly controlling style of leadership and management might well be problematic. Still, for whatever the constellation of reasons, most of Holmes's followers missed the signals. They hung in from the beginning to the end. Until they could no longer deny that Theranos was little more than smoke and mirrors—and that Holmes was herself little better than a fraudster.

To understand how so many signed on to Theranos for so long, it is helpful to see Elizabeth Holmes as a charismatic leader—someone who had no obvious source of power and precious little authority, but who was able nevertheless to get others to follow her down the garden path. Holmes could not compel members of her tribe to fall into line, nor did she reward them in extravagant ways. Moreover, she could not draw on her impeccable credentials, for she had none. She was not a scientist, a physician, or an expert of any kind. She was not even a college graduate.

What, then, *did* she have? The answer is that she was preternaturally gifted at exercising influence. Because she had a singularly compelling persona—it was her look, her speech, her manner, her indomitable determination and extravagant vision—she was able for years to persuade people to do what she wanted when and how she wanted it. Of course, her subordinates at Theranos were treated differently: Holmes got them to fall into line simply because she was their superior. But the rest were, effectively, volunteers. They volunteered or at least agreed to do Holmes's bidding because they were in her thrall and under her influence—and because she asked.

The word "charisma" has long been carelessly used, bandied about without much thought given to what it means. Of course, it meant something specific to Max Weber, the German sociologist who early in the twentieth century first applied the word "charisma" to leaders who had an extraordinary, almost hypnotic effect on their followers. It means something quite different now. Now the word is used more casually, applied to any leader endowed with some sort of special appeal. So far as Elizabeth Holmes is concerned, the notion of charisma is appropriate. For if she had nothing else, she had, at a minimum, a special appeal to those who followed where she led simply because they wanted to. She was, it's fair to say, inspirational—she inspired others to freely and voluntarily join in her quest for the holy grail.

So much for followers who were members of Elizabeth Holmes's tribe. What about members of her team? Oddly, from everything we know, most of the time it was a team of only one. Only Sunny Balwani belonged. Only he and Holmes were fully privy to what transpired at Theranos. Which is why he ultimately was judged at least as responsible as she for all those years of wrongdoing. Recall that in July 2022, a California jury found Balwani guilty on twelve counts of fraud. The lawyer prosecuting Balwani said in his closing argument that Balwani "is not the victim—he is the perpetrator of the fraud."[14]

In some cases, followers follow their leader because they feel forced to. With Elizabeth Holmes, followers followed not because they were compelled or obliged to, but because they wanted to. She was a pied piper, a charismatic leader who attracted, enticed, inspired people to follow of their own free will. She even got some of her followers to give her things of great value, such as large sums of money and large amounts of time, as well as a level of commitment and dedication that was often extravagant.

Xi Jinping

During Phase I, when he first became party chair and a year later president, Xi Jinping promised his people that he would lead them to a better place. Take them from where they were then to higher levels of success and prosperity, and to where China would take its rightful place as the equal of any great power in the world. For the entirety of his presidency Xi sought to imbue his followers with a new sense of confidence, to where they believed what he repeatedly said, "The East is rising, and the West is declining."[15]

China's accomplishments during the decades before Xi came to power had already been stupendous. They included lifting the country out of poverty, making it a manufacturing colossus, and building new skyscrapers, subways, highways, and railways, some among the best in the world. Xi aimed to imbue his followers with an even greater sense of possibility. He wanted to prove to them and to the world that China's model of governance, a model of reliable stability and rigorous security, was superior to that of any Western nation—especially to that of the United States.

Xi's promise to the Chinese people, of a future even better than their present and better than all but their distant past, was one part of a two-part strategy designed to keep his followers in line. This part was the carrot—a gift on which Xi in many ways delivered. For most of his first decade as president, China thrived. It became more prosperous and successful, more consequential, and more powerful. The other part was the stick. Those who refused to follow where the president led were even at the outset threatened with punishment. The first was enticing, the second menacing. The first was effective, the second very effective. Which is why most of the Chinese people most of the time obeyed and continue to obey the dictates of the Chinese president.

I describe Phase II as one in which followers join in because leaders make a concerted, deliberate effort to expand and secure their support. In the case of Xi Jinping this effort was enormous in its breadth and depth, and endless in its quest for total subservience and complete obedience. Which is to say that while the strenuous effort at recruitment and commitment began in Phase II, it never let up, and over time that resulted in a high price to pay. Civil society was destroyed; recalcitrant and resistant individuals and groups were endangered, imprisoned, or even eliminated; and Chinese people in every walk of life were socialized to conform to the prevailing norms.

During Xi's reign different groups of people were, of course, treated differently. Ethnic minorities were pressured, by force, if necessary, to follow the Chinese model. This applied most obviously to the Uyghurs, to whom drastic measures were applied to compel them to identify with China and to follow the dictates of the Chinese Communist Party. Others—such as top executives who were perceived by the authorities as having grown too big for their britches—were gradually brought to heel by other measures. For example, by 2020 the once highly visible and relatively vocal Jack Ma, the billionaire cofounder of Alibaba, had effectively disappeared, no doubt on account of his criticisms of the government, specifically government regulators. (Ma resurfaced in 2023, reportedly to teach in Japan.) By the time of the 20th Congress of the Chinese Communist Party in 2022, Xi was going full force not only after individuals but also after institutions and corporations. Didi Global, a ride-hailing giant, was hit with a record $1.2 billion fine for data breaches, part of what soon became a sweeping campaign to strengthen the state's control over the economy and to signal to China's internet companies that "their free-wheeling days were over."[16]

China's educational system was similarly caught in his ever-tightening grip. Party schools and academies were especially affected by his insistence that reenergized party rule was essential to China's continuing ascent. Just a few years earlier these same institutions had tolerated some level of individualism and freedom of thought. But by the third decade of the twenty-first century, Xi's ideas had become core to their curricula, conformity was demanded, and a single theme pervaded: "China's success story is the success story of the Chinese Communist Party." Even young children were taught to be vigilant. "In defending national security, nobody is an outsider or bystander," said a presenter at an elementary school in northwest China. Students were reminded to report anything they thought suspicious—and were given the phone number of the Ministry of State Security.[17]

Finally, perhaps most tellingly, President Xi tried to ensure that China would remain stable and his followers loyal by gradually establishing a surveillance state of unparalleled size and scope. In 2022 the *New York Times* published the results of its investigation into the Chinese government's program to collect a "staggering amount of personal data from everyday citizens." Here are four symptoms of the totalitarian disease: (1) the authorities trying to "ensure that facial recognition cameras capture as much activity as possible"; (2) the authorities "using phone trackers to link people's digital lives to their physical movements"; (3) the authorities collecting DNA, iris scan samples, and voiceprints even from people with no connection to crime; and (4) the authorities connecting "all of these data points to build comprehensive profiles" of people, profiles intended to be accessible to every arm of government.[18]

China's population is over 1.4 billion—which is to say that President Xi has undertaken a Herculean as well as Orwellian task. As the *Times* summarized it, "The Chinese government's goal is clear: designing a system to maximize what the state can find out about a person's [identity and activities], which could ultimately help the government maintain its authoritarian rule."[19] Or, more precisely, its totalitarian rule.

For Xi to exercise such a high degree of control over his people, he required—in both his roles, as head of the party and as head of state—a slate of subordinates on whom he could completely rely. This is not to say that this team was without strife, or willing to follow his every command without question. Nor is it to say that in the future his subordinates will be as subservient to him as they have been in the past. Rather, it is to point out that for at least the first decade of his tenure as president and party chair, his closest comrades, his most significant aides, his key followers have been, in general, both highly competent and reliably loyal.

By the time the 2022 Party Congress was over, however, China experts detected a small but important shift. It was revealed that the Politburo Standing Committee, the Chinese Communist Party's most powerful decision-making body, had been revamped. Instead of representing minimally different interests and ideas, all seven of the standing committee members were now men widely known to be not just fiercely loyal to Xi but fiercely loyal *only* to Xi. Of course, this was just before a small crack appeared in Xi's edifice: a series of protests against the government for its punishing COVID lockdowns, protests that revealed to both Chinese citizens and those outside China that not all of the Chinese people were willing blindly to follow Xi all of the time. These relatively very few brave souls at least were no longer willing to be shut in and they were no longer willing to be shut up.

Warning Signs

By now the train has left the station. By the end of Phase II, on the cusp of Phase III, the progression from bad leadership to worse has gained momentum. For whatever their various reasons, and in whatever their various ways, followers have already joined in and signed on. They have agreed, either explicitly or implicitly, to follow a leader who is bad—unethical, ineffective, or both.

In the next chapter I will address how it is that being in a certain situation, or a certain group, can get us to behave badly, in ways that otherwise we would not. But there is another reason we behave badly—because we are incentivized as individuals. *Sometimes we follow bad leaders because we are directly rewarded for following or because we are directly punished for not following.*

In addition to my book, *The Enablers*, two others—one titled *Why We Did It*, the other *Thank You for Your Servitude*—explore how Donald Trump, who "contained not a single honorable attribute," was able to marshal such large and loyal cadres of followers.[20] Especially among those who should have known better: longtime and in many cases well-known establishment Republicans who were elected officials, such as governors and members of the House and Senate, in addition to members of Trump's cabinet and administration. What were their individual rewards for being Trump toadies?

To be clear, some of the reasons we follow are unconscious. Sometimes we make bad choices unwittingly, and then we try to justify them, to rationalize our way out of them. But some of our reasons for following bad leaders are completely conscious. They are deliberate. We don't have to rationalize them, because we think them rational. We follow because we assess that we personally are more likely to gain by doing so, or are less likely to lose. Here are six examples of "rational" rewards for going along with a bad leader:

- *Individual Reward #1: Power.* Following the bad leader is likely to get us more power.
- *Individual Reward #2: Money.* Following the bad leader is likely to get us more money.
- *Individual Reward #3: Success.* Following the bad leader is likely to facilitate and accelerate our advancement.
- *Individual Reward #4: Access.* Following the bad leader is likely to facilitate our proximity to power, fame, and fortune.
- *Individual Reward #5: Acceptance.* Following the bad leader is likely to facilitate and accelerate our membership in a group(s) we deem desirable.
- *Individual Reward #6: Avoidance.* Following the bad leader is likely to enable us to escape disappointment, derision, and defeat.

This returns us to the question of which followers of bad leaders are themselves bad. We know now that not all of them are bad. Is there a way, then, for us to distinguish between followers who are obviously bad and those who appear less bad or not at all bad?

Here is a preliminary attempt to answer the question. If someone follows a bad leader for good reason, we cannot say they are bad. Which necessarily raises another question: What in this case would be a good reason? As always, it's impossible in these matters to reply with precision, "good" and "bad" being always in the eye of the beholder. But in general, we might say that venal rewards such as money and power do not justify following a leader who obviously is bad. Conversely, we might say that ensuring safety and security—either one's own or that of others considered important, such as family members—do excuse following a leader who is bad. The bottom line is that we know, intuitively and experientially, that there are some circumstances that justify going along with a leader who obviously is bad. However, it's inevitable that some of us will disagree about what those circumstances are.

I noted that sometimes we follow bad leaders because we have no other choice, or we think we have no other choice. As in, for example, this situation: "I have a terrible boss, but I need this job." Still others of us follow bad leaders because we do not think they are bad, or because we do not know they are bad. Finally, there is this: Many if not most of us incline some of the time to follow bad leaders because we are on automatic pilot. Because obeying authority is what we are programmed to do. Moreover, in a country and culture such as China's, most people follow their leaders because that is what they are taught to do throughout their lives. In China, dutifully following is taught first at home (parents), then at school (teachers), and then in the workplace (superiors), whether in a factory or in the military, whether in a small group or a large organization. Life in China is, and traditionally has been, structured hierarchically.

Having said that not all followers of bad leaders can reasonably be called bad, I argue that some followers can. They can be called bad because they are knowingly, and for insufficiently good reason, enabling a leader who is behaving badly. Martin Winterkorn's underlings, specifically those among his subordinates who were consciously complicit in installing what they knew full well was a device intended to cheat, were bad followers. Similarly, what Sunny Balwani did was by every measure wrong. For years he went to great lengths to enable Elizabeth Holmes, a leader he knew full well was deceptive if not also delusional.

Followers of political leaders are differently situated than followers of corporate leaders, so they should be differently assessed, certainly in some cases. What were Turkish nationals to do, even those who were liberals, as Recep Tayyip Erdogan evolved from a democratic leader to an authoritarian one? Openly resist, even as resisters were at risk? Move to Canada or Argentina? Maybe. But the answer is neither easy nor obvious. Similarly, what about Chinese nationals living under Xi as he evolved from being an authoritarian leader to being a totalitarian one? Should they have openly resisted, even as resisters were at risk? Moved to Canada or Argentina? Maybe. Again, the answer is neither easy nor obvious.

What we can say for certain is this. Leadership and followership are not static. They fluctuate. When the fluctuation or transition is from bad to worse, it is in four phases that progress inexorably from one to the next over time.

In 2022 foreign affairs columnist Thomas Friedman admitted that he had long been wrong about China. "I confess," he wrote, "that I've been too optimistic. I plead guilty." He was guilty of having been blindsided by changes he did not foresee. "It is hard to believe now," he wrote in 2022, "but back in the 1990s and early 2000s, I was able to lecture freely at Chinese universities, do bookstore talks in Beijing and Shanghai, and even travel around." Since then, he conceded—since Xi Jinping became head of the Chinese Communist Party in 2012 and president in 2013—there had been "a pronounced reversal in trajectory."[21] But Friedman was not guilty of having been too optimistic about China. What he was "guilty" of is failing to appreciate how much people and places change. History is as replete with reversals in trajectories as it is with all sorts of other changes—including leaders who go from bad to worse, their followers in tow.

11

Phase III: Leaders Start In

Leaders and Their Followers Embark On or Continue a Course That in Some Way Is Bad

This is the phase during which bad becomes unambiguously clear. As we have seen, this does not suggest there is no evidence of unethical or ineffectual leadership and followership earlier, during Phases I and II. What it does mean is that in Phase III there's no mistaking it. To some, many, or most, bad is now blindingly clear. Additionally, this is the phase during which, if bad is to be stopped or at least slowed, it is past time to do so. For the more weeks, months, years that go by, the deeper bad leadership and followership dig in, which means they become that much more difficult to uproot.

This raises the question, again, of why we fail to act early on. If bad leadership is easiest to uproot in the early stages, why don't we uproot it sooner rather than later? Why don't we stop bad leaders immediately, as soon as they start behaving badly? Well, if humankind knew the answer to this question, humankind would have spared itself a lot of grief. More precisely, we, or at least I, would like to think that if we knew for certain that a leader who was bad would, if left unimpeded, get worse, we would do what we could to stop them. To preclude that leader from getting to Phase III and then progressing to Phase IV.

As I have already made clear, we know more than we think we do about bad leadership and why we allow it to fester, to linger, to go from bad to worse. It's one of the reasons for this book. Not only do I want to generate more knowledge about how and why bad leadership and bad followership happen, but I want to get the knowledge that we do have out there. To have it become common knowledge.

In the decade or two after the Second World War there were a number of studies specifically about bad followership. How did it happen that in a country such as Germany millions of people followed where Adolf Hitler led? Not only did many if not most Germans follow, but they followed the Nazis eagerly, often even wildly enthusiastically during the years immediately after Hitler became chancellor—and for a decade thereafter, even after the Nazis started a global war. This was despite his bad leadership—or was it because of it?

A somewhat similar, if obviously less lethal, case is that of Donald Trump. As mentioned, in the years since he left office there have been a few books that focused on Trump's followers, and specifically about why his followers followed a leader who, even when he first ran for president, was known to be inexperienced and inexpert in government and governance. In fact, he was known to be more of a huckster and even a fraudster than a serious man of serious purpose. And yet. Notwithstanding his blatant shortcomings and character flaws, Trump was able from his first day in political life to gratify and satisfy the many millions of Americans who constituted what came to be called his base. He was further able to get strong support from large swaths of America's financial and political elite. Rich and powerful Americans who saw fit, for their own reasons, to follow his lead—even as it became clear to many other Americans that their democracy was being threatened.

I already addressed the subject of why people follow bad leaders—they do so for reasons of their own, for rewards they get as individuals. I will have more to say about this shortly; suffice it for now to say that followers who follow leaders during Phase III, when their leaders clearly are bad, are likely (though not necessarily) themselves bad, complicit in the wrongdoing. We saw this in Chapter 4 regarding Hitler, a leader who famously let no grass grow under his feet. Who almost as soon as he became chancellor set about realizing his vision and implementing his program. By 1935, just two years after he came to power, the Nazis were able to pass the infamous Nuremberg Laws, the laws drafted specifically to address "the Jewish question." There's no mistaking what, certainly in retrospect, seems obvious: the Nuremberg Laws were a precursor to the Holocaust. This is not to say that Germans who supported Hitler in 1935 could have foreseen the genocide. But it is to say that even in Phases I and II, not to speak of in Phase III, Hitler and his supporters were demonstrating the proclivity to toxicity that in time became their hallmark.

Martin Winterkorn

Toward the end of 2006 was an all-important meeting attended by about fifteen of Volkswagen's top executives. This was the meeting, as we saw, during which it was decided to install a defeat device, which disabled emissions controls under real-world driving conditions—in this case to allow the vehicle to pass formal emissions testing.[1]

Martin Winterkorn was not at that meeting. He was still formally CEO at Audi. But even then he was a member of the board of management of Volkswagen AG, and just a few weeks later he became CEO of Volkswagen. This means it was inconceivable that he did not know from day one of his tenure at the top that Volkswagen's leadership group had recently decided to commit fraud on a regular basis—though, of course, we cannot prove he knew. It further means that all along Winterkorn presided over a company whose global ambitions bumped up against the immutable laws of physics. Recall that he was highly experienced in and deeply knowledgeable about every aspect of the auto business—including how cars were assembled.

Years later Volkswagen admitted that its engineers were never able to reconcile the conflicting goals of fuel economy and emissions control, at least not "within the allocated time frame and budget." Thus, to go "onward and upward" as rapidly and remarkably as Winterkorn had promised, Volkswagen would have had no choice but to engage in wrongdoing—and to continue to engage in wrongdoing until there was an engineering breakthrough.

Under Winterkorn's leadership Volkswagen deceived and defrauded a wide range of people. People who worked at the company. People who were part of the car industry. People in government charged with monitoring emissions controls. People who bought Volkswagen vehicles precisely because they thought they were buying a (relatively) clean car. And people who constituted the public, a public that assumed that by keeping emissions lower than its competitors Volkswagen was being a good corporate citizen.

It was during this phase—Phase III, "Leader Starts In"—that Winterkorn began to use the defeat device as his secret weapon. He began to tout Volkswagen's singular accomplishments on emissions control, pointing out that his car company was able to accomplish something that the other car companies were not. At the Vienna Motor Symposium in April 2008, Volkswagen's presentation was titled "Volkswagen's New 2.0-Liter TDI Engine Fulfills the Most Stringent Emission Standards." Moreover, in his speech in Vienna Winterkorn lashed himself to his company's fraudulent practices by boasting that Volkswagen, and Volkswagen alone, was positioned to "set new benchmarks for high fuel economy and environmentally sound motoring." In other words, Winterkorn's ability to satisfy his own personal and professional ambitions, as well as to at least ostensibly fulfill the promises he made to his followers both within the company and outside it, came to depend entirely on Volkswagen's deliberate deception.

During Phase III of Winterkorn's progression from bad to worse he became wedded to his own rhetoric, rhetoric that he had started to spew beginning in Phase I. Even in his first year as CEO of Volkswagen, he had boasted to the board of his vaulting ambition. Within a decade, he declared at the time, he would increase sales of Volkswagen's cars and trucks to 10 million a year—up from 6 million. Of course, to ensure that he could clear the extremely high bar he had set for himself, he would have to do what he should not have done. He would have to cheat. He would have to make sure that Volkswagen continued indefinitely to secretly install the device that would allow it to beat the competition.

Soon after becoming Volkswagen's CEO, Winterkorn was locked into a process that psychologists call entrapment. The phenomenon of entrapment is like that of sunk costs. Entrapment is when one "makes increasing commitments to a failing course of action or an unattainable goal in order to justify the amount of time and effort already invested, feeling helpless to do otherwise."[2] Implicit in entrapment is an element of irrationality. In Winterkorn's case, as soon as he signed on to become CEO of Volkswagen, which had just committed to engaging in a fraudulent practice, he was investing his time and energy, his heart and soul, in what was nearly certain at some point in the future to prove a "failing course of action."

Did Winterkorn think that Volkswagen's dirty not-so-little secret would never come out? Did he think that he would never be found out? Hard to say for sure, obviously, but the evidence suggests that during Phase II, and maybe even during Phase III, he did not think much if at all about getting caught. There is in any case not a shred of evidence that he ever once considered reversing course. To the contrary, to all appearances, Winterkorn saw the defeat device as an opportunity, as a way for him to realize his outsized ambition.

Winterkorn was a leader who lusted for success. Again, lust is "a psychological drive that produces intense wanting, even desperately needing, to obtain an object or to secure a circumstance. When the object has been obtained, or the circumstance secured, there is relief, but only briefly, temporarily."[3] Winterkorn's lust for success was such that even if the risk of committing corporate fraud year after year after year was high, he would not be stopped. He could not stop—until he was forced to.

Lust is akin to an addiction, and leaders who lust for success have an irresistible and unstoppable need to achieve. That Winterkorn was driven was already in evidence during Phase I—and repeatedly reconfirmed during nearly the entirety of his time as Volkswagen's CEO. By Phase III he and his team were fully and irrevocably committed to bad leadership. They did not lead; they *mis*led.

Recep Tayyip Erdogan

After a few years in office Turkish prime minister Recep Tayyip Erdogan paid less attention to striking a political balance between secularists and Islamists and more attention to keeping his core constituents, Islamists, happy. This meant that he gradually became less concerned about the niceties of democracy and more comfortable with the habits of autocracy.

Early in his life as a leader Erdogan was able to do what he wanted to do because he was demonstrably capable. Specifically, he was a good leader and manager: relatively effective and ethical. As a result, he and his party, the AKP, had an appeal that extended well beyond his base; it included many secularists and democrats, satisfied at that early point that Erdogan was able to deliver on many of his most important promises. These included but were not limited to expanding the size of Turkey's middle class and raising their living standards.

It further mattered that Erdogan's early successes came not only at home but abroad as well. For example, both the United States and the European Union welcomed Erdogan, and they embraced his political and economic reforms. The country's status at the crossroads of Europe and the Middle East was further enhanced, with Turkey's prime minister increasingly seen as a regional leader with whom other leaders in the area had to reckon. It was the Middle East, not Europe, that during the "Golden Years," from 2004 to 2007, became the arena within which Erdogan sealed his status as a global leader with whom other national leaders had to reckon.[4]

The prime minister's accomplishments enabled him to taste power—and it turned out he liked it. He liked it so much that he decided he did not want to give it up. His appetite grew with eating. Which brings us to Phase III, "Leaders Start In," during which, as is typical of bad leaders who get worse, Erdogan started to show his true self, or at least his later self, which in his case revealed a proclivity to autocracy. In June 2011 Erdogan and the AKP won a record third term in the general election—which raised the all-important issue of the length of a leader's tenure. Specifically, of how many years a leader *is* in power, versus how many years a leader *ought to be* in power.

When Erdogan ran for and won a third term as prime minister of Turkey, he sent an unmistakable signal. Giving up power without a struggle was not in his playbook. Think of the analogues: dictators such as Russia's president Vladimir Putin and China's president Xi Jinping, both leaders who manipulated the facts on the ground to enable them to be leaders indefinitely. This is not to compare Erdogan to either Putin or Xi. Rather, it is to make the point that leaders who for long periods of time, very long periods of time, have great power, authority, and influence, change. Power usually corrupts, and over time it usually corrupts more.

There are, of course, as the word "usually" suggests, exceptions to this rule. But in general, leaders who are reluctant to or, worse, refuse to leave their posts after about a decade should be considered suspect. This applies especially, though by no means exclusively, to political leaders. Curiously, notwithstanding what should be their importance, the norms associated with leader tenure are weak or even nonexistent. It's true that some countries have some laws on the books that relate. The United States, for instance, limits presidents to serving no more than two terms in office. However, the United States has no similar restrictions on justices of the Supreme Court, on members of Congress, or on most other elected officials. Nor are other leaders, such as corporate, educational, or religious leaders, typically subject to term limits. Even the leadership industry is largely silent on the subject. It has little or nothing to say about how over the years (again, more than, say, ten) leaders tend to get sclerotic. Increasingly they lose touch, they self-protect, they dissuade dissent, and they become rigid, self-aggrandizing, and controlling. Sometimes, in addition, they get old, too old to serve with maximum energy to maximum effect.

With Erdogan tendencies to the deficits of longevity in office were clearly in evidence during Phase III, when concerns about his high-handed ways started to surface regularly. These concerns were, predictably, found more among secularists than among Islamists, especially secularists who identified as liberal democrats. Evidence that Erdogan was becoming more emboldened, less willing to tolerate his opponents and more willing to target them, was starting to accumulate. As Erdogan began to dismantle constitutional checks and balances, doubts about his commitment to democracy started to rise. What began under his leadership as a debate about the role of Islam in public life morphed toward the end of his first decade in office into a different question entirely: what, specifically in Turkey, constitutes a healthy democracy?

As Erdogan changed over the years from a democratic leader to an autocratic one, some Turks began to openly challenge his increasingly obvious and irksome transition. Key members of the political elite were unhappy with his overreach, specifically the degree to which the executive branch began to impinge on the courts, the civil service, and the media. To take perhaps the most notable example, the man who was president of Turkey from 2007 to 2014, Abdullah Gul, warned that "democracy is not just the ballot box." Most people, though, didn't care. By 2013 Gul had been sidelined, while then prime minister, Erdogan, along with his party held the reins of power more tightly with every passing year. To be sure, there were protests, most importantly the one around Istanbul's Taksim Square. But these were beaten back and beaten down by the government, unceremoniously and in some cases brutally.

Taksim Square was a turning point, a foretaste of what was to come, evidence that from that point on "Erdogan would tolerate no opposition to his rule." The days of his party as a broad-based movement were over and "the break with liberal fellow travelers was a done deal."[5] It also signaled that Erdogan was now thumbing his nose at democratic leaders in the United States and Europe, instead throwing in his lot with autocrats not only in the Middle East but elsewhere in the world as well.

To be clear, at this point Erdogan was still in Phase III. He and his followers were not yet in Phase IV. But the ways in which he had changed from what he was earlier in his political career were becoming apparent; in fact, now they were impossible to miss. Dimitar Bechev summarized the trajectory: "The story of the AKP's second and third terms (2007–15) boils down to how a Machiavellian leader grabbed power, dismantling institutional constraints that checked his unbridled ambition. *Erdogan did not miraculously turn from an exemplary democrat to a Putin lookalike overnight in the summer of 2013. He evolved over the years.* What the [Taksim Square] episode did was to hammer home the fact that, following a period of consolidation, Turkish democracy was eroding" (italics added).[6]

Elizabeth Holmes

To grasp the full extent of Elizabeth Holmes's personal and professional deceptions it's helpful to go back in time, to the years before her claims were even remotely suspected of being untethered to reality. For given what we later found out—that nearly nothing she claimed about Theranos was true—it's still mind-boggling to be reminded of the successes of her swindle.

This is not to parse the difference, if any, between what she said was true and what she thought was true. Was Holmes deceptive or delusional? It's not apparent, at least not to me. All I know for certain is that many people believed what she said. They swallowed whole the lies that she fed them. In fact, she was able to go from Phase I to Phases II and III precisely because she was so skilled at pitching her wares to those ready and willing to buy what she was selling.

In 2013, before suspicions about her came to light publicly, a story about Holmes in the *Wall Street Journal* did her work for her. The fictions of Theranos were presented as facts. Though exactly what Holmes was doing remained unclear—recall that she was using nondisclosure claims to protect her "trade secrets," and was forbidding any sort of peer review—the *Journal* nevertheless reported that Theranos was now "refining" devices that "automate and miniaturize more than 1,000 laboratory tests, from routine blood work to advanced genetic analyses." The devices themselves were described as revolutionary, as promising improvements in medical testing that would change American health care forever. "Theranos's products," the *Journal* breathlessly if prematurely concluded, "are faster, cheaper, and more accurate than the conventional methods." Further, they putatively required only microscopic blood volumes, not "vial after vial of the stuff."[7]

It's clear, if only in retrospect, that during Phase III Holmes's bad leadership was in full throttle, going from bad to worse. She had developed habits of bad leadership and management that even then should have raised red flags. They included: (1) exaggerating, fabricating, lying; (2) insisting on extreme secrecy; (3) forbidding dissension; (4) failing to communicate; (5) refusing to encourage and empower; (6) manifesting extreme rigidity; (7) resisting collaboration and delegation; and (8) forbidding objective evaluations and peer reviews. Each of these tendencies and proclivities became worse over time, and each continued to be inflicted on those Holmes led and managed until she was finally stopped by the revelations of John Carreyrou, the reporter who ultimately got to the bottom of what really was (and was not) happening.

Given that so much of what Holmes said and did was in some way fabricated or false, the question is how exactly she compelled such compliance. To which there is one all-important answer. She was a charismatic leader and an astonishing pitchwoman who, from beginning to bitter end, sold herself and her product successfully and relentlessly. For example, when Holmes persuaded Walgreens to become her customer, she pulled off an amazing feat. It was a humongous sale to a humongous company, one of the largest drugstore chains in America. The deal amounted to a giant step toward Holmes's goal—which was to make Theranos services available "within five miles of virtually every American home."[8]

Holmes was known for her unusual self-discipline, for her fierce determination to improve and if possible perfect both herself and her company. Her routine was the same every day, and it was spartan: she got up very early, exercised, meditated, prayed, and ate a banana. She had similarly rigid patterns of behavior at work. She was never late. She never showed excitement. She was not impulsive. She did not hesitate. "I speak rarely," she once said. "I call bullshit immediately."[9] Given her personal rigidity and self-control, it's no great surprise that professionally she was resistant to change, or even incapable of it. Change, it became clear during Phase III, would never come from within, from within her. Nor would it ever come from her partner, Sunny Balwani, to whom she remained joined at the hip. Such change as there would be, then, had to come from someone or something outside. Which is of course what ultimately happened. Change finally came because an outsider brought bad leadership to light.

In a perfect world, someone from inside Theranos would have stopped the fraud, the craziness earlier on, in, say, Phase II—years before Carreyrou came on the scene. But in this imperfect world, a decade or so passed during which no one who was at Theranos or associated with the company called Holmes out. For years nearly every follower who was subjected to, even victimized by Elizabeth Holmes's penchant for lying and secrecy, harshness, and rigidity was willing to stay the course. Moreover, until Erika Cheung and Tyler Shultz came on the scene, none of the few who quit her orbit of their own volition—because they knew or strongly suspected that something was wrong—ever in any effective way blew the whistle. Which is why what happened at Theranos was permitted to proceed unimpeded for so long.

Xi Jinping

Before further discussing China's president Xi Jinping during Phase III, let's take a step back, to two topics touched on earlier. The first is making meaning of being bad. The second is differences in culture—especially political culture and organizational culture—that inevitably impact on how we judge bad, on how we identify, define, and describe bad leadership and followership.

In Chapter 3 I wrote about how elusive a concept "bad" is, notably when it is used as an adjective before the word "leadership." In fact, I argued that the complexities associated with researching and writing about bad leadership, even calling it out as such, are so daunting they appear to have discouraged most academics as well as the leadership industry more generally from taking the subject on. To take perhaps the most obvious examples, people in democracies have a hard time agreeing on who is a good political leader and who is a bad one. And the differences of opinion on what constitutes good leadership and bad are even greater between those who live in democracies and those who live in autocracies.

Case in point: After President Vladimir Putin invaded Ukraine in February 2022, he was considered by large majorities in the United States and Europe to be extremely, unambiguously "bad." A leader who was immoral, amoral. After all, what quickly came to be called "Putin's war" was as unprovoked as it was destructive and deadly. However, in the months after the invasion, Putin's approval ratings within Russia soared to levels he had not enjoyed for years. While in times of war this "rally round the flag" effect is common, and while polling numbers in Russia are not exactly highly reliable, it is nevertheless striking that in a poll taken a month after the invasion, a whopping 83 percent of Russians reportedly approved of Putin's leadership.[10] Nor did this figure abate as the conflict ground on and more about the war became known, even within Russia. In October 2022 about 80 percent of Russians still approved of their leader.[11]

Differences of opinion such as these—our views on who is a good leader and who is a bad one—are characteristic not only of the public sector but of the private sector as well. In business the metric of success generally is money. How able is the leader, the CEO, to show a handsome profit and, if it's a publicly traded company, raise the price of its stock? But sometimes there are other criteria that pertain, such as, for example, stewardship of the environment, social responsibility, and good governance (ESG).

Lee Raymond was CEO of ExxonMobil from 1993 to 2005. As good as he was at making the company money, that's how bad he was on the environment. Before it was publicly an issue, Exxon's scientists had discovered that climate change was real and that it was dangerous. Notwithstanding, Raymond joined with others in the oil industry to cover up the truth, In fact, he has the dubious distinction of having given the "single most audacious speech of the era." In 1997 Raymond told an audience at the World Petroleum Congress that "the planet was cooling" and that acting on the environment was in any case not urgent.[12] Was Raymond a good leader or a bad one? Or is it impossible to describe a leader such as Raymond with a single modifier? Maybe so, though as I argue throughout this book complexity should not ever stop us from taking bad on. In fact, it's of the utmost importance that we do.

The judgments Americans make when they assess the "goodness" or "badness" of a leader such as China's president Xi Jinping are necessarily fraught. For where anyone stands on a leader like him will depend on where they were born and raised, on what they have done, and on what their interests are. Ray Dalio, the wildly successful American asset manager, ran into trouble on just this issue. While his hedge fund, Bridgewater Associates, managed billions of dollars for companies partly owned by the Chinese government, Dalio seemed to focus nearly exclusively on what the Chinese president had accomplished, such as building China's capacities in industry and technology. Additionally, Dalio repeatedly warned against the dangers of judging leaders of countries and cultures entirely different from our own.[13] But his reputation was tarnished when he seemed to dismiss as not especially important China's miserable record on human rights, likening its government to a "strict parent."[14]

Whatever the complexities, it's not possible (or, for that matter, desirable) to completely withhold judgment. Which returns us to Xi during Phase III. It was the phase during which he made clear that to reach his goals he would tighten the screws on his people in ways that most in the West would find objectionable or even abhorrent. It was also the phase during which it became clear that he had accrued more power than any of his immediate predecessors. A decade into Xi's presidency, his only rival for supremacy in Communist China was the legendary revolutionary and founder of the People's Republic of China, Mao Zedong.

Xi's progression from autocratic to totalitarian leader was relatively swift, and it was sweeping. No stone was left unturned, which is to say that not a single aspect of Chinese society was left untouched by Xi's heavy hand. His control over the military was especially important as his appetite for foreign adventure grew. In 2023 political scientist Michael Mandelbaum concluded that Xi's appetite for more territory was increasing, and that Xi had his eye on "much of the Pacific Ocean as well as the now de facto independent . . . island of Taiwan."[15] Xi's control over the Chinese Communist Party was equally important. As his zeal for domestic surveillance grew, the tentacles of the Party gradually reached into every aspect of Chinese society, including government and education at all levels as well as organizations and corporations of every size and stripe.

By 2016, the level of Xi's ambition was amply in evidence. Already regarded as "China's most powerful leader in decades," he developed a personality cult intended to boost not the power of party and the state generally but his power particularly. As a March 2016 article in *Foreign Policy* pointed out, Xi's name started to appear with unusual frequency in Communist Party publications. He was increasingly called a "core" leader, a descriptor reserved for only the most vaunted of Chinese leaders. And songs and videos in praise of Xi were going viral. While the ultimate impact of Xi's personality cult remains an open question, by 2016 China watchers in the West were already claiming that its "successful cultivation" had been a "political gain."[16]

Xi's presidency has been in keeping with an age-old Chinese culture in which it is presumed that decisions are made from the top down. Leaders are expected to lead. And, as importantly, followers are expected to follow. This belief—that people should organize themselves hierarchically and that everyone should know their place and behave accordingly—can be traced back to Confucius. These lines are from his *Analects*: "A man who respects his parents and his elders would hardly be inclined to defy his superiors. A man who is not inclined to defy his superiors will never foment a rebellion. . . . To respect parents and elders is the root of humanity."[17]

How people in China generally think is obviously in strong contrast to how people in the United States generally think. In the former the collective comes first; in the latter it is the individual. In the former hierarchies are being maintained and even strengthened; in the latter they are being flattened and even weakened. I acknowledge the contextual differences—while at the same time taking a stand. The extent to which President Xi Jinping expanded his power, authority, and influence in Phase III was questionable at best, reprehensible at worst.

Danger Ahead

I concluded the chapter immediately preceding this one, on Phase II, with a section titled "Warning Signs." Now, in Phase III, the word "warning" no longer applies. Now evidence of the progression from bad leadership to worse is overwhelming—danger clearly looms. Moreover, stopping the progression is extremely difficult at this point, or even effectively impossible. How does it happen, this transition from bad to worse? How do we get caught in a web that seems not of our own making?

As indicated in the preceding chapter, the answers to these questions are on two levels: internal, located within us; and external, located outside us, in the group to which we belong. Earlier I discussed the former, here the latter. To sum up: It's impossible to exaggerate the impact of the situation and of the group on the individual. We have our personal reasons for doing what we do. But these are in tandem with other reasons, ones that are social and situational.

To start with, there is our innate proclivity to obey authority, which is strengthened or weakened depending on the context, on the situation in which we find ourselves. Since the 1960s the phrase "obedience to authority" has had a rather sinister connotation. It was made famous/infamous in the 1960s as a consequence of an experiment in social psychology that had daunting implications. Yale professor Stanley Milgram sought to understand how it happened that so many Germans were willing to kill so many Jews during the Second World War. So he devised a laboratory experiment in which he manipulated his subjects to get them to inflict physical pain on another person. Suffice it here to say that the way Milgram manipulated his subjects was to create situations in which they were prompted to do as instructed. What Milgram's experiment demonstrated was how, in certain circumstances and in certain contexts—in this case being told what to do by an authority figure in a laboratory setting—people will behave in reprehensible and even terrible ways. Ways in which they never would normally.

Somewhat similarly, psychologist Robert Cialdini described the impact on us of the group, in this case society writ large. A widely accepted system of authority, Cialdini wrote, "confers an immense advantage upon a society . . . Consequently, we are trained from birth that obedience of proper authority is right and disobedience is wrong. This essential message fills the parental lessons, the schoolhouse rhymes, stories, and songs of our childhood and is carried forward in the legal, military, [organizational] and political systems we encounter as adults. Notions of submission and loyalty to legitimate rule are accorded much value in each."[18]

When we're in groups, then, we are socialized and incentivized to follow. *Most of the time we follow bad leaders because the group seems to us to dictate or at least encourage it.* Because to follow is our default position, the position we assume when we're on automatic pilot. All our lives we are told what to do by those designated our superiors—our parents, our teachers, our bosses—which is why all our lives we tend to do what we are told to do with little or no conscious deliberation. The fact is that most of the time not only we but the groups and organizations to which we belong *benefit* from our obedience to authority. Here are five examples of how:

- *Group Benefit #1: Stability.* The groups to which we belong are more likely to be stable if most members go along with what the leader wants and intends. Refusals to conform usually are disruptive.
- *Group Benefit #2: Security.* The groups to which we belong are more likely to be secure if most members agree to protect and defend them. Refusals to protect and defend usually put the group at risk.
- *Group Benefit #3: Productivity.* The groups to which we belong are more likely to be productive if most members let the leader lead. Refusals to let the leader lead usually result in hesitation and confusion.
- *Group Benefit #4: Community and Comity.* The groups to which we belong are more likely to be agreeable and compatible if most members refrain from resisting. Resistance usually results in frustration and fractiousness.
- *Group Benefit #5: Survival of the Fittest.* Groups that avoid constant divisiveness and infighting are more likely to survive long-term. Joining hands is healthier for both individuals and groups than throwing fists.

To be sure, as I pointed out earlier, because of changes in cultures and technologies, leaders in democracies have generally gotten weaker and followers stronger. Still, to say that followers are less likely to go along is not to say that they are unlikely to go along. Moreover, while democracies have gone in one direction, autocracies have, for the same underlying reasons, gone in the other. Precisely because in the last decade or two followers in the former have become more empowered, followers in the latter have become less empowered. Specifically, people who live in autocracies, from China to Russia, from Egypt to Venezuela and beyond, are more oppressed and suppressed now than they were ten, fifteen years ago. This is because autocratic/totalitarian leaders understand that if they do not rule with an iron fist or close to it, it is unlikely they will rule at all.

The shift from Phase II to Phase III is significant. The previous chapter did not end on an extremely pessimistic note. By the end of Phase III, in contrast, it has become clear that it's as hard to fight human nature as it is to fight Mother Nature. Human nature programs us, as individuals and as members of groups, to go along to get along. To go along rather than to resist, especially when resistance is likely to be costly.

Volkswagen has long employed hundreds of thousands of people. When Martin Winterkorn was CEO nearly none had any idea that on his watch the company regularly equipped its cars with a defeat device. But some did know. Which means that as Winterkorn progressed from Phase II to Phase III, so did those of his followers who were wise to his ways. All those years their leader went rogue, mum was the word.

Not so with Recep Tayyip Erdogan. During Phase III some of his followers did object; some even took to the streets to protest publicly. Indeed, some risked their safety and security by demonstrating against Erdogan's increasingly autocratic ways. But their numbers, though considerable, were too small and the government was too strong for the protesters to have a significant impact. Most Turks continued to support Erdogan, even if only by doing nothing. The trouble is that to do nothing is to do something. To do nothing to resist the bad leader is, effectively, to support the bad leader. To this general rule most of Erdogan's followers were, for two decades, no exception.

Once Elizabeth Holmes started the progression from bad leadership to worse, she did not stop—she apparently could not stop. Not because she sought from the start to swindle her investors, deceive her partners, or hoodwink her subordinates. Rather, it was because she herself was persuaded by the power of her fever dream. The evidence is that for years—certainly through Phase III—Holmes genuinely believed that she could and would do what she said she could and would do.

Finally, China's Xi Jinping. Once he progressed from Phase II to Phase III, it was too late for anyone or anything to stop his transformation from authoritarian to totalitarian. Given how far he had already advanced, given his ambition to be ruler for life, and given China's history and culture, it was hard to imagine where significant resistance, resistance that threatened his hold on power, would come from. To be sure, protesters did apparently trigger Xi's about-face on what had been for nearly three years his draconian COVID policy. But for various reasons, including China's measurably declining economy, Xi must have been prepared for this reversal. Further, it is one thing for demonstrators to challenge a specific policy. It is quite another for them to challenge the party, the government, or the supreme leader.

Early on it was clear that Xi fully intended to break from the pattern of the recent past, during which leadership was exercised by a group. It was equally clear that so long as he was hell-bent on becoming and remaining king of the hill, it was unlikely—not impossible, but unlikely—that anyone or anything could stop him.

12

Phase IV: Bad to Worse

Leaders and Their Followers Extend and Expand Their Commitment to Being Bad

It's over. The progression from bad to worse ends at Phase IV because there's no place else to go. Bad has become worse, and worse has become entrenched. Nor can we bank on bad backtracking. It doesn't happen. Leaders virtually never, of their own volition, reverse course and go from being bad to being good. Can you imagine Martin Winterkorn, Recep Tayyip Erdogan, Elizabeth Holmes, or Xi Jinping waking up one morning after many years of being bad and deciding to change their ways? Of course not. To the contrary. In each case, over time the leader's commitment to being bad—their identification with the character they created—became stronger.

Of course, it's always possible to go from worse to even worse. While Jews were persecuted, prosecuted, and incarcerated by the Nazis soon after Adolf Hitler came to power, attacks on Jews—and other groups such as communists, socialists, and homosexuals—became more vicious as time went on. Moreover, the systematic killing of Jews, the genocide, began only in 1942, nine years after Hitler became chancellor.[1]

Nor is going from worse to even worse limited to people in government, to the public sector. The same thing happens to people in business, in the private sector. For example, leaders at Boeing were given license to get worse when, after the first deadly crash of a Boeing 737 Max airliner in October 2018, neither the company nor its watchdog, the U.S. Federal Aviation Administration, required the airliner to be grounded until the accident had been fully investigated. It took a second, nearly identical fatal accident—by then 346 people had been killed in the two separate crashes—for the plane to be taken out of service.

Still, worse is worse, which is to say that once bad has reached Phase IV, once it has become awful or even catastrophic, it has come to the end of the line. This is not to say that the degrees of difference between worse and even worse are insignificant. Rather, it is to say that bad at the end is a dead end. Sometimes figuratively, sometimes literally.

Each of the three parts of the leadership system—leaders, followers, and contexts—is of equal importance. And each is dependent on the others, independent of the others, and interdependent with the others. For instance, how followers react to leaders depends on who the followers are, who the leaders are, and the contexts within which they are situated. Context, remember, is key. For when the context changes (which it always does, if only over time), so will the leaders and followers situated within them.

How Ukrainians responded to their president, Volodymyr Zelensky, in June 2022 was dramatically different from how they had responded to him in June 2021—not because he had changed, or because they had changed, but because their situation had changed. Their country had been attacked by Russia. Ukraine was at war. Of a different magnitude but still in some ways similar was how employees at Goldman Sachs responded to their chief executive officer, David Solomon, in 2022 compared to a couple of years earlier. The response was different not because he had changed dramatically, or because they had changed dramatically, but because the situation had changed dramatically. After the pandemic Solomon's mandate to get his employees back to the office full-time was experienced differently than it would have been if COVID had never happened.

The leadership system constitutes its own ecosystem. Which means, among other things, that it resists intrusion from anything or anyone outside. This is not to say that the ecosystem—whether Volkswagen or Theranos, Turkey or China—is entirely impervious and impenetrable, because it is not. Consider, for example, the impact of John Carreyrou on Theranos. Rather, it is to say that interfering with that ecosystem, intruding on it, is difficult, sometimes effectively impossible, at least not without incurring enormous costs. Whatever the sanctions the West has imposed on Russia, and whatever the assistance the West has provided Ukraine, Putin's Russia, which is its own ecosystem, has proved a very difficult nut to crack.

The implications of this for bad leadership are profound. Because leaders and their followers are largely sealed off, they are hard to change because they are hard to reach. Change is possible in only three ways. First, it can be triggered by a person or persons inside the ecosystem—for example, by a whistleblower. Second, it can be triggered by a person or persons outside the ecosystem—for example, by a regulator, an investigative reporter, a

competitor, or an enemy. Third, change can happen in reaction to an exogenous event—for example, a natural disaster.

Whistleblowers attempt to stop bad leadership from the inside. But they
succeed only rarely. Usually they put themselves at personal and professional risk while failing to do what they are trying to do. Another example
of attempting to create change from within is when a group of followers—
small, large, or somewhere in between—becomes so angry and unhappy
with their leader(s) or manager(s) that they join forces to rebel. By 2022
labor unions had formed at more than two hundred Starbucks stores. Why?
Because Starbucks baristas were fed up with their employer, especially with
Howard Schultz, Starbucks's founder and, for decades, its CEO. In Israel in
March 2023, so many people were so furious at Prime Minister Benjamin
Netanyahu—specifically over his plan to overhaul the judiciary, which they
saw as a power grab—that they took to the streets in numbers enormous
enough to effectively paralyze the country. Netanyahu was forced to retreat,
to delay, at least temporarily.

Someone who tries to bring about change from outside the leadership
system is, by definition, engaging in a hostile act. When the United States
declared war against Nazi Germany in 1941, it was a hostile act. When the
authorities started to go after Volkswagen, it was certainly perceived by the
carmaker, notwithstanding its being a corporate behemoth, to be a challenge
not just to its integrity but to its way of doing business. And when investigative work by *Wall Street Journal* reporter John Carreyrou revealed that
Theranos was smoke and mirrors, Elizabeth Holmes saw it, correctly, as an
effort to bring her down, which ultimately it did.

An example of how an exogenous event can impact a leadership system
was Hurricane Katrina. The storm hit the Gulf Coast in 2005. It spread
across a four-hundred-mile stretch with sustained winds of up to 125 miles
per hour and was accompanied by a storm surge so high it resulted in widespread flooding and the displacement of hundreds of thousands of people
in Louisiana, Mississippi, and Alabama. America's president at the time was
George W. Bush, who happened, when Katrina hit, to be on an extended vaca-
tion, which seemed to slow his response. Fairly or unfairly, he was perceived
to have paid the disaster only belated and inadequate attention—a lapse or
mistake from which neither his reputation nor his administration ever fully
recovered.

Of course, not every exogenous event—including a catastrophic natural
disaster—shakes up the leadership system in a major way. We saw this in

Turkey, where it seemed that Erdogan's long tenure in power might finally be over on account of the major earthquake in early 2023. Especially since he bore some responsibility for much of the shoddy construction that had contributed to the widespread damage—and since he was already bracing for his toughest election in two decades. But whatever the political damage to him, it was certainly not lethal. Instead, when the election results were in, it was clear that the president had retained the loyalty of most of his faithful followers, winning, for example, eight out of the eleven provinces in the earthquake zone.

This book makes clear that the success of an attempt to upend bad leadership depends to an extent on *when* the attempt is made. As a general principle, the more time passes, the more bad leadership and followership become entrenched the more difficult they are to uproot. Therefore, the more years that went by during which Winterkorn and his minions freely installed Volkswagen's cheat device, the less likely it became that any of them would break the code of silence. The more years that went by during which Erdogan was given license to lead as an authoritarian, the more difficult it became for anyone to effectively resist him. The more years that went by during which Holmes engaged in militant management and fraudulent practices, the less likely it was that anyone on the inside would dare to speak up. The more years that went by during which Xi Jinping ruled China with an iron fist, the harder it became for the Chinese people, inside and outside the government and the party, to do anything but fall into line.

This does not mean that resistance to Winterkorn, Erdogan, Holmes, or Xi was impossible. Just that it became harder to do as more time passed. Similarly, this does not mean that resistance to other bad leaders even well into their tenures is impossible. It is not. For many years Robert Mugabe, who was prime minister or president of Zimbabwe for nearly forty years, was widely acknowledged as a leader who had long since gone from bad to worse. Finally he was ousted—though by then he was in his nineties.

How, then, do bad leadership and followership end? We know that sometimes they do. We also know that sometimes bad leaders and followers are obliged to pay a price for their wrongdoing. Moreover, there are times when history is their judge. Which is to say that there are times when bad leaders escape the consequences of their actions during their lifetimes—but after they are gone their reputations are destroyed and their names forever blackened. The bottom line is that how bad leadership and followership end, if they ever do, depends on the usual multiplicity of factors. These include whoever and whatever is relevant within the leadership system, and whoever and whatever is relevant outside it.

In a perfect world, we would know precisely how to end bad leadership and how to hold bad leaders and followers accountable. But in this imperfect world all we have are tentative conclusions and preliminary recommendations. Still, it helps to know that some of the time wrongs are righted. And that some of the time wrongs are righted because we right them.

Martin Winterkorn

In 2021 four former Volkswagen employees charged with fraud finally went on trial in Germany. They were accused of being aware of the illegal software but deciding to say nothing, opting instead to protect their posts and profits by staying silent. Some of the four insisted that they never even knew about the manipulation. Others admitted that they did know, and swore they told their superiors. But then, they acknowledged, they left it at that. Their excuse was that they were pressured to keep quiet.[2]

One of the four defendants, Hanno Jelden—a Volkswagen manager who was accused of overseeing the illegal software that was at the heart of the fraudulent scheme—blamed his years-long silence and subsequent cover-up on Volkswagen's corporate culture. He described it as one in which "problems were to be solved quickly rather than analyzed." Jelden further maintained that he never would have remained silent had he "known the legal consequences this could have."[3] What he failed to understand was that the right thing to do would have been to call out the fraud in any case, whatever the dictates of the law. After all, the company spent years deceiving countless customers, regulators, and of course the general public, all of whom believed that Volkswagen vehicles were one thing when in fact they were another.

As we have seen, Martin Winterkorn was forced, finally, to pay up (or at least to pay something) for his "breaches of due diligence." Additionally, he was formally charged with having lied to the German parliament about when exactly he learned about the cheat device. (He claimed it was in September 2015; the state charged it was in May.) This was all farce, of course, because to anyone even remotely familiar with the case, the idea that Winterkorn learned about the defeat device only in 2015 was ludicrous, unbelievable. On what planet was Volkswagen's tyrannical CEO and micromanager between

2007, when the cheat device was first installed, and 2015, when it was finally exposed?

By Phase IV the cheat device had become so deeply and completely entrenched at Volkswagen the company knew no other way. This was what Volkswagen did. This was how it made cars, advertised cars, sold cars. How it ostensibly shone where other carmakers did not. How it beat the competition by claiming to be a cleaner, more caring, and more careful steward of the environment. Of course, so far as Winterkorn was concerned, this was all about money and power. By claiming to be cleaner and more careful, Volkswagen was becoming richer and more powerful—and so was he.

Never in a million years would the truth about Volkswagen have come out had it not been for outsiders who revealed it. As mentioned, the agents of change were a handful of graduate students at West Virginia University and a little-known independent nonprofit organization called the International Council on Clean Transportation (ICCT). According to a detailed account of the unraveling in the *Financial Times*, it was a senior fellow at the ICCT, ironically named John German, who led the charge against the car company. When it became apparent at least to him that there was no good explanation for why Volkswagen's vehicles were passing their emissions tests in the laboratory but not on the road, where they had nitrogen oxide emissions up to thirty-five times allowed levels, he concluded that something was off. "It had to be a defeat device," he said later. "There was no other explanation." Initially German was careful about presenting his findings. He thought accusing a multibillion-dollar company of deliberately lying was "just way too dangerous." So he kept his mouth shut—not about his findings, but about suggesting that installing the "defeat device" was a deliberate deception.

It took over a year for U.S. regulators to confirm that Volkswagen was cheating intentionally. Some of the delay was on account of the caution exercised by people like German. And some of it was on account of Volkswagen itself, which, according to a court document, "intentionally made . . . false and fraudulent statements" to make the discrepancies between vehicle emissions in the laboratory and on the road appear as if they were "innocent mechanical and technological problems." Only in 2015—when a Volkswagen employee "disclosed, in direct contravention of instructions from his management," that some cars could detect when they were in the laboratory as opposed to on the road—was the truth finally revealed.[4] And only in 2015 did Winterkorn finally fall. He finally fell because he was finally pushed—not by insiders but by outsiders.

Recep Tayyip Erdogan

Erdogan's is a textbook case. He is a perfect example of how leaders and their followers can and sometimes do change over time. Experts on Turkey confirm the point. They confirm that under Erdogan's skillful if baleful leadership his country shifted from being one thing, a democracy, to being another, an autocracy.

- In 2022 Tony Barber wrote, "Erdogan's . . . methods and style of rule have acquired ever more authoritarian features, including a militarized foreign policy, the longer he has stayed in power."[5]
- In 2022 Gideon Rachman remembered his first encounter with Erdogan, in 2004. Then the fledgling prime minister replied to questions in ways that were "well suited to liberal western sensibilities." But eighteen years later, "the idea that Erdogan shares a liberal set of values with the EU would be regarded as absurd in both Turkey and Brussels." Erdogan had become "increasingly authoritarian and stridently anti-western." He had also become imperial, now dominating his country from a "huge new presidential palace constructed for him in Ankara."[6]
- In 2022 Dimitar Bechev concluded that Erdogan had taken "advantage of electoral democracy to seize ever more authority and eventually install a one-man regime."[7]

People who try to explain how Turkey changed from an electoral democracy to a "one-man regime" tend to focus on Erdogan. He is, after all, the "one man" at the center of the action. Moreover, during his time in office there were several turning points. In 2010 he permanently expanded his control over the judiciary. In 2013 he used the protests in Gezi Park as an excuse to stifle and intimidate those whom he perceived as his political enemies. In 2016, after a failed attempt at a coup, he engaged in a widespread purge of the military and judiciary. And in 2017 he arranged changes to the Turkish constitution that bestowed on the president, on him, significantly greater power.

Still, this is a story not just about Erdogan, or his followers, or even the context that is Turkey. It is also about the larger context within which Turkey is situated—specifically, the global context. As I indicated in Chapter 1, in recent years Freedom House has focused on what it referred to in 2022 as the "global expansion of authoritarian rule." After careful study it concluded that democracy's opponents "have succeeded in shifting global incentives, in jeopardizing the consensus that democracy is the only viable path to prosperity and security, and in encouraging more authoritarian approaches to governance." Freedom House's conclusion is not an abstraction. Erdogan and his minions simply exemplify (and, for that matter, typify) what has been for sixteen consecutive years the decline of global freedom.[8] Put directly, because strongmen have "become a central fixture of global politics" over the last two decades, Turkey's shift to authoritarian rule has not exactly been an outlier.[9]

Erdogan's strongman strategies are in evidence not only at home but abroad as well. Turkey is a member of the North Atlantic Treaty Organization (NATO), but Turkey's president has driven most of his fellow members crazy. He has been an infuriating and unreliable ally, playing off West against East and, when it suits him, cozying up to Vladimir Putin even after the start of Putin's war. (Erdogan and Putin have a complicated relationship; each has something the other wants and needs.) Turkey's president has gone against NATO not only by initially opposing the admission of Sweden and Finland. He has also objected to NATO's position on the issue of human rights, especially as it pertains to the Kurds, a largely Muslim ethnic group that constitutes about one-fifth of Turkey's population. Most Kurds want greater autonomy, and many want independence—which is precisely why Erdogan has long seen them as being threatening and has long sought to marginalize them.

None of this is to say that Recep Tayyip Erdogan is guaranteed to live in his enormous, ostentatious presidential palace indefinitely. The 2023 presidential elections were held during a period when, even before the awful earthquake, Turkey was struggling—reeling from among other things a collapsing currency and runaway inflation (an annual rate of 85 percent in fall 2022).[10] Moreover, the president's party, the AKP, has become more fractious and less popular, and the Kurds could conclude the time is ripe for them to seek some sort of retaliation or revenge. Finally, so successfully has the president isolated himself from his critics that the only voices he hears echo his own—never a way to make smart decisions. Still, Turkey's president is not likely to go quietly into the night. Preceding the elections, his government spent billions of dollars in state funds to bolster both him and his party, and it unleashed a slew of legal threats to weaken those who posed any risk of unseating him.

Turkey is a large and powerful state that constitutes its own ecosystem. This means that when Erdogan does finally leave office it will be because of what happens within. He will have surrendered power of his own volition—or he will have been pushed from power by a competitor. But pushing him out will not be easy, and it could be risky. Authoritarians hate being told what to do, and they hate being told when to do it.

Elizabeth Holmes

Companies similarly constitute their own ecosystem, and Theranos was no exception. This meant that while it was possible for wrongdoing to be exposed from inside, that was unlikely given Elizabeth Holmes's penchant for militant concealment and complete control. No surprise, then, that what was going on inside Theranos—a scam based on a lie—was ultimately exposed by someone outside Theranos, John Carreyrou, whose first article investigating the company appeared in the fall of 2015. It became a sensational story almost immediately.

In the wake of its publication, Holmes remained true to form, which meant she followed her instinct. She hid out, avoided the press, and said nothing. Instead, she holed up in a company conference room, surrounded only by a few lawyers, consultants, and members of her very, very small inner circle. She and Sunny Balwani were determined to keep the company going, no matter how obvious had become the discrepancy between Theranos fantasy and Theranos reality. There was talk of bringing a lawsuit against Carreyrou, on the false charge that his reporting was flawed. But after another few days of procrastination, it became clear that if Elizabeth Holmes was to have even a shot at saving herself and her company, she had no choice but to go on a public relations offensive.

Her first public appearance after the *Journal* story appeared was on CNBC's *Mad Money*. "This is what happens when you work to change things," Holmes told the host, Jim Cramer. "First, they think you're crazy, then they fight you, and then all of a sudden you change the world."[11] After that she returned to California—following a brief trip to Cambridge, Massachusetts, to pick up an award from Harvard—to finally speak to her hundreds of employees about what was threatening to become a serious scandal. *Vanity Fair* described what happened after a company-wide email instructed them all to gather in the cafeteria. "There, Holmes, with Balwani at her side, began an eloquent speech in her typical baritone, explaining to her loyal colleagues that they were changing the world. . . . The *Journal*, she said, had gotten the story wrong. Carreyrou, she insisted, with a tinge of fury, was simply picking a fight. She handed the stage to Balwani, who echoed her sentiments." After they finished their presentation, a chant erupted, Holmes's still faithful followers joining in unison to repeat over and over again, "Fuck you, Carreyrou! Fuck. You. Carreyrou!"[12]

As the truth gradually began to emerge, Carreyrou was able to get some seventy former Theranos employees to speak with him.[13] It was they who allowed him to finally piece together the complex story of how and why the company had gone so badly wrong. But the House of Theranos did not fall overnight. It took months and finally years for everything that could possibly collapse to collapse: the company, the board, the investors, the partnerships, the publicity machine, the media machine, the legal defenses, Holmes's near-singular status as a female tech icon, and her relationship with the preternaturally stalwart, even slavishly dedicated Sunny Balwani. Ultimately, not only was Holmes's professional dream destroyed, but she herself metamorphosed from citizen in good standing to convicted felon.

After *Bad Blood* came out, Carreyrou reflected on the experience of researching and writing it. He remembered meeting "so many smart, competent, capable people among [Theranos] former employees who had integrity." It was not they who were to blame for what happened, he clearly believed. Rather, the wrongdoing was "really committed chiefly by two people," Holmes and Balwani.[14] The rest were followers who, with a few notable and finally critical exceptions, continued obediently, and essentially silently, to follow until the end was evident.[15]

I of course take issue with the idea that followers are exempt from responsibility. I believe that followers who know better, and who can speak up without incurring significant cost, should do so.

The longer and more successfully Elizabeth Holmes peddled her wares, the more havoc she wreaked. We will never know what was in her head in, say, 2014. Did she honestly think that any day now things would turn around, that if only she hung in a bit longer the Edison would right itself? Or did she know by Phase IV that her venture was a failure even as she continued to insist the opposite?

One thing is clear: if Carreyrou's reporting had not brought Theranos to an ignominious end, the company would have gone from worse to still worse. It would have continued to do harm and then more harm until someone on the inside blew the whistle, or until someone else on the outside did what he did: peel the outside and expose the inside.

Xi Jinping

In 2017 I put up a blog post titled "The Gradualism of Totalitarianism." Here is a short excerpt: "One of the most interesting things about totalitarianism is how it comes to pass. It does not happen in an instant with, say, a sudden seizure of power. It is not in the least like a train wreck that, in a split second, destroys everything in its path. Rather totalitarian states are crafted gradually. They are heralded both in advance and along the way, so that the process proceeds with minimal disruption."[16]

Even Adolf Hitler and Joseph Stalin tightened the noose only over time, over a period of years. Nazi Germany and the Soviet Union were not totalitarian states from the get-go, and neither was China. In the years immediately after Xi Jinping became president many experts in the West expressed what we now recognize as wishful thinking—that Xi's looser economic controls would be followed by looser political controls. A decade later it had become all too clear that he was more in the vein of his dictatorial predecessor, Mao Zedong, than of his more liberal one, Deng Xiaoping. Xi, like Mao, was intent on being in complete control and on his followers being completely compliant.

President Xi had planned for years to be crowned at the Chinese Communist Party's 20th Party Congress in 2022. To this end—to secure for himself an unprecedented third five-year term in power—he arranged to have the regime's key power centers directly beholden to him. He orchestrated a "methodical campaign of highly personalized aggrandization of his position."[17] And shortly before the congress, he instigated yet another crackdown on graft—as well as on dissent and disloyalty—by having Chinese courts orchestrate another in the series of high-profile corruption trials, this time of senior officials from the state's policy and security apparatus. (Death sentences were imposed on three former top managers, and jail terms of more than ten years were issued to at least three other former police and security chiefs.)[18] What had finally become unmistakably and irretrievably clear was that Xi's increasing insistence on centralization, and on leadership from the top down, meant that what since Deng had been touted as greater transparency and more open competition for leadership posts was, for the indefinite future, dead.

It would be difficult to exaggerate the global response to the 20th Party Congress. In the West, at least, it was uniform: Xi was now seen as the "eternal emperor" who had remade every corner of China in his image. "The president presides alone in a way that no other 'paramount leader' has done since Mao," concluded an article in the *Financial Times*.[19] "In ten years of ruling China," noted a piece in the *New York Times*, "Xi Jinping has expunged political rivals, replacing them with allies. He has wiped out civil society, giving citizens no recourse for help but his government. He has muzzled dissent, saturating public conversation with propaganda about his greatness. Now . . . Mr. Xi is posed to push his vision of a swaggering, nationalist China even further, with himself at the center."[20] Finally, according to China expert Yuen Yuen Ang, the party congress effectively certified "Xi's unchallenged authority and plans for China that revolve around his obsession with control and security."[21] His obsession even extended into arts and culture: over the years, especially beginning in 2022, increasing pressure was put on artists to align their own ambitions with the goals of the CCP.

Again, this is not to imply that Xi's political position is impregnable. It is not. Even the most controlling of leaders is not immune to troubles, upheavals, and uprisings from within. Further, China is by no means impervious to what happens outside it. It is not, for example, protected against the exigencies of unanticipated pandemics, or the vagaries of capital markets, or the uncertainties of world politics. For example, during 2022 and into 2023 China's problems multiplied. A partial list:

COVID in China continued for a time to linger; the economy slowed and there was a real estate crisis; there were unprecedented runs on several Chinese banks and local governments were awash in debt; the Belt and Road Initiative suffered a series of blows including bad loans; Chinese tech giants reported their worst earnings ever (a result of Xi's extreme effort to control COVID); youth unemployment was reported to be sky-high; the clamor to punish China for its "crimes" against the Uyghurs continued; and it became clear that Putin's war in Ukraine was not going as either of the two declared allies, Putin and Xi, initially anticipated.

Moreover, all leaders tend over time to get sclerotic, tired, and rigid. Worse, leaders who are dictators tend over time to get monomaniacal, ossified, and paranoid. Their decision-making ability deteriorates, and their openness to new information and ideas diminishes. Which is not to suggest, of course, that when Xi warns the United States against providing further support to Taiwan, as he did during a recent party congress and repeatedly since then, American officials should ignore what he says. Nor should they ignore the director of national intelligence, Avril Haines, who, while maintaining that she did not consider war with China to be imminent, nevertheless testified before the Senate Intelligence Committee in March 2023 that China "posed the most consequential threat to U.S. national security."[22]

Mostly Xi focused on domestic affairs during his first several years in office, though he invested heavily in China's military. He tended to avoid situations that could escalate tensions either with China's neighbors or with its adversaries. But experts in the West are increasingly nervous about the future. Will his foreign policy now much more strongly resemble his domestic policy, which for years has been extremely assertive? Will he seek to control what happens outside China as he already controls what happens inside the country? More specifically, will China's grip on the oceans and the skies around Taiwan continue to tighten?

In 2022 America's anxiety about the direction in which Xi was heading went from intermittent to consistent and became palpable. Two experts on China published a book titled *Danger Zone: The Coming Conflict with China* and wrote an article for the *Wall Street Journal* headlined "The Coming War over Taiwan."[23] Another wrote an essay for *Foreign Affairs* titled "What to Expect from a Bolder Xi Jinping—Get Ready for a More Ambitious Chinese Foreign Policy."[24] And still another penned a piece for *Project Syndicate* headlined "Xi Jinping's Guns of August."[25] The point was made. Among those who studied Xi most closely, the fear was that his transition from authoritarian to totalitarian would sooner rather than later have serious implications for the international system.

Xi has a lust for power. He has a drive to acquire power that can be satisfied only temporarily.[26] So while we have seen that even Xi is not entirely immune to political pressure—to wit, his reversal on COVID—the West has reason to believe that his intent to exert complete control within China will extend beyond the country's borders. Unless and until, that is, someone or something intervenes—an event that seems highly improbable though not altogether impossible.

Which explains why U.S.–China relations is one of the few subjects on which congressional Democrats and Republicans are in approximate alignment—for better and worse. Elected officials in both parties support a more muscular American foreign policy, specifically as it pertains to China. The Republican chair of the House Foreign Affairs Committee titled his spring 2023 hearings on China "Combatting the Generational Challenge of CCP Aggression." And he spoke in no uncertain terms about what he perceived to be nothing short of "a struggle for the global balance of power."[27]

Danger!

Too late now—or almost too late—to do anything. More precisely, by the time bad leaders and followers are in Phase IV, they have already gone from bad to worse. From the four cases in point—Winterkorn, Erdogan, Holmes, and Xi—we can extrapolate this simple but all-important proposition: *Given that bad leaders and followers do not stop being bad on their own, of their own volition, to stop them getting worse there must be an intervention before worse is set in stone.*

We have seen that deconstructing bad leadership, even agreeing on what it is, is inordinately difficult if not impossible. First, humans are not widgets. Second, the word "bad" can be defined in different ways. Third, and most problematically, "bad" can be judged in different ways. Your "bad" could very well be my "good." Likely this is less of an issue as it pertains to efficacy than ethics. Specifically, we are more likely to agree on who is an effective leader than on who is an ethical one. Context also matters. It might well be easier to concur on who is a bad leader in business than in politics. The criterion for excellence in business is often no more than (though also no less than) profit. You are a "good" corporate leader if earnings soar at the company of which you are in charge. Business is also less fraught an enterprise, less vulnerable than government is to personal preferences and partisan passions.

For example, I am guessing that most of us would agree that Martin Winterkorn was a bad leader. First, he was callous. Second, and more importantly, he was corrupt. He was corrupt because he and some of his followers were fully aware that Volkswagen was, over a long period of time, deliberately installing a cheat device in its vehicles. Similarly, probably most of us would concur that Elizabeth Holmes was a bad leader, that she was rigid. Why did Holmes commit fraud? Because she could not or would not absorb, accept, the truth—that her devices for testing blood were failing abysmally at doing what they were purported to do.

Assessing a leader like Erdogan is a gnarlier enterprise. Among other reasons, his strong supporters will argue that he did no wrong, or at least not much, whereas his strong opponents will say that he did no right, or at least not much. Interestingly, likely most of us would agree that Erdogan continued to crave power, always more power than he already had. Where people will disagree is over whether this was a good thing or a bad thing. Over whether it was good or bad that Erdogan was intemperate, that he gradually gave up on being a democrat to become instead an autocrat. Presumably if you were a strong supporter of Erdogan's and I was not, we would disagree over precisely this issue.

Which brings us finally to Xi Jinping. His case raises the question of whether totalitarian leadership is by definition evil leadership, and whether he is therefore an evil leader. I will not even try to address this question here, at least not in depth. I will, however, reiterate that there is overwhelming evidence that, apart from being generally repressive, under Xi the Chinese government has treated its Turkic Muslim minority, the Uyghurs, cruelly and that this cruelty has been perpetrated for years.

A scathing 2022 report issued by the United Nations is, tragically, largely retrospective. It found that China had committed "serious human rights violations" against its Uyghur Muslim community, pointing to mass incarcerations and forced sterilizations, and concluding that the deprivation of Uyghur rights "may constitute crimes, in particular crimes against humanity."[28]

What is to be done given this report? It is clearly well-intentioned. But is it much too little much too late? It cannot change the past, obviously. But what about the present and the future? A "scathing" UN report is something. It is better than nothing. In fact, there is evidence that China's treatment of the Uyghurs is less harsh than it was a few years ago. But let's be clear. Of itself, a report will not suffice. Of itself—in this imperfect world—a report will not reverse China's policy toward the Uyghurs.

As I wrote at the start of this chapter, the progression from bad to worse ends here, at Phase IV. There is nowhere else to go. Bad became worse because bad was permitted to proceed unimpeded. Which leads us finally to this question: What more precisely are the costs of doing nothing? Of allowing bad to begin in Phase I and then continuing to allow it to metastasize, to grow and to spread from Phase II to Phase III and finally to Phase IV? Based only on the evidence presented in this book—though Putin and Trump were referenced only briefly—, these costs include:

- *Cost #1: Death and Destruction.* Had Russian president Vladimir Putin been stopped earlier—for example, in 2014, when Russia seized Crimea—the likelihood of his launching an unprovoked attack on Ukraine in 2022 would have been greatly diminished. And Ukraine, would have been spared widespread death and destruction.

- *Cost #2: Dishonesty and Dissension.* Had Donald Trump been stopped by his Republican enablers from continuing to lie compulsively—had he, for example, been convicted in one of his two impeachment trials—the decline of democracy would have been slowed or maybe even stopped.[29] Americans would certainly have been spared the years-long dramas and traumas of his multiple criminal indictments.
- *Cost #3: Retribution and Reputation.* Had Martin Winterkorn been stopped at the start or even early on from being complicit in a corporate culture that sanctioned cheating (on emissions, no less), he, the company he led, and numberless others would have been saved from humiliations, sanctions, and various other costs both literal and figurative.
- *Cost #4: Repression and Dysfunction.* Had Recep Tayyip Erdogan been stopped earlier from accruing power and then still more power—to the point where he was able to punish, sometimes severely, those he considered his political enemies—Turkey likely would have avoided the transition from a reasonably well-functioning democracy to a measurably less well-functioning autocracy.
- *Cost #5: Disappointment and Punishment.* Had Elizabeth Holmes been stopped earlier from deluding herself, from lashing herself to a technology that was failing to deliver anywhere near what she had promised, she (and Sunny Balwani) would not have been sentenced to more than a decade in prison—and her followers at every level would have been spared significant financial, professional, and personal harm (and in some cases ruin).
- *Cost #6: Loss of Freedom, Compulsory Conformity.* Had Xi Jinping been stopped earlier—stopped from accumulating so much power, from aggrandizing his standing at the expense of everyone else, from obsessively monitoring and controlling everything and everyone, and from effectively naming himself leader for life—the Chinese people, on the mainland and in Hong Kong, would have been able to breathe more freely, express themselves more openly, and avoid the fear and loathing that are inevitable byproducts of totalitarian leadership.

Do we have it in us to learn from history? Or from experience, or from bearing witness? Do we have the will and skill to detect bad leadership early on? To detect it—*and* to act on it to stop it or at least to slow it?

Epilogue

The Future

To repeat what I wrote at the start of this book: *Bad leadership and its conjoined twin, bad followership, are as ubiquitous as they are pernicious. They are everywhere: in business and government, in religion and education and in the military, in democracies as well as autocracies.*

But despite the pervasiveness and balefulness of bad leadership, our will to stop or at least slow bad leaders, and our skill at doing so, remains meager. There are some theories that explore the dark side of the human condition. And there are some practices that bring bad leaders down. But the work pales in comparison with the magnitude of the problem. Leaders who act largely or even entirely in their self-interest, as opposed to in our interest, the public interest, are part of everyday life.

Bad leadership is a social disease—or, if you prefer, a sociological one. But unlike diseases that are physical or psychological, bad leadership remains at the margins of our collective concerns. We fret about it; sometimes we even fixate on it. However, we think long and hard about bad leaders only when they directly affect us, such as a callous manager, inept administrator, corrupt mayor, greedy chief executive officer, or feckless president. But precisely because we fail to see bad leadership as an affliction affecting the human condition, we continue to suffer it not so much in silence as in ignorance.

Cancer has been studied for decades, which is why more people now survive it than ever before. Similarly, great progress has been made in tackling schizophrenia. New antipsychotic drugs come on the market all the time, and brain research has markedly advanced our understanding of the roots of mental illness.[1] There have been, in short, massive investments over a period of many years that have advanced our ability to address diseases such as these. But no such luck with what should be considered a different sort of plague, bad leadership.

I have no illusions. This book is a drop in a near-bottomless pit. But a drop is not nothing. It is something. The book then serves two purposes. First, to further our theoretical understanding of how bad leadership and followership, and then worse leadership and followership, happen. Second, to have a practical impact on mitigating them, especially early on. We now know that the longer and deeper bad digs in, the harder it is to uproot. Therefore, when we break bad leadership and followership into phases—each worse than the one before—their progression will be easier to predict and detect, and therefore easier to stop or at least slow before they turn toxic.

Ideally, we would have a checklist. A list of how to know when a leader begins to go bad and what specifically to watch for. Checklists and lists have long proved useful. There was one in my book *Hard Times: Leadership in America*, where I chronicled what you need to know about America if you want to lead in America. Historian Timothy Snyder had a list in his small, influential treatise *On Tyranny: Twenty Lessons from the Twentieth Century*.[2] And diplomat Richard Haass compiled one for his book *The Bill of Obligations: The Ten Habits of Good Citizens*.[3] In *The Checklist Manifesto: How to Get Things Right*, author Atul Gawande points out that precisely because they are so simple, checklists are reliably helpful.[4] They provide an easy, efficient way of managing enormous amounts of information and of decoding complex contexts.

But is a list of what to know and how to respond reasonable or even feasible in the case of bad leadership? For we are dealing here not with a single individual but with a system—the leadership system, which has three separate and equally important parts: leaders, followers, and contexts. This means the variables are almost infinite. For that reason, what would be considered bad leadership in one context or culture or circumstance is not necessarily bad leadership in another. As a general principle, then, hard and fast rules do not here apply, nor is there a handy-dandy guide to indicate when things begin to go wrong or what steps to take when they do.

Still, disclaimers notwithstanding, I cannot *not* try to fix some of what's broken. We promote good leadership not by ignoring bad leadership, nor by presuming it immutable. To the contrary, our only hope is to take it on, to decode and decipher it, and then to attack it as we would any disease that damages, debilitates, and sometimes even destroys.

This book about leadership from bad to worse concludes, then, with a list. A list of twelve steps to take to forestall or, if necessary, interrupt an otherwise inexorable process. *How?* By educating and training us to detect and attack bad leadership early on. *Why?* Because leaders who go bad nearly never self-correct. Because this leaves followers—or, on occasion, other leaders—to do the heavy lifting, the course-correcting. Because if they do not, they all become bystanders. Because if they do not, they all become complicit. Because if they do not, they all become enablers. Because if they do not, they all become bad.

I have written before about intervening when things go wrong. Even earlier in this book I highlighted one of my axioms: "To oppose a leader who is bad—ineffective and/or unethical—is to be a good follower." Nor am I the only one to prompt people to prevent and, if necessary, to confront bad. I already mentioned the work of Stanley Milgram and Philip Zimbardo. More recently, in his book *Complicit: How We Enable the Unethical and How to Stop*, psychologist Max Bazerman suggests how to be "less complicit" when things go wrong, such as acknowledging your blind spots.[5] Additionally, a few people, like Snyder and Haass, make plain what people can and should do to defend against bad leaders, to be not just reactive but proactive.

My twelve steps bear some resemblance to other action steps that preceded them, but not much. For mine are intended to be not general but specific. *The purpose of this list is particularly to provide ideas, information, and instructions on how to know when bad leadership threatens, and on what to do when it happens.*

> *Step 1:* Pay attention to the distinction between good and bad. Between a good leader and a bad one—and between a good follower and a bad one.
>
> *Step 2:* Pay attention to the distinction between bad as in unethical and bad as in ineffective.
>
> *Step 3:* Pay attention to the leader. The leader's nature and character, beliefs and behaviors, preferences and proclivities, style and substance, friends and enemies.
>
> *Step 4:* Pay attention to everyone else. If you're thinking of challenging a bad leader, remember that some people might be your allies, others might be your opponents or even your enemies, and still others are nearly certain to remain neutral.
>
> *Step 5:* Pay attention to the context. Be contextually conscious. Contextually informed. Contextually intelligent.
>
> *Step 6:* Know that to oppose a bad leader is generally to do the right thing.

Step 7: Know that not to oppose a bad leader is generally to do the wrong thing.

Step 8. Don't be impetuous. Assess your risks, Weigh the costs and benefits of doing something to take on a bad leader versus the costs and benefits of doing nothing. Similarly, weigh the costs and benefits of doing one thing to challenge a bad leader versus the costs and benefits of doing another.

Step 9: Don't be reckless. Some bad leaders are dangerous and must be handled with care—or maybe not at all. Other bad leaders are more amenable to being questioned or challenged, even to being changed.

Step 10: Don't act alone—at least not if you can help it. Acting alone against a bad leader is harder and certainly riskier than acting in tandem with others.

Step 11: Don't be automatically allegiant or blindly obedient.

Step 12: Pay attention to the progression—the invariable, inexorable progression. Bad leaders who are not slowed or stopped during Phase I will proceed to Phase II. Bad leaders who are not slowed or stopped during Phase II will proceed to Phase III. Bad leaders who are not slowed or stopped during Phase III will proceed to Phase IV.

I began this book with a chapter titled "Democracy in Decline and Capitalism in Question." I cannot stress enough the relationship between the two. As *Financial Times* columnist Martin Wolf put it in a recent book, politics and economics "are necessarily symbiotic."[6] This means that leaders in government and business must cooperate, collaborate, and compromise to secure for their followers reasonable political equality and sufficient economic security. Leaders' failure in recent years to do so—their tolerance for high inequality and low security in countries and companies that profess otherwise—has eroded our trust in them and in the political and economic systems of which they are largely in charge.

Why does this matter? Because bad leadership and followership tend to flourish when the contexts within which they are situated are perceived as unfair and unequal, as strongly favoring the richer and more powerful at the expense of the poorer and weaker. Moreover, to see democracy and capitalism as inextricably entwined is to see leaders in politics and business as *equally* responsible for what's gone wrong, and *equally* responsible for making it right.

To repeat the old saw, we get the leaders we deserve. If we continue too long to tolerate stupidities and inefficiencies, lying and cheating, voraciousness and intemperance, indignities, inequities, and cruelties, usually—though, admittedly, not always—it's on us.

In the end, then, this is a book about time. About what happens, and does not happen, when leaders begin to go bad and then get worse. About how time is finite. About how time is of the essence.

Notes

Prologue

1. In Barbara Kellerman and Larraine Matusak, *Cutting Edge: Leadership 2000* (College Park, MD: Center for the Advanced Study of Leadership, University of Maryland, 2000).
2. Barbara Kellerman, *Bad Leadership: What It Is, How It Happens, Why It Matters* (Boston: Harvard Business School Press, 2004).
3. Barbara Kellerman, *The Enablers: How Team Trump Flunked the Pandemic and Failed America* (New York: Cambridge University Press, 2021).
4. Andrei Soldatov and Irina Borogan, "Putin's New Police State," *Foreign Affairs*, July 27, 2022, https://www.foreignaffairs.com/russian-federation/putins-new-police-state.
5. Quoted in Roger Cohen, "The Making of Vladimir Putin," *New York Times*, March 26, 2022, https://www.nytimes.com/2022/03/26/world/europe/vladimir-putin-rus sia.html.
6. Kellerman, *Bad Leadership*.
7. John Haltiwanger, "Historians Rank Trump Among Worst Presidents in US History, New C-SPAN Survey Shows," Insider, June 30, 2021, https://www.businessinsider.com/historians-rank-trump-among-worst-presidents-us-history-c-span-2021-6.
8. Lydia Saad, "Do Americans Like or Dislike 'Big Business'?," Gallup, June 27, 2022, https://news.gallup.com/poll/270296/americans-dislike-big-business.aspx.
9. "Americans' Views of Government: Decades of Distrust, Enduring Support for Its Role," Pew Research Center, June 6, 2022, https://www.pewresearch.org/politics/2022/06/06/americans-views-of-government-decades-of-distrust-enduring-support-for-its-role/.
10. Natalie Sachmechi, "New Study Shows American's Dwindling Faith in Leaders," *Forbes*, September 19, 2019, https://www.forbes.com/sites/nataliesachmechi/2019/09/19/new-study-shows-americans-dwindling-faith-in-leaders/?sh=4eba71bb7a4d.
11. For a thorough analysis of Congress's "botched impeachments of Donald Trump," see Rachel Bade and Karoun Demirjian, *Unchecked* (New York: HarperCollins, 2022). The quote is on xvi.
12. Kellerman, *The Enablers*, 1.
13. Julia Manchester, "Majority of Young Adults in US Hold Negative View of Capitalism: Poll," *The Hill*, June 28, 2021, https://thehill.com/homenews/campaign/560493-majority-of-young-adults-in-us-hold-negative-view-of-capitalism-poll/.

Chapter 1

1. Andrew Van Dam and Heather Long, "The Post-Covid Luxury Spending Boom Has Begun. It's Already Reshaping the Economy," *Washington Post*, June 18, 2021, https://www.washingtonpost.com/business/2021/06/18/luxury-boom-recovery/.

2. Sam Jones, "Patrick Odier: 'Switzerland Cannot Hide Behind Neutrality,'" *Financial Times*, February 17, 2023, https://www.ft.com/content/6e03ab7f-6430-4256-b137-ed34a3989bca.

3. "New Report Highlights U.S. 2020 Gun-Related Deaths: Highest Number Ever Recorded by CDC, Gun Homicides Increase by More Than One-Third," Bloomberg School of Public Health, Johns Hopkins University, April 28, 2022,

    https://publichealth.jhu.edu/2022/new-report-highlights-us-2020-gun-related-deaths-highest-number-ever-recorded-by-cdc-gun-homicides-increase-by-more-than-one-third.

4. Douglas Heaven, "The Uncertain Future of Democracy," BBC, March 30, 2017, https://www.bbc.com/future/article/20170330-the-uncertain-future-of-democracy.

5. Sarah Repucci and Amy Slipowitz, "Democracy Under Siege," Freedom House, 2021, https://freedomhouse.org/report/freedom-world/2021/democracy-under-siege. All the Freedom House quotes in this section are from this report.

6. Jacob Lew, Gary Roughead, Jennifer Hillman, and David Sacks, *China's Belt and Road: Implications for the United States* (New York: Council on Foreign Relations, 2021), 2.

7. Timothy Snyder, *On Tyranny: Ten Lessons from the Twentieth Century* (New York: Tim Duggan Books, 2017).

8. Timothy Snyder, "The American Abyss," *New York Times Magazine*, June 9, 2021, https://www.nytimes.com/2021/01/09/magazine/trump-coup.html.

9. Ann Applebaum, *Twilight of Democracy: The Seductive Lure of Authoritarianism* (New York: Doubleday, 2020), 185, 186.

10. "2024 Republican Primary Polling," RacetotheWH, https://www.racetothewh.com/2024/rep. As of September 2023 Trump led the second-place contender for the Republican nomination for president, Ron DeSantis, by almost 40 points. https://thehill.com/homenews/campaign/4190222-trump-holds-wide-lead-among-california-republicans-desantis-support-slips-in-new-poll/.

11. Steven Levitsky and Daniel Ziblatt, *How Democracies Die* (New York: Crown, 2018).

12. Steven Levitsky and Daniel Ziblatt, *Tyranny of the Minority* (Penguin, 2023).

13. Shoshana Zuboff, "The Coup We Are Not Talking About," *New York Times*, January 29, 2021, https://www.nytimes.com/2021/01/29/opinion/sunday/facebook-surveillance-society-technology.html.

14. Tom Nichols, *Our Own Worst Enemy: The Assault from Within on Modern Democracy* (New York: Oxford University Press, 2021), 91.

15. Barbara Kellerman, *The End of Leadership* (New York: HarperCollins, 2012).

16. Anat R. Admati, "Capitalism, Laws, and the Need for Trustworthy Institutions," European Corporate Governance Institute, Law Working Paper No. 598/2021, July 19, 2021, https://papers.ssrn.com/sol3/papers.cfm?abstract_id=3886969.

17. Jennifer Szalai, "Is the Marriage Between Democracy and Capitalism on the Rocks?," *New York Times*, February 15, 2023, https://www.nytimes.com/2023/02/15/books/review/books-democracy-capitalism.html.

18. Blake Hounshell and Max Fisher, "Why the U.S. Is Being Ominously Compared to Hungary and Turkey," *New York Times*, September 12, 2022, https://www.nytimes.com/2022/09/12/us/politics/democracy-united-states.html.

19. Willy Staley, "How Many Billionaires Are There, Anyway?," *New York Times Magazine*, April 7, 2022, https://www.nytimes.com/2022/04/07/magazine/billionaires.html.

20. Rachel Tillman, "Report: Hate Crimes Rose 44% Last Year in Study of Major Cities," Spectrum News/NY1, February 15, 2022, https://www.ny1.com/nyc/all-boroughs/news/2022/02/14/hate-crime-increase-2021-asian-american-.

21. Haley Cohen, "Hate in New York: Antisemitic Attacks Increased 41% in 2022," *Jerusalem Post*, January 11, 2023, https://www.jpost.com/diaspora/article-728192.

22. Rana Foroohar, "Talk of Doing Good Rings Hollow at Davos," *Financial Times*, May 30, 2022, https://www.ft.com/content/6a53a74e-f0a6-45c4-84cf-bb4da6e603cd.

23. Howard Schneider and Chris Kahn, "Majority of Americans Favor Wealth Tax on Very Rich: Reuters/Ipsos Poll," Reuters, January 10, 2020, https://www.reuters.com/article/us-usa-election-inequality-poll/majority-of-americans-favor-wealth-tax-on-very-rich-reuters-ipsos-poll-idUSKBN1Z9141.

24. Binyamin Appelbaum, "The Tax Pirates Are Us," *New York Times*, June 13, 2021, https://www.nytimes.com/2021/06/13/opinion/us-corporate-tax-rate-biden.html.

25. Martin Hellwig, "'Capitalism: What Has Gone Wrong?': Who Went Wrong? Capitalism? The Market Economy? Governments? 'Neoliberal' Economics?," *Oxford Review of Economic Policy* 37, no. 4 (2021): 664–677, https://academic.oup.com/oxrep/article/37/4/664/6423494.

26. Jesse Eisinger, Jeff Ernsthausen, and Paul Kiel, "The Secret IRS Files: Trove of Never-Before-Seen Records Reveal How the Wealthiest Avoid Income Tax," ProPublica, June 8, 2021, https://www.propublica.org/article/the-secret-irs-files-trove-of-never-before-seen-records-reveal-how-the-wealthiest-avoid-income-tax.

27. "Diamonstein-Spielvogel Project on the Future of Democracy," Council on Foreign Relations, https://www.cfr.org/diamonstein-spielvogel-project-future-democracy. This project was launched in 2021.

28. "The State of America's Children 2021: Income and Wealth Inequality," Children's Defense Fund, 2021, https://www.childrensdefense.org/state-of-americas-children/soac-2021-income-inequality/. For information on the reduction in childhood poverty, see Jason DeParle, "Expanded Safety Net Drives Sharp Drop in Child Poverty," *New York Times*, September 11, 2022, https://www.nytimes.com/2022/09/11/us/politics/child-poverty-analysis-safety-net.html.

29. "Global Inequality Data—2020 Update," World Inequality Database, November 10, 2020, https://wid.world/news-article/2020-regional-updates/.

30. Rana Foroohar, "The Rise of Kitchen Table Economics," *Financial Times*, February 19, 2023, https://www.ft.com/content/e53e4b14-4653-4b6e-a72f-d50f75e97cb7.

31. Peter Eavis, "Meager Rewards for Workers, Exceptionally Rich Pay for C.E.O.s," *New York Times*, June 11, 2021, https://www.nytimes.com/2021/06/11/business/ceo-pay-compensation-stock.html.

32. Economic Policy Institute, "CEO-to-Worker Pay Ratio Hits All-Time High," The Stand, October 5, 2022, https://www.thestand.org/2022/10/ceo-to-worker-pay-ratio-hits-all-time-high/.

33. Jeff Cox, "CEOs See Pay Grow 1,000% in the Last 40 Years, Now Make 278 Times the Average Worker," CNBC, August 16, 2019, https://www.cnbc.com/2019/08/16/ceos-see-pay-grow-1000percent-and-now-make-278-times-the-average-worker.html.

34. The statistic in this sentence is from Jeff Yang, "The Problem with the Genius Billionaire Philanthropist Superhero," New York Times, June 20, 2021, https://www.nytimes.com/2021/06/20/opinion/rich-musk-gates-bezos-comics.html.

35. E. Tammy Kim, "Amazon Transformed Seattle. Now, Its Workers Are Poised to Take It Back," New York Times, July 5, 2021, https://www.nytimes.com/2021/07/05/opinion/bezos-amazon-bessmer-labor.html.

36. Greg Bensinger, "A Final Word Before Mr. Bezos Blasts Off," New York Times, June 27, 2021, https://www.nytimes.com/2021/06/27/opinion/jeff-bezos-amazon-ceo.html.

37. David Gelles, "Hubert Joly Turned Around Best Buy. Now He's Trying to Fix Capitalism," New York Times, July 15, 2021, https://www.nytimes.com/2021/07/15/business/hubert-joly-corner-office-best-buy.html.

38. Jodi Kantor, Karen Weise, and Grace Ashford, "Power and Peril: 5 Takeaways on Amazon's Employment Machine," New York Times, June 15, 2021, https://www.nytimes.com/2021/06/15/us/politics/amazon-warehouse-workers.html.

39. Jen McAndrew and Robin Smyton, "Half of Young People Voted in 2020, Major Increase from 2016," Tufts Now, April 29, 2021, https://now.tufts.edu/2021/04/29/half-young-people-voted-2020-major-increase-2016; Rana Foroohar, "Saving Capitalism," Time, May 12, 2016, https://time.com/4327419/american-capitalisms-great-crisis/.

40. John Bitzan and Clay Routledge, "College Kids Don't Understand Socialism—or Capitalism. Our Research Proves It," Newsweek, July 12, 2021, https://www.newsweek.com/college-kids-dont-understand-socialism-capitalism-our-research-proves-it-opinion-1608876.

41. Jaime Lowe, "With 'Stealth Politics,' Billionaires Make Sure Their Money Talks," New York Times, April 6, 2022, https://www.nytimes.com/2022/04/06/magazine/billionaire-politics.html.

42. For more on leaders, see Barbara Kellerman and Todd Pittinsky, Leaders Who Lust: Power, Money, Sex, Success, Legitimacy, Legacy (New York: Cambridge University Press, 2020).

43. For an article on the depressing consequences and complexities of this, see Dorothy S. Lund and Leo E. Strine Jr., "Corporate Political Spending Is Bad Business," Harvard Business Review, January–February 2022, https://hbr.org/2022/01/corporate-political-spending-is-bad-business.

44. Foroohar, "Saving Capitalism."

45. Jonathan Levy, Ages of American Capitalism: A History of the United States (New York: Random House, 2021), 739.

46. Chris Melore, "Just 56% of Americans Can Name All Three Branches of Government—That's Actually a 15-Year High," WANE (Fort Wayne, IN), September

21, 2021, https://www.wane.com/news/national-world/just-56-of-americans-can-name-all-three-branches-of-government-thats-actually-a-15-year-high/.

47. Laura Silver, Christine Huang, Laura Clancy, Aidan Connaughton, and Sneha Gubbala, "What Do Americans Know About International Affairs?," Pew Research Center, May 25, 2022, https://www.pewresearch.org/global/wp-content/uploads/sites/2/2022/05/PG_2022.05.25_international-knowledge_REPORT.pdf.

48. "Americans' Views of Government: Low Trust, but Some Positive Performance Ratings," Pew Research Center, September 14, 2020,
    https://www.pewresearch.org/politics/2020/09/14/americans-views-of-government-low-trust-but-some-positive-performance-ratings/.

49. Drew DeSilver, "Turnout in U.S. Has Soared in Recent Elections but by Some Measures Still Trails That of Many Other Countries," Pew Research Center, November 1, 2022,
    https://www.pewresearch.org/fact-tank/2022/11/01/turnout-in-u-s-has-soared-in-recent-elections-but-by-some-measures-still-trails-that-of-many-other-countries/.

50. The Europeans have done far more than the Americans to rein in and monitor big tech. See, for example, Agence France-Presse, "Europe's Battle to Rein In Big Tech," *Barron's*, September 13, 2022, https://www.barrons.com/news/europe-s-battle-with-big-tech-billions-in-fines-and-tough-laws-01663126807.

Chapter 2

1. Chip Cutter and Kathryn Dill, "Remote Work Is the New Signing Bonus," *Wall Street Journal*, June 26, 2021, https://www.wsj.com/articles/remote-work-is-the-new-signing-bonus-11624680029.

2. I have written about these changes before. See, for example, Barbara Kellerman, *The End of Leadership* (New York: HarperCollins, 2012).

3. Tara Adhikari, "BLM and Floyd Protests Were Largely Peaceful, Data Confirms," *Christian Science Monitor*, July 8, 2021, https://www.csmonitor.com/USA/Politics/2021/0708/BLM-and-Floyd-protests-were-largely-peaceful-data-confirms.

4. Tess Thackara, "'It's About Time.' Museums Make Bids for Their Communities," *New York Times*, May 21, 2021, https://www.nytimes.com/2021/05/21/arts/museums-communities.html.

5. Baurzhan Rakhmetov, "The Putin Regime Will Never Tire of Imposing Internet Control: Developments in Digital Legislation in Russia," Council on Foreign Relations blog post, February 22, 2021, https://www.cfr.org/blog/putin-regime-will-never-tire-imposing-internet-control-developments-digital-legislation-russia.

6. William A. Galston, "Biden Tries to Save the Infrastructure Bill," *Wall Street Journal*, June 29, 2021, https://www.wsj.com/articles/biden-tries-to-save-the-infrastructure-bill-11624981835.

7. John Delaney, "Congressman: 97% of Americans Want One Kind of Gun Control. Here's Why Congress Hasn't Acted," *Time*, April 13, 2018, https://time.com/5233748/gun-control-background-checks-gerrymandering-policy/.

8. "Public Trust in Government: 1958–2022," Pew Research Center, June 6, 2022, https:// www.pewresearch.org/politics/2022/06/06/public-trust-in-government-1958-2022/.

9. "Public Trust in Government: 1958–2022."

10. Rebecca Winthrop, "The Need for Civic Education in 21st-Century Schools," Brookings Institution, June 4, 2020, https://www.brookings.edu/policy2020/bigid eas/the-need-for-civic-education-in-21st-century-schools/.

11. The quotes in this paragraph are from Pippa Norris, "Voters Against Democracy: The Roots of Autocratic Resurgence," *Foreign Affairs*, April 20, 2021, https://www.foreign affairs.com/reviews/voters-against-democracy.

12. Anton Troianovski, " 'My Conscience Is Clean. And Yet They Came for Me,' " *New York Times*, June 4, 2021, https://www.nytimes.com/2021/06/04/world/europe/ pavlov-navalny-russia-putin.html.

13. Yascha Mounk, "Democracy on the Defense," *Foreign Affairs*, February 16, 2021, https://www.foreignaffairs.com/articles/united-states/2021-02-16/democracy-defense.

14. Quoted in Barbara Kellerman, *Leadership: Essential Selections* (New York: McGraw-Hill, 2010), 83.

15. Andrew Atkinson, "Brexit Is Costing the UK £100 Billion a Year in Lost Output," Bloomberg, January 30, 2023, https://www.bloomberg.com/news/articles/2023-01-31/brexit-is-costing-the-uk-100-billion-a-year-in-lost-output#xj4y7vzkg.

16. Ellen Barry, "Drained by a Year of Covid, Many Mayors Head for the Exit," *New York Times*, April 11, 2021, https://www.nytimes.com/2021/04/11/us/covid-burnout-may ors.html.

17. Geoffrey Skelley, "There Was a Lot of Turnover in the House in the 2018 Cycle," FiveThirtyEight, November 13, 2018, https://fivethirtyeight.com/features/retireme nts-resignations-and-electoral-losses-the-104-house-members-who-wont-be-back-next-year/.

18. Mitchell Hartman, "U.S. Firms Dealing with High CEO Turnover," Marketplace, February 13, 2020, https://www.marketplace.org/2020/02/13/ceo-turnover-report-challenger-gray-christmas/.

19. "October 2021 CEO Turnover Report: The Great Resignation Hits the Top Spot," Challenger, Gray, and Christmas, Inc., November 22, 2021, https://www.challengerg ray.com/blog/october-2021-ceo-turnover-report-the-great-resignation-hits-the-top-spot/.

20. "September 2022 CEO Turnover: CEO Exits Rise 17%; Ages & Tenures of Exiting CEOs Fall," Challenger, Gray, and Christmas, Inc., October 26, 2022, https://www. challengergray.com/blog/september-2022-ceo-turnover-ceo-exits-rise-17-ages-tenu res-of-exiting-ceos-fall/.

21. "Leadership Turnover Creates Surge in Searches for College Presidents," Hunt Scanlon Media, January 18, 2019, https://huntscanlon.com/leadership-turnover-crea tes-surge-in-searches-for-college-presidents/.

22. Justin Zackal, "Riding the Wave of College President Turnover," Higher Ed Jobs, April 5, 2022, https://www.higheredjobs.com/Articles/articleDisplay.cfm?ID=

3013&Title=Riding%20the%20Wave%20of%20College%20Presidential%20T
urnover.

23. Stephanie Saul, "At N.Y.U., Students Were Failing Organic Chemistry. Who Was to Blame?," New York Times, October 3, 2022, https://www.nytimes.com/2022/10/03/us/nyu-organic-chemistry-petition.html.

24. The discussion on authority is to an extent drawn from Kellerman, *The End of Leadership*.

25. Kevin Crowley and Scott Deveau, "Tiny Activist Investor Forces Exxon CEO to Chart a Greener, More Diversified Course," World Oil, May 27, 2021, https://www.worldoil.com/news/2021/5/27/tiny-activist-investor-forces-exxon-ceo-to-chart-a-greener-more-diversified-course.

26. "Bernie Sanders vs. Howard Schultz: Longtime Starbucks CEO Grilled on Company's Union-Busting Tactics," *Democracy Now*, March 30, 2022, https://www.democracynow.org/2023/3/30/starbucks_union_busting.

27. Audrey Carlsen, Maya Salam, Claire Cain Miller, Denise Lu, Ash Ngu, Jugal K. Patek, and Zach Wichter, "#MeToo Brought Down 201 Powerful Men. Nearly Half of Their Replacements Are Women," *New York Times*, October 23, 2018, https://www.nytimes.com/interactive/2018/10/23/us/metoo-replacements.html.

28. Elaine Godfrey, Lena Felton, and Taylor Hosking, "The 25 Candidates for 2018 Sunk by #MeToo Allegations," *The Atlantic*, July 26, 2018, https://www.theatlantic.com/politics/archive/2018/07/the-25-candidates-for-2018-sunk-by-metoo-allegations/565457/.

29. David Yaffe-Bellany, "McDonald's CEO Fired over a Relationship That's Becoming Taboo," *New York Times*, November 4, 2019, https://www.nytimes.com/2019/11/04/business/mcdonalds-ceo-fired.html.

30. Chip Cutter, "Rich Lesser, CEO Whisperer, on His Toughest Moments," *Wall Street Journal*, June 25, 2021, https://www.wsj.com/articles/rich-lesser-ceo-whisperer-on-his-toughest-moments-11624618800.

Chapter 3

1. Barbara Kellerman, *Bad Leadership: What It Is, How It Happens, Why It Matters* (Boston: Harvard Business School Press, 2004), 29ff.

2. Peter Robison, *Flying Blind: The 737 Max Tragedy and the Fall of Boeing* (New York: Doubleday, 2021), 178.

3. Andrew J. Hawkins, "Everything You Need to Know About the Boeing 737 Max Airplane Crashes," The Verge, March 22, 2019, https://www.theverge.com/2019/3/22/18275736/boeing-737-max-plane-crashes-grounded-problems-info-details-explained-reasons.

4. Robison, *Flying Blind*, 199.

5. Bill George, "Have We Lost Sight of Integrity?," Harvard Business School, January 27, 2023, https://hbswk.hbs.edu/item/have-we-lost-sight-of-integrity.

6. Robison, *Flying Blind*, 6.

7. Deborah Rhode, *Moral Leadership: The Theory and Practice of Power, Judgement, and Policy* (San Francisco: Jossey-Bass, 2006), 4, 20.

8. Barbara Kellerman, *Followership: How Followers Are Creating Change and Changing Leaders* (Boston: Harvard Business School Press, 2008), 230.

9. Dominic Gates and Mike Baker, "Engineers Say Boeing Pushed to Limit Safety Testing in Race to Certify Planes, Including 737 Max," *Seattle Times*, May 5, 2019, https://www.seattletimes.com/business/boeing-aerospace/engineers-say-boeing-pushed-to-limit-safety-testing-in-race-to-certify-planes-including-737-max/.

10. Robison, *Flying Blind*, 169. Relatives of people who died in the 2018 and 2019 crashes went on to challenge Boeing on several fronts. It was only years later, in 2023, that a federal judge issued a ruling requiring Boeing to be arraigned on a previously settled criminal charge that related to the two crashes. He also gave permission to the victim's relatives to speak in court about an agreement that had allowed Boeing to avoid being indicted or to plead guilty. Andrew Tangel and Dave Michaels, "Boeing 737 Max Families May Weigh In on DOJ's Criminal Settlement, Judge Rules," *Wall Street Journal*, January 19, 2023, https://www.wsj.com/articles/boeing-737-max-families-may-weigh-in-on-dojs-criminal-settlement-judge-rules-11674170929.

11. Glenn Kessler, "Trump Made 30,573 False or Misleading Claims as President. Nearly Half Came in His Final Year," *Washington Post*, January 23, 2021, https://www.washingtonpost.com/politics/how-fact-checker-tracked-trump-claims/2021/01/23/ad04b69a-5c1d-11eb-a976-bad6431e03e2_story.html.

Chapter 4

1. Stephanie Langmaid, "Stages of Cancer," WebMD, March 8, 2021, https://www.webmd.com/cancer/cancer-stages.

2. Mark Barton, "What Is the Difference Between 'Stage,' 'Phase' and 'Level'?," Quora, https://www.quora.com/What-is-the-difference-between-stage-phase-and-level. Accessed September 10, 2023.

3. Barbara Kellerman, "Leadership—It's a System, Not a Person!," *Daedalus* 145, no. 3 (2016): 83–94, https://direct.mit.edu/daed/article/145/3/83/27116/Leadership-It-s-a-System-Not-a-Person.

4. Ian Kershaw, *Hitler, 1889–1936: Hubris* (New York: Norton, 1998), 316.

5. "Hitler Speech on Enabling Act 1933," March 13, 1933, World Future Fund, http://www.worldfuturefund.org/Reports2013/hitlerenablingact.htm.

6. Robert Gellately, *Backing Hitler: Consent and Coercion in Nazi Germany* (Oxford: Oxford University Press, 2001), 13.

7. This paragraph is based on material in Frederic Spotts, *Hitler and the Power of Aesthetics* (Woodstock, NY: Overlook Press, 2003), 44, 45.

8. For more on the different types of followers, see Barbara Kellerman, *Followership: How Followers Are Creating Change and Changing Leaders* (Boston: Harvard Business School Press, 2008).

9. Kershaw, *Hitler*, 468.
10. Excerpts from both these speeches are in Barbara Kellerman, *Leadership: Essential Selections on Power, Authority, and Influence* (New York: McGraw-Hill, 2010), 244ff.

Chapter 5

1. Jack Ewing, *Faster, Higher, Farther: The Volkswagen Scandal* (New York: Norton, 2017), 14. Ewing reported on the Volkswagen scandal for the *New York Times*, and his book is an excellent source on the subject.
2. Jill Lepore, "Moving Right Along," *New Yorker*, July 25, 2022, 26, https://www.newyor ker.com/magazine/2022/07/25/the-vw-bus-took-the-sixties-on-the-road-now-its-getting-a-twenty-first-century-makeover.
3. Ewing, *Faster, Higher, Farther*, 50.
4. "Ferdinand Piëch," Wikipedia, September 10, 2023, https://en.wikipedia.org/wiki/Anton_Pi%C3%Abch.
5. "Ferdinand Piëch."
6. N. Craig Smith and Erin McCormick, "Volkswagen's Emissions Scandal: How Could It Happen?," INSEAD case study, May 2018.
7. Ewing, *Faster, Higher, Farther*. See ch. 9 for more on the relatively brief tenure of Bernd Pischetsreider.
8. Barbara Kellerman and Todd Pittinsky, *Leaders Who Lust: Power, Money, Sex, Success, Legitimacy, Legacy* (New York: Cambridge University Press, 2020).
9. Bertel Schmitt, "Volkswagen's Strategy 2018. With Generous Support from GM and Toyota," The Truth About Cars, February 3, 2010, https://www.thetruthaboutcars.com/2010/02/volkswagen%e2%80%99s-strategy-2018-with-generous-support-from-gm-and-toyota/.
10. Schmitt, "Volkswagen's Strategy 2018."
11. Danny Hakim, Aaron M. Kessler, and Jack Ewing, "As Volkswagen Pushed to Be No. 1, Ambitions Fueled a Scandal," *New York Times*, September 26, 2015, https://www.nytimes.com/2015/09/27/business/as-vw-pushed-to-be-no-1-ambitions-fueled-a-scandal.html.
12. Ewing, *Faster, Higher, Farther*, 118.
13. Andreas Cremer and Tom Bergin, "Fear and Respect: VW's Culture Under Winterkorn," Reuters, October 10, 2015.
14. Smith and McCormick, "Volkswagen's Emissions Scandal," 6.
15. Chris Bryant and Richard Milne, "Volkswagen's 'Uniquely Awful' Governance at Fault in Emissions Scandal," *Financial Times*, October 4, 2015.
16. This paragraph draws on Ewing, *Faster, Higher, Farther*, 125.
17. Michael Schrage, "VW's Problem Is Bad Management, Not Rogue Engineers," *Harvard Business Review*, October 15, 2015.
18. Ewing, *Faster, Higher, Farther*, 119.
19. Smith and McCormick, "Volkswagen's Emissions Scandal," 7.
20. Smith and McCormick, "Volkswagen's Emissions Scandal," 13.

21. Leah McGrath Goodman, "Why Volkswagen Cheated," *Newsweek*, December 15, 2015, https://www.newsweek.com/2015/12/25/why-volkswagen-cheated-404891.html. All the quotes in this section are from this article.

22. Quotes in this paragraph are from Goodman, "Why Volkswagen Cheated."

23. This paragraph is based on Ewing, *Faster, Higher, Farther*, 128.

24. "Plausible Deniability," Wikipedia, September 10, 2023, https://en.wikipedia.org/wiki/Plausible_deniability.

25. Ewing, *Faster, Higher, Farther*, 112.

26. Peter Stanwick and Sarah Stanwick, "Volkswagen Emissions Scandal: The Perils of Installing Illegal Software," *International Review of Management and Business Research*, March 2017. The case study by Smith and McCormick describes a somewhat different sequence. But both case studies attribute the initial discovery of Volkswagen's defeat device to the researchers at West Virginia University.

27. Smith and McCormick, "Volkswagen's Emissions Scandal," 11.

28. Jack Ewing, "Volkswagen C.E.O. Martin Winterkorn Resigns amid Emissions Scandal," *New York Times*, September 23, 2015, https://www.nytimes.com/2015/09/24/business/international/volkswagen-chief-martin-winterkorn-resigns-amid-emissions-scandal.html.

29. William Boston, Hendrik Varnholt, and Sarah Sloat, "Volkswagen Blames 'Chain of Mistakes' for Emissions Scandal," *Wall Street Journal*, December 10, 2015, https://www.wsj.com/articles/vw-shares-up-ahead-of-emissions-findings-1449740759.

30. Jack Ewing, "Inside VW's Campaign of Trickery," *New York Times*, May 6, 2017, https://www.nytimes.com/2017/05/06/business/inside-vws-campaign-of-trickery.html.

31. Rupert Neate, "VW CEO Was Told About Emissions Crisis a Year Before Admitting to Cheat Scandal," *The Guardian*, March 2, 2016, https://www.theguardian.com/business/2016/mar/02/vw-ceo-martin-winterkorn-told-about-emissions-scandal.

32. Ewing, "Inside VW's Campaign of Trickery." The quotes in this paragraph and the substance of it are based on this article.

33. Smith and McCormick, "Volkswagen's Emissions Scandal," 12.

34. "Volkswagen Emissions Scandal," Wikipedia, For more details on the scandal see, https://en.wikipedia.org/wiki/Volkswagen_emissions_scandal (accessed September 10, 2019).

35. Lepore, "Moving Right Along," 24.

36. The information on Oliver Schmidt and the related quotes are all in Roger Parloff's excellent piece, "How VW Paid $25 Billion for Dieselgate—and Got Off Easy," ProPublica, February 8, 2018, https://www.propublica.org/article/how-vw-paid-25-billion-for-dieselgate-and-got-off-easy.

37. Smith and McCormick, "Volkswagen's Emissions Scandal," 20.

38. Marianne Jennings, "When the CEO 'Didn't Know,'" *Corporate Finance Review* 20, no. 3 (November–December 2015). The previous quote is also from this article.

Chapter 6

1. Soner Cagaptay, *Erdogan's Empire: Turkey and the Politics of the Middle East* (London: I. B. Tauris, 2021).
2. Cagaptay, *Erdogan's Empire*, 30.
3. Deborah Sontag, "The Erdogan Experiment," *New York Times Magazine*, May 11, 2003, https://www.nytimes.com/2003/05/11/magazine/the-erdogan-experiment.html.
4. "Recep Tayyip Erdogan," Wikipedia, September 11, 2023. https://en.wikipedia.org/wiki/Recep_Tayyip_Erdo%C4%9Fan.
5. Cagaptay, *Erdogan's Empire*, 35.
6. Cagaptay, *Erdogan's Empire*, 36.
7. "White Turks," Wikipedia, September 11, 2023. https://en.wikipedia.org/wiki/White_Turks.
8. Sontag, "The Erdogan Experiment."
9. Mark Tran, "The Rise of Recep Tayyip Erdogan," *The Guardian*, February 24, 2009, https://www.theguardian.com/world/2009/feb/24/erdogan-turkey, .
10. Dimitar Bechev, *Turkey Under Erdogan* (New Haven, CT: Yale University Press, 2022), 49ff.
11. Ihsan D. Dagi, "The Justice and Development Party," in *The Emergence of a New Turkey: Democracy and the AK Parti*, edited by M. Hakan Yavuz (Salt Lake City: University of Utah Press, 2006), 88–106.
12. David Gardner, "Conciliatory Gul Makes His Mark in Turkey's Taksim Uprising," *Financial Times*, June 6, 2013, https://www.ft.com/content/aa39ad2c-ceb7-11e2-8e16-00144feab7de.
13. Bechev, *Turkey Under Erdogan*, 59.
14. Taner Dogan, *Communications Strategies in Turkey: Erdogan, the AKP and Political Messaging* (London: I. B. Tauris, 2021), 153.
15. Cagaptay, *Erdogan's Empire*, 34.
16. This paragraph draws on Cagaptay, *Erdogan's Empire*, 39–40.
17. Jenny B. White, "The Turkish Complex," *The American Interest*, February 2, 2015, http://www.the-american-interest.com/2015/02/02/the-turkish-complex/.
18. Dogan, *Communications Strategies in Turkey*, 156.
19. Raquel dos Santos Fernandes and Isabel Estrada Carvalhais, "Understanding Erdogan's Leadership in the 'New Turkey,'" *Janus.net, e-Journal of International Relations* 9, no. 1 (2018): 88–102.
20. Berk Esen and Sebnem Gumuscu, "Building a Competitive Authoritarian Regime: State-Business Relations in the AKP's Turkey," *Journal of Balkan and Near Eastern Studies* 20, no. 4 (2018): 349–372.
21. Bechev, *Turkey Under Erdogan*, 49ff.
22. Dagi, "The Justice and Development Party."

23. Gareth Jenkins, "Symbols and Shadow Play: Military-JDP Relations, 2002–2004," in *The Emergence of a New Turkey: Democracy and the AK Parti*, edited by M. Hakan Yavuz (Salt Lake City: University of Utah Press, 2006), 201.

24. Cagaptay, *Erdogan's Empire*, 62.

25. "Recep Tayyip Erdogan."

26. Peter Beaumont, "Recep Tayyip Erdogan: Is 'Papa' Still a Father Figure to Turks?," *The Guardian*, June 4, https://www.theguardian.com/theobserver/2011/jun/05/observer-profile-recep-erdogan-turkey.

27. Simon Tisdall, "Recep Tayyip Erdogan: Turkey's Elected Sultan or an Islamic Democrat?," *The Guardian*, October 24, 2012, https://www.theguardian.com/world/2012/oct/24/recep-tayyip-erdogan-turkey.

28. Steven Cook, "How Erdogan Made Turkey Authoritarian Again," *The Atlantic*, July 21, 2016.

29. This paragraph is based on Cook, "How Erdogan Made Turkey Authoritarian Again."

30. Tony Barber, "When Democratic Spin Conceals a Descent into Dictatorship," *Financial Times*, May 15, 2022, https://www.ft.com/content/ff757408-d955-433b-af8d-f58085998c1b.

31. All quotes in this paragraph are from Ceylan Yeginsu and Sebnem Arsu, "Turkey's Premier Is Proclaimed Winner of Presidential Election," *New York Times*, August 10, 2014, https://www.nytimes.com/2014/08/11/world/europe/erdogan-turkeys-premier-wins-presidential-election.html.

32. Tim Arango and Ceylan Yeginsu, "Turkey Rounds Up Thousands of Military Personnel," *New York Times*, July 16, 2016, https://www.nytimes.com/2016/07/17/world/europe/turkey-attempted-coup-erdogan.html.

33. Suzy Hansen, "Inside Turkey's Purge," *New York Times Magazine*, April 13, 2017, https://www.nytimes.com/2017/04/13/magazine/inside-turkeys-purge.html.

34. Patrick Kingsley, "Erdogan Claims Vast Powers in Turkey After Narrow Victory in Referendum," *New York Times*, April 16, 2017, https://www.nytimes.com/2017/04/16/world/europe/turkey-referendum-polls-erdogan.html.

35. Carlotta Gall, "Erdogan, Flush with Power, Seizes New Powers in Turkey," *New York Times*, July 19, 2018, https://www.nytimes.com/2018/07/19/world/asia/turkey-erdogan.html.

36. Carlotta Gall, "A Canal Through Turkey? Presidential Vote Is a Test of Erdogan's Building Spree," *New York Times*, June 21, 2018, https://www.nytimes.com/2018/06/21/world/europe/turkey-election-ergodan-canal-megaprojects.html.

37. Sinem Adar and Gunter Seufert, "Turkey's Presidential System After Two and a Half Years," German Institute for International and Security Affairs, Berlin, 2021.

38. David Gardner, "Erdogan's Strongman Rule Is Beginning to Fray," *Financial Times*, July 22, 2021, https://www.ft.com/content/b807e28f-f7e3-4629-8cdc-1d30e622773e.

39. Carlotta Gall, "As Biden Meeting Nears, Erdogan Softens His Stance," *New York Times*, June 13, 2021, https://www.nytimes.com/2021/06/13/world/europe/biden-erdogan-turkey-nato.html.

40. For more on the lust for power, see Barbara Kellerman and Todd Pittinsky, *Leaders Who Lust: Power, Money, Sex, Success, Legitimacy, Legacy* (New York: Cambridge University Press, 2021).

41. "Turkey Could Be on the Brink of Dictatorship," *The Economist*, January 19, 2023, https://www.economist.com/leaders/2023/01/19/turkey-could-be-on-the-brink-of-dictatorship.

42. Lydia Polgreen, "The State Failed These People. They Didn't Have to Die Like This," *New York Times*, March 10, 2023, https://www.nytimes.com/2023/03/10/opinion/erdogan-turkey-earthquake.html.

43. All quotes in this paragraph are from Soner Cagaptay, "Erdogan's Russian Victory," *Foreign Affairs*, May 29, 2023, https://www.foreignaffairs.com/russian-federation/erdogans-russian-victory.

Chapter 7

1. Andrew Edgecliffe-Johnson, "The Cult of We—WeWork, Weed and Wild Ambition," *Financial Times*, July 15, 2021, https://www.ft.com/content/08750ef4-c0ed-4c82-a8e2-473d2ad499b9.

2. Neumann quote is in Edgecliffe-Johnson, "The Cult of We"; Zuckerberg quote is in Casey Newton, "Facebook Just Changed Its Mission, Because the Old One Was Broken," The Verge, February 16, 2017, https://www.theverge.com/2017/2/16/14642164/facebook-mark-zuckerberg-letter-mission-statement; Page quote is in Asad Meah, "35 Inspirational Larry Page and Sergey Brin Quotes on Success," Awaken the Greatness Within, August 2023, https://www.awakenthegreatnesswithin.com/35-inspirational-larry-page-sergey-brin-quotes-on-success/.

3. Joseph Fuller and John Masko, "Theranos: The Unicorn That Wasn't," Harvard Business School, September 6, 2019.

4. John Carreyrou, *Bad Blood: Secrets and Lies in a Silicon Valley Startup* (New York: Knopf, 2018), 9.

5. Ken Auletta, "Blood, Simpler," *New Yorker*, December 15, 2014, https://www.newyorker.com/magazine/2014/12/15/blood-simpler.

6. Auletta, "Blood, Simpler."

7. Carreyrou, *Bad Blood*, 14.

8. Ben Popken and Cyrus Farivar, "Elizabeth Holmes Testifies College Rape, Partner's Control Fueled Her Drive at Theranos," NBC News, November 29, 2021, https://www.nbcnews.com/business/business-news/elizabeth-holmes-testifies-college-rape-partners-control-fueled-drive-rcna6925.

9. Carreyrou, *Bad Blood*, 15.

10. Carreyrou, *Bad Blood*, 16.

11. Fuller and Masko, "Theranos," 3.

12. Erin Griffith, "What Red Flags? Elizabeth Holmes Trial Exposes Investors' Carelessness," *New York Times*, November 4, 2021, https://www.nytimes.com/2021/11/04/technology/theranos-elizabeth-holmes-investors-diligence.html.

13. The descriptions—and the relevant quotes—of the relationships between Holmes/ Theranos and Walgreens, Safeway, and the U.S. Department of Defense are based on Fuller and Masko, "Theranos."

14. Paul Farhi, "The Magazine Story That Made Elizabeth Holmes Famous Could Now Help Send Her to Prison," *Washington Post*, December 16, 2021, https://www.washing tonpost.com/lifestyle/media/elizabeth-holmes-fortune-cover-theranos/2021/12/15/ f2332ed8-5841-11ec-a808-3197a22b19fa_story.html.

15. This account and the relevant quotes are from Carreyrou, *Bad Blood*, 206ff.

16. Nick Bolton, "The Secret Culprit in the Theranos Mess," *Vanity Fair*, May 2, 2016, https://www.vanityfair.com/news/2016/05/theranos-silicon-valley-media.

17. Benjamin Wallace, "Tech vs. Journalism," *New York Magazine*, May 12, 2021, https:// nymag.com/intelligencer/2021/05/tech-vs-journalism-silicon-valley-reporters.html.

18. Sara Randazzo, "Former Lab Worker Erika Cheung Testifies Theranos Cut Corners," *Wall Street Journal*, September 15, 2021, https://www.wsj.com/livecoverage/elizab eth-holmes-trial-theranos/card/XHIzfm9StO3sW1NIfQm3.

19. Auletta, "Blood, Simpler."

20. The term "cult of secrecy" was used in Fuller and Masko, "Theranos," 4.

21. Carreyrou, *Bad Blood*, 25, 26.

22. Fuller and Masko, "Theranos," 5.

23. Quoted in Carreyrou, *Bad Blood*, 40.

24. Quoted in "The Enforcer," episode 2 of the podcast *The Dropout*, https://abcaudio. com/podcasts/the-dropout/.

25. Carreyrou, *Bad Blood*, 237.

26. This paragraph is based on John Carreyrou, "Theranos Whistleblower Shook the Company—and His Family," *Wall Street Journal*, November 18, 2016, https://www. wsj.com/articles/theranos-whistleblower-shook-the-companyand-his-family-147 9335963.

27. Ben Popken and Cyrus Farivar, "Elizabeth Holmes Admits Whistleblower Was Right and Reporter Was 'Mishandled,' " NBC News, November 30, 2021, https://www.nbcn ews.com/business/business-news/elizabeth-holmes-admits-whistleblower-was-right-reporter-was-mishandle-rcna7123.

28. Ernesto Dal Bó and Guo Xu, "Theranos: How Did a $9 Billion Health Tech Startup End Up DOA?," Berkeley Haas Case Series, February 1, 2021, https://cases.haas.berke ley.edu/2021/02/theranos/.

29. Soo Kim, "What Is Theranos CEO Elizabeth Holmes' Net Worth as Founder Faces Federal Charges?," *Newsweek*, November 5, 2021, https://www.newsweek.com/elizab eth-holmes-theranos-net-worth-fraud-charges-federal-trial-1646242.

30. Christopher Weaver and John Carreyrou, "Craving Growth, Walgreens Dismissed Its Doubts About Theranos," *Wall Street Journal*, May 25, 2016, https://www.wsj. com/articles/craving-growth-walgreens-dismissed-its-doubts-about-theranos-146 4207285.

31. Nien-Hê Hsieh, Christina R. Wing, Emilie Fournier, and Anna Resman, "Theranos: Who Has Blood on Their Hands?," Harvard Business School Case Study,

February 13, 2020, https://www.hbs.edu/faculty/Pages/item.aspx?num=55760. Quotes in this paragraph are from the case study.

32. Kevin Loria, "Scientists Are Skeptical About the Secret Blood Test That Has Made Elizabeth Holmes a Billionaire," *Yahoo Finance*, April 25, 2015, https://finance.yahoo.com/news/scientists-skeptical-secret-blood-test-100000161.html.

33. Reed Abelson and Julie Creswell, "Theranos Founder Faces a Test of Technology, and Reputation," *New York Times*, December 19, 2015, https://www.nytimes.com/2015/12/20/business/theranos-founder-faces-a-test-of-technology-and-reputation.html.

34. Carreyrou, *Bad Blood*, 273.

35. John Carreyrou, "Hot Startup Theranos Has Struggled with Its Blood-Test Technology," *Wall Street Journal*, October 16, 2015, https://www.wsj.com/articles/theranos-has-struggled-with-blood-tests-1444881901.

36. John Carreyrou and Christopher Weaver, "Theranos Devices Often Failed Accuracy Requirements," *Wall Street Journal*, March 31, 2016, https://www.wsj.com/articles/theranos-devices-often-failed-accuracy-requirements-1459465578.

37. Fuller and Masko, "Theranos."

38. Nick Bolton, "'She Never Looks Back': Inside Elizabeth Holmes's Chilling Final Months at Theranos," *Vanity Fair*, February 20, 2019, https://www.vanityfair.com/news/2019/02/inside-elizabeth-holmess-final-months-at-theranos.

39. Erin Griffith, "Silicon Valley Can't Escape Elizabeth Holmes," *New York Times*, January 4, 2022, https://www.nytimes.com/2022/01/04/technology/elizabeth-holmes-verdict.html.

40. Christopher Weaver, "Court Documents Shed Light on Theranos Board's Response to Crisis," *Wall Street Journal*, May 30, 2017, https://www.wsj.com/articles/court-documents-shed-light-on-theranos-boards-response-to-crisis-1496136600.

41. Ron Leuty, "'Ultimately, Elizabeth Made the Decisions': A Look Inside Theranos' Ineffective Board," *San Francisco Business Times*, August 8, 2018, https://www.bizjournals.com/sanfrancisco/news/2018/08/07/theranos-elizabeth-holmes-board-kovacevich-shultz.html.

42. Ellen Pao, "The Elizabeth Holmes Trial Is a Wake-up Call for Sexism in Tech," *New York Times*, September 15, 2021, https://www.nytimes.com/2021/09/15/opinion/elizabeth-holmes-trial-sexism.html.

43. Erin Griffith, "They Still Live in the Shadow of Theranos's Elizabeth Holmes," *New York Times*, August 24, 2021, https://www.nytimes.com/2021/08/24/technology/theranos-elizabeth-holmes.html.

Chapter 8

1. Paul Mozur, Muyi Xiao, and John Liu, "'An Invisible Cage': How China Is Policing the Future," *New York Times*, June 25, 2022, https://www.nytimes.com/2022/06/25/technology/china-surveillance-police.html.

2. Anne Applebaum, *Iron Curtain: The Crushing of Eastern Europe 1944–1956* (Random House, 2012), p. xxi.

3. Chris Buckley, "'Uncle Xi' to Exalted Ruler: China's Leader Embodies His Authoritarian Era," *New York Times*, October 14, 2022, https://www.nytimes.com/2022/10/14/world/asia/china-xi-jinping-communist-party.html.

4. Barbara Kellerman and Todd L. Pittinsky, *Leaders Who Lust: Power, Money, Sex, Success, Legitimacy, Legacy* (New York: Cambridge University Press, 2021).

5. Barbara Kellerman, *The Enablers: How Team Trump Flunked the Pandemic and Failed America* (New York: Cambridge University Press, 2021).

6. This paragraph is based on Cheng Li, *Chinese Politics in the Xi Jinping Era* (Washington, DC: Brookings Institution Press, 2016), 9.

7. Li, *Chinese Politics in the Xi Jinping Era*, 11.

8. Li, *Chinese Politics in the Xi Jinping Era*, 11.

9. Nargiza Salidjanova and Iacob Koch-Weser, "Third Plenum Economic Reform Proposals: A Scorecard," U.S.-China Economic and Security Review Commission, November 19, 2013, https://www.uscc.gov/sites/default/files/Research/Backgrounde r_Third%20Plenum%20Economic%20Reform%20Proposals--A%20Scorecard%20 (2).pdf.

10. Jacob Lew, Gary Roughhead, Jennifer Hillman, and David Sacks, *China's Belt and Road: Implications for the United States* (New York: Council on Foreign Relations, 2021), 2.

11. Ryan Dube and Gabriele Steinhauser, "China's Global Mega-Projects Are Falling Apart," *Wall Street Journal*, January 20, 2023, https://www.wsj.com/articles/china-glo bal-mega-projects-infrastructure-falling-apart-11674166180.

12. Lew et al., *China's Belt and Road*, 9.

13. Chun Han Wong, "Xi Jinping's Quest for Control over China Targets Even Old Friends—WSJ," EnergiesNet.com, October 17, 2022, https://energiesnet.com/xi-jinpi ngs-quest-for-control-over-china-targets-even-old-friends-wsj/.

14. This paragraph draws from Elizabeth Economy, "China's Neo-Maoist Moment: How Xi Jinping Is Using China's Past to Accomplish What His Predecessors Could Not," *Foreign Affairs*, October 1, 2019, https://www.foreignaffairs.com/articles/china/2019-10-01/chinas-neo-maoist-moment.

15. Sun Yu, "China's Marxism Majors Prosper amid Labour Market Woes," *Financial Times*, June 28, 2022, https://www.ft.com/content/36d34b2f-7f69-4224-8322-87d99 a820f64.

16. Scholar cited by Economy in "China's Neo-Marxist Moment."

17. Hudson Lockett and Mercedes Ruehl, "No 'Adults in the Room': Xi Jinping Catches Global Investors Off Guard," *Financial Times*, October 27, 2022, https://www.ft.com/content/6589ecaa-b609-4714-b966-d498b03a2d88.

18. Kellerman and Pittinsky, *Leaders Who Lust*, 39.

19. Li, *Chinese Politics in the Xi Jinping Era*, 304.

20. Li, *Chinese Politics in the Xi Jinping Era*, 309.

21. Kellerman and Pittinsky, *Leaders Who Lust*, 40.

22. Li, *Chinese Politics in the Xi Jinping Era*, 347.

23. Applebaum, *Iron Curtain*, xxxvi.

24. Zheng Yongnian and Weng Cuifen, "The Development of China's Formal Political Structures," in *China in the Era of Xi Jinping: Domestic and Foreign Policy Challenges*, edited by Robert Ross and Jo Inge Bekkevold (Washington, DC: Georgetown University Press, 2016), 43.

25. See discussion of Xi in Kellerman and Pittinsky, *Leaders Who Lust*, 31ff.

26. Kellerman and Pittinsky, *Leaders Who Lust*, 35.

27. Kellerman and Pittinsky, *Leaders Who Lust*, 36.

28. Kellerman and Pittinsky, *Leaders Who Lust*, 36.

29. Economy, "China's Neo-Maoist Moment."

30. Quoted in Kellerman and Pittinsky, *Leaders Who Lust*, 39, 40.

31. Stein Ringer, *The Perfect Dictatorship: China in the 21st Century* (Hong Kong: Hong Kong University Press, 2016), 79.

32. Kellerman and Pittinsky, *Leaders Who Lust*, 36.

33. Richard McGregor, "Party Man: Xi Jinping's Quest to Dominate China," *Foreign Affairs*, August 14, 2019, https://www.foreignaffairs.com/china/party-man.

34. Elizabeth C. Economy, "China's New Revolution: The Reign of Xi Jinping," *Foreign Affairs* 97, no. 3 (May/June 2018).

35. Nury Turkel and Beth Van Schaack, "What America Owes the Uyghurs: A Plan for Stopping China's Genocide," *Foreign Affairs*, July 16, 2021, https://www.foreignaffairs.com/articles/china/2021-07-16/what-america-owes-uyghurs.

36. Sean R. Roberts, "The Roots of Cultural Genocide in Xinjiang: China's Imperial Past Hangs over the Uyghurs," *Foreign Affairs*, February 10, 2021, https://www.foreignaffairs.com/articles/china/2021-02-10/roots-cultural-genocide-xinjiang.

37. Grace Tsoi and Lam Cho Wai, "Hong Kong National Security Law: What Is It and Is It Worrying?," BBC, June 28, 2022, https://www.bbc.com/news/world-asia-china-52765838.

38. Timothy McLaughlin, "How China Weaponized the Press," *The Atlantic*, September 9, 2021, https://www.theatlantic.com/international/archive/2021/09/hong-kong-china-media-newspaper/620005/.

39. Mark L. Clifford, "China's Ambitions and the Fate of a Hong Kong Daily," *Wall Street Journal*, January 27, 2022, https://www.wsj.com/articles/chinas-ambitions-and-the-fate-of-a-hong-kong-daily-11643296501.

40. Primrose Riordan, Andy Lin, Chan Ho-him, and Gloria Li, "The Reinvention of Hong Kong," *Financial Times*, June 30, 2022, https://www.ft.com/content/36df0106-3a83-4076-82ae-0fb298456800.

41. Austin Ramzy and Vivian Wang, "Xi Tells a Muted Hong Kong That Political Power Is for Patriots," *New York Times*, July 1, 2022, https://www.nytimes.com/2022/07/01/world/asia/xi-jinping-hong-kong-china.html.

42. Steven Lee Myers, Keith Bradsher, and Tariq Panja, "China's Games: How Xi Jinping Is Staging the Olympics on His Own Terms," *New York Times*, January 1, 2022, https://www.nytimes.com/2022/01/22/world/asia/winter-olympics-china-beijing-xi-jinping.html.

43. Hudson Lockett, "How Xi Jinping Is Reshaping China's Capital Markets," *Financial Times*, June 13, 2022, https://www.ft.com/content/d5b81ea0-5955-414c-b2eb-886dfed4dffe.

44. "China's Xi Calls for Wealth Redistribution and Crackdown on High Incomes," *Financial Times*, August 17, 2021, https://www.ft.com/content/87c3aa02-f970-48c8-b795-82768c9f7634.

45. Chris Buckley, Vivian Wang, and Keith Bradsher, "Living by the Code: In China, Covid-Era Controls May Outlast the Virus," *New York Times*, January 30, 2022,

https://www.nytimes.com/2022/01/30/world/asia/covid-restrictions-china-lockd
own.html.

46. Lingling Wei, "Xi Jinping Aims to Rein In Chinese Capitalism, Hew to Mao's Socialist Vision," *Wall Street Journal*, September 20, 2021, https://www.wsj.com/articles/xi-jinping-aims-to-rein-in-chinese-capitalism-hew-to-maos-socialist-vision-1163 2150725.

47. Chun Han Wong, "China's Xi Mimics Mao's Crisis Response in Sweeping Indoctrination Drive," *Wall Street Journal*, May 21, 2023, https://www.wsj.com/artic les/chinas-xi-mimics-maos-crisis-response-in-sweeping-indoctrination-drive-b8941652.

48. In "The World According to Xi Jinping" in *Foreign Policy*, November/December 2022.

49. Lingling Wei, "China's Forgotten Premier Steps Out of Xi's Shadow as Economic Fixer," *Wall Street Journal*, May 11, 2022, https://www.wsj.com/articles/china-prem ier-li-keqiang-xi-jinping-11652277107.

50. James Kynge and Sun Yu, "China and Big Tech: Xi's Blueprint for a Digital Dictatorship," *Financial Times*, September 7, 2021, https://www.ft.com/content/ 9ef38be2-9b4d-49a4-a812-97ad6d70ea6f.

51. Ezekiel J. Emanuel, "China's Let-It-Rip Covid Reopening," *Wall Street Journal*, December 22, 2022, https://www.wsj.com/articles/china-goes-from-zero-to-epide mic-in-no-time-covid-vaccines-spread-180-mrna-pfizer-new-year-11671716102.

52. Lynette H. Ong, "China's Epidemic of Mistrust: How Xi's COVID-19 U-Turn Will Make the Country Harder to Govern," *Foreign Affairs*, January 11, 2023, https://www. foreignaffairs.com/china/china-epidemic-mistrust-xi-jinping-covid-19.

53. Jonathan Tepperman, "China's Dangerous Decline: Washington Must Adjust as Beijing's Troubles Mount," *Foreign Affairs*, December 19, 2022, https://www.foreign affairs.com/china/chinas-dangerous-decline.

54. Vivian Wang and Zixu Wang, "In China's Crackdown on Protesters, a Familiar Effort to Blame Foreign Powers," *New York Times*, January 26, 2023, https://www.nytimes. com/2023/01/26/world/asia/china-protests-arrests.html.

55. Elizabeth Economy, "Xi Jinping's New World Order: Can China Remake the International System?," *Foreign Affairs*, December 9, 2021, https://www.foreignaffa irs.com/china/xi-jinpings-new-world-order.

Chapter 9

1. "Hitler's Speeches Key," Teaching Literacy Through Historical Inquiry Project, University of North Carolina–Pembroke, n.d., https://www.uncp.edu/sites/default/ files/2019-01/Hilter%26%23039%3Bs%20Speeches%20Key.pdf.

2. "Martin Winterkorn Named 'Man of the Year 2008' in Paris," press release, Auto123, April 16, 2009, https://www.auto123.com/en/news/martin-winterkorn-named-man-of-the-year-2008-in-paris/24677/.

3. Alvin Powell, "Erdogan Calls for Cooperation," *Harvard Gazette*, February 5, 2004, https://news.harvard.edu/gazette/story/2004/02/erdogan-calls-for-cooperation/.

4. This paragraph is based on Ditmar Bechev, *Turkey Under Erdogan: How A Country Turned from Democracy and the West* (New Haven, CT: Yale University Press, 2022), 50–54.

5. "President Bush Welcomes Prime Minister Erdogan of Turkey to the White House," press release, The White House, October 2, 2006, https://georgewbush-whitehouse. archives.gov/news/releases/2006/10/20061002-5.html.

6. Bechev, *Turkey Under Erdogan*, 4.

7. Jasmine D. Adkins, "The Lifesaver," *Inc.*, June 22, 2006, https://www.inc.com/30unde r30/holmes.html.

8. "Elizabeth Holmes," https://www.medscape.com/viewarticle/814233_2.

9. James Leung, "Xi's Corruption Crackdown: How Bribery and Graft Threaten the Chinese Dream," *Foreign Affairs*, April 20, 2015, https://www.foreignaffairs.com/ china/xis-corruption-crackdown. The last quote in this paragraph is from Elizabeth Economy, cited in the Leung article.

10. Alexandra Fiol-Mahon, "Xi Jinping's Anti-Corruption Campaign: The Hidden Motives of a Modern-Day Mao," Foreign Policy Research Institute, August 17, 2018, https://www.fpri.org/article/2018/08/xi-jinpings-anti-corruption-campaign-the-hid den-motives-of-a-modern-day-mao/.

11. James Palmer, "The Resistible Rise of Xi Jinping," *Foreign Policy*, October 19, 2017, https://foreignpolicy.com/2017/10/19/the-resistible-rise-of-xi-jinping/.

12. Ministry of Foreign Affairs of the People's Republic of China, "Xi Jinping Attends Welcome Ceremony Held by US President Barack Obama at White House," September 26, 2015, https://www.fmprc.gov.cn/mfa_eng/topics_665678/2015zt/ xjpdmgjxgsfwbcxlhgcl70znxlfh/201509/t20150930_705347.html#:~:text=On%20Se ptember%2025%20local%20time,to%20seek%20win%2Dwin%20cooperation.

13. "Remarks by President Obama and President Xi of the People's Republic of China in Joint Press Conference," press release, The White House, September 25, 2015, https:// obamawhitehouse.archives.gov/the-press-office/2015/09/25/remarks-president- obama-and-president-xi-peoples-republic-china-joint.

Chapter 10

1. Henry Kissinger, *Leadership: Six Studies in World Strategy* (New York: Penguin, 2022), xv.

2. Barbara Kellerman, *The Enablers: How Team Trump Flunked the Pandemic and Failed America* (New York: Cambridge University Press, 2021), 11.

3. Kellerman, *The Enablers*, 1.

4. Robert L. Leahy, "Letting Go of Sunk Costs," *Psychology Today*, September 24, 2014, https://www.psychologytoday.com/us/blog/anxiety-files/201409/letting-go-sunk- costs.

5. Philip Zimbardo, *The Lucifer Effect: Understanding How Good People Turn Evil* (New York: Random House, 2007).

6. Zimbardo, *The Lucifer Effect*, 278.

7. Zimbardo, *The Lucifer Effect*, 260.

8. Dimitar Bechev, *Turkey Under Erdogan: How a Country Turned from Democracy and the West* (New Haven, CT: Yale University Press, 2022).
9. Bechev, *Turkey Under Erdogan*, 6, 7.
10. Laura Pitel, "Will the Ailing Turkish Economy Bring Erdogan Down?," *Financial Times*, November 1, 2021, https://www.ft.com/content/0563fbba-9fc7-4779-a6a5-bd013293661d.
11. Pitel, "Will the Ailing Turkish Economy Bring Erdogan Down?"
12. Pitel, "Will the Ailing Turkish Economy Bring Erdogan Down?"
13. Steven Cook, "Turkish Governance Model May Ruin Economy," Ahval, December 14, 2021, https://ahvalnews.com/turkey-politics/turkish-governance-model-may-ruin-economy-steven-cook.
14. Erin Griffith, "No. 2 Theranos Executive Found Guilty of 12 Counts of Fraud," *New York Times*, July 7, 2022, https://www.nytimes.com/2022/07/07/technology/ramesh-balwani-theranos-fraud.html.
15. Li Yuan, "Why China's Confidence Could Turn Out to Be a Weakness," *New York Times*, August 9, 2022, https://www.nytimes.com/2022/08/09/business/china-xi-jinping-united-states-taiwan.html.
16. Paul Mozur and John Liu, "China Fines Didi $1.2 Billion as Tech Sector Pressures Persist," *New York Times*, July 21, 2022, https://www.nytimes.com/2022/07/21/business/china-fines-didi.html.
17. Chris Buckley and Steven Lee Myers, "In Turbulent Times, Xi Builds a Security Fortress for China, and Himself," *New York Times*, August 6, 2022, https://www.nytimes.com/2022/08/06/world/asia/xi-jinping-china-security.html.
18. Isabelle Qian, Muyi Xiao, Paul Mozur, and Alexander Cardia, "Four Takeaways from a Times Investigation into China's Expanding Surveillance State," *New York Times*, June 21, 2022, https://www.nytimes.com/2022/06/21/world/asia/china-surveillance-investigation.html.
19. Qian et al., "Four Takeaways."
20. The quote is from Tim Miller, *Why We Did It* (New York: HarperCollins, 2022), 97. See also Mark Leibovich, *Thank You for Your Servitude* (New York: Penguin, 2022).
21. Thomas L. Friedman, "I Was Wrong About Chinese Censorship," *New York Times*, July 21, 2022, https://www.nytimes.com/2022/07/21/opinion/thomas-friedman-china.html.

Chapter 11

1. "Defeat Device," Wikipedia, September 14, 2023, https://en.wikipedia.org/wiki/Defeat_device.
2. *APA Dictionary of Psychology*, s.v. "entrapment," https://dictionary.apa.org/entrapment
3. Barbara Kellerman and Todd L. Pittinsky, *Leaders Who Lust: Power, Money, Sex, Success, Legitimacy, Legacy* (New York: Cambridge University Press, 2020. The quote is on 2.

4. Dimitar Bechev, *Turkey Under Erdogan: How a Country Turned from Democracy and the West* (New Haven, CT: Yale University Press, 2022), 57.

5. Bechev, *Turkey Under Erdogan*, 132.

6. Bechev, *Turkey Under Erdogan*, 116.

7. Joseph Rago, "Elizabeth Holmes: The Breakthrough of Instant Diagnosis," *Wall Street Journal*, September 8, 2013, https://www.wsj.com/articles/SB100014241278873241 23004579055003869574012.

8. Rago, "Elizabeth Holmes."

9. David Streitfeld, "The Epic Rise and Fall of Elizabeth Holmes," *New York Times*, March 31, 2022, https://www.nytimes.com/2022/01/03/technology/elizabeth-hol mes-theranos.html.

10. Ivan Nechepurenko, "Faced with Foreign Pressure, Russians Rally Around Putin, Poll Shows," *New York Times*, January 3, 2022, https://www.nytimes.com/2022/03/31/ world/europe/putin-approval-rating-russia.html.

11. "Do You Approve of the Activities of Vladimir Putin as the President (Prime Minister) of Russia?," Statista, August 1, 2023, https://www.statista.com/statistics/896 181/putin-approval-rating-russia/.

12. Bill McKibben, "Big Oil's Reign Is Finally Weakening," *New Yorker*, May 7, 2020, https://www.newyorker.com/news/annals-of-a-warming-planet/big-oils-reign-is-finally-weakening.

13. Ray Dalio, *Principles for Dealing with the Changing World Order* (New York: Simon and Schuster, 2021), 416, 417.

14. Rob Copeland and Maureen Farrell, "Hedge Fund Billionaire Extracts Billions More to Retire," *New York Times*, February 20, 2023, https://www.nytimes.com/2023/02/ 20/business/bridgewater-ray-dalio-retire.html.

15. Michael Mandelbaum, "The Sources of Chinese Conduct," American Purpose, January 24, 2023, https://www.americanpurpose.com/articles/the-sources-of-chin ese-conduct/.

16. Jiayang Fan, Taisu Zhang, and Ying Zhu, "Behind the Personality Cult of Xi Jinping," *Foreign Policy*, March 8, 2016, https://foreignpolicy.com/2016/03/08/the-personal ity-cult-of-xi-jinping-china-leader-communist-party/.

17. Barbara Kellerman, *Leadership: Essential Selections on Power, Authority, and Influence* (New York: McGraw-Hill, 2010), 9.

18. Robert Cialdini, *Influence: The Psychology of Persuasion* (New York: William Morrow, 1984), 216.

Chapter 12

1. Operation Reinhard, the largest single murder campaign of the Holocaust, took place from 1942 to 1943. Lewi Stone, "Quantifying the Holocaust: Hyperintense Kill Rates During the Nazi Genocide," *Science Advances* 5, no. 1 (2019), https://www.science. org/doi/10.1126/sciadv.aau7292.

2. "Four Former VW Employees Go on Trial in Dieselgate Lawsuit," Reuters, September 16, 2021, https://www.reuters.com/business/autos-transportation/four-former-vw-employees-go-trial-dieselgate-lawsuit-2021-09-16/.

3. "VW Culture to Blame for Silence over Emissions Scandal, Ex-Manager Says in Trial," Reuters, September 23, 2021, https://www.reuters.com/business/autos-transportation/vw-culture-blame-silence-over-emissions-scandal-ex-manager-says-trial-2021-09-23/.

4. This paragraph and the one previous are based on Patrick McGee, "How VW's Cheating on Emissions Was Exposed," Financial Times, January 11, 2017, https://www.ft.com/content/103dbe6a-d7a6-11e6-944b-e7eb37a6aa8e.

5. Tony Barber, "The Tipping Point of Tyranny," Financial Times, May 15, 2022, https://www.ft.com/content/ff757408-d955-433b-af8d-f58085998c1b.

6. Gideon Rachman, "Strongman Syndrome," Financial Times, April 3, 2022.

7. Dimitar Bechev, Turkey Under Erdogan: How a Country Turned from Democracy and the West (New Haven, CT: Yale University Press, 2022), 3, 5.

8. "Freedom in the World 2022: The Global Expansion of Authoritarian Rule," Freedom House, February 2022, https://freedomhouse.org/sites/default/files/2022-02/FIW_2022_PDF_Booklet_Digital_Final_Web.pdf.

9. Rachman, "Strongman Syndrome."

10. Liz Alderman, "Turkey's Reeling Economy Is an Added Challenge for Erdogan," New York Times, February 19, 2023, https://www.nytimes.com/2023/02/19/business/turkey-earthquake-economy-erdogan.html.

11. Avery Hartmans, Sarah Jackson, Azmi Haroun, and Sam Tabahriti, "The Rise and Fall of Elizabeth Holmes, the Former Theranos CEO Whose Prison Term Has Been Shortened by 2 Years," Business Insider, July 11, 2023, https://www.businessinsider.com/theranos-founder-ceo-elizabeth-holmes-life-story-bio-2018-4.

12. Nick Bilton, "Exclusive: How Elizabeth Holmes's House of Cards Came Tumbling Down," Vanity Fair, October 2016, https://www.vanityfair.com/news/2016/09/elizabeth-holmes-theranos-exclusive.

13. Kate Knibbs, "How John Carreyrou Exposed the Theranos Scam," The Ringer, May 22, 2018, https://www.theringer.com/2018/5/22/17378494/bad-blood-theranos-john-carreyrou-interview.

14. Knibbs, "How John Carreyrou Exposed the Theranos Scam."

15. "Theranos Exec Sunny Balwani Convicted of Fraud," BBC, July 7, 2022, https://www.bbc.com/news/world-us-canada-61902378.

16. "Theranos Exec Sunny Balwani Convicted of Fraud."

17. Christopher K. Johnson, "Raising the Curtain on China's 20th Party Congress: Mechanics, Rules, 'Norms,' and the Realities of Power," Asia Society Policy Institute, August 2022, https://asiasociety.org/policy-institute/raising-curtain-chinas-20th-party-congress-mechanics-rules-norms-and-realities-power.

18. Edward White, "Xi Crackdown Signals Warning on Disloyalty," Financial Times, October 7, 2022, https://www.ft.com/content/ad65cbdb-5c51-43f5-b936-1a50e7433546.

19. Tom Mitchel, "China's Eternal Emperor Awaits His Third Term," *Financial Times*, October 16, 2022, https://www.ft.com/content/2f5ae8b7-b42c-49e4-8d49-225cd 2b6107c.

20. Agnes Chang, Pablo Robles, Vivian Wang, and Isabelle Qian, "How Xi Jinping Remade China in His Image," *New York Times*, October 23, 2022, https://www.nyti mes.com/interactive/2022/10/23/world/asia/xi-propaganda.html.

21. Yuen Yuen Ang, "An Era Just Ended in China," *New York Times*, October 26, 2022, https://www.nytimes.com/2022/10/26/opinion/china-communist-xi-economy.html.

22. Danielle Wallace, "DNI Haines Deems Chinese Communist Party 'Leading and Most Consequential Threat to US National Security,'" Fox News, March 8, 2023, https:// www.foxnews.com/politics/dni-haines-deems-chinese-communist-party-leading-most-consequential-threat-us-national-security.

23. Hal Brands and Michael Beckley, *Danger Zone: The Coming Conflict with China* (New York: Norton, 2022); Hal Brands and Michael Beckley, "The Coming War over Taiwan," *Wall Street Journal*, August 4, 2022, https://www.wsj.com/articles/the-com ing-war-over-taiwan-11659614417.

24. Yun Sun, "What to Expect from a Bolder Xi Jinping—Get Ready for a More Ambitious Chinese Foreign Policy," *Foreign Affairs*, July 28, 2022, https://www.foreignaffairs. com/china/what-expect-bolder-xi-jinping.

25. Richard Haass, "Xi Jinping's Guns of August," Project Syndicate, August 11, 2022, https://www.project-syndicate.org/commentary/explainning-xi-harsh-response-to-pelosi-taiwan-visit-by-richard-haass-2022-08.

26. Barbara Kellerman and Todd Pittinsky, *Leaders Who Lust: Power, Money, Sex, Success, Legitimacy, Legacy* (New York: Cambridge University Press, 2020), 2.

27. Phelim Kine, "What It Looks Like When Congress Takes on China," Politico, March 2, 2023, https://www.politico.com/newsletters/politico-china-watcher/2023/03/02/ what-it-looks-like-when-congress-takes-on-china-00085100.

28. Stuart Lau, "China's Uyghur Abuses 'May Constitute Crimes Against Humanity,' UN Finds," September 1, 2022, https://www.politico.eu/article/chinas-uyghur-abuses-may-constitute-crimes-against-humanity-un-finds/.

29. Glenn Kessler, Salvador Rizzo, and Meg Kelly, "Trump's False or Misleading Claims Total 30,573 over 4 Years," *Washington Post*, January 24, 2021, https://www.washing tonpost.com/politics/2021/01/24/trumps-false-or-misleading-claims-total-30573-over-four-years/.

Epilogue

1. "Schizophrenia Prognosis," WebMD, April 19, 2022, https://www.webmd.com/schizo phrenia/schizophrenia-outlook.

2. Timothy Snyder, *On Tyranny: Twenty Lessons from the Twentieth Century* (New York: Tim Duggan Books, 2017).

3. Richard Haass, *The Bill of Obligations: The Ten Habits of Good Citizens* (New York: Penguin, 2023).

4. Atul Gawande, *The Checklist Manifesto: How to Get Things Right* (New York: Metropolitan Books, 2009).
5. Max Bazerman, *Complicit: How We Enable the Unethical and How to Stop* (Princeton, NJ: Princeton University Press, 2022), 180, 181.
6. Martin Wolf, *The Crisis of Democratic Capitalism* (New York: Penguin, 2023), 13.

Index

For the benefit of digital users, indexed terms that span two pages (e.g., 52–53) may, on occasion, appear on only one of those pages.